BROKEN WORLD™

Frank J. Barbiere
Christopher Peterson
Marissa Louise

BOOM! STUDIOS

BROKEN WORLD, July 2016. Published by BOOM! Studios, a division of Boom Entertainment, Inc. Broken World is ™ & © 2016 Frank J. Barbiere and Christopher Peterson. Originally published in single magazine form as BROKEN WORLD No. 1-4. ™ & © 2015 Frank J. Barbiere and Christopher Peterson. All rights reserved. BOOM! Studios™ and the BOOM! Studios logo are trademarks of Boom Entertainment, Inc., registered in various countries and categories. All characters, events, and institutions depicted herein are fictional. Any similarity between any of the names, characters, persons, events, and/or institutions in this publication to actual names, characters, and persons, whether living or dead, events, and/or institutions is unintended and purely coincidental. BOOM! Studios does not read or accept unsolicited submissions of ideas, stories, or artwork.

A catalog record of this book is available from OCLC and from the BOOM! Studios website, www.boom-studios.com, on the Librarians Page.

BOOM! Studios, 5670 Wilshire Boulevard, Suite 450, Los Angeles, CA 90036-5679. Printed in China. First Printing.

ISBN: 978-1-60886-856-8, eISBN: 978-1-61398-527-4

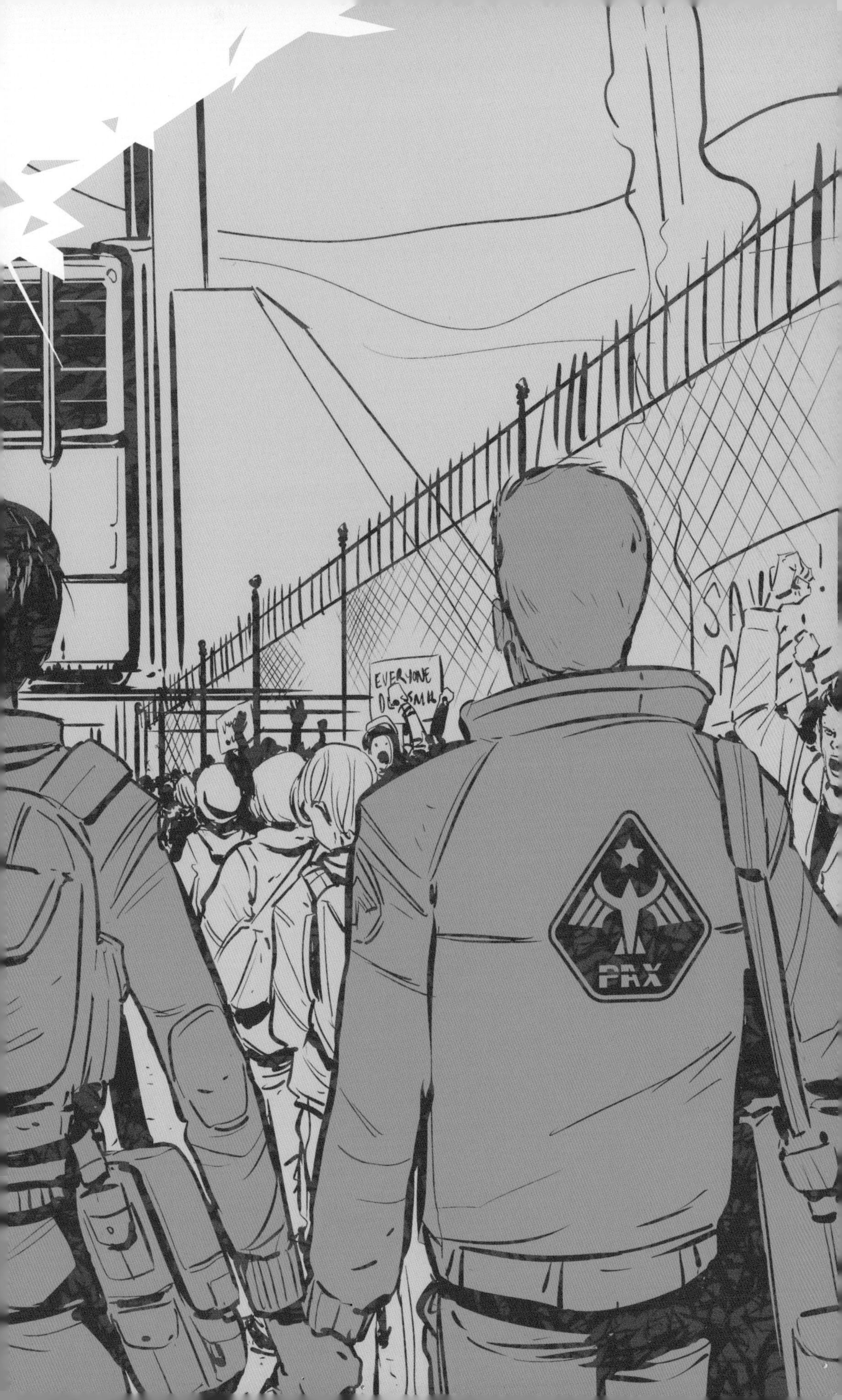
EVERYONE
PAX

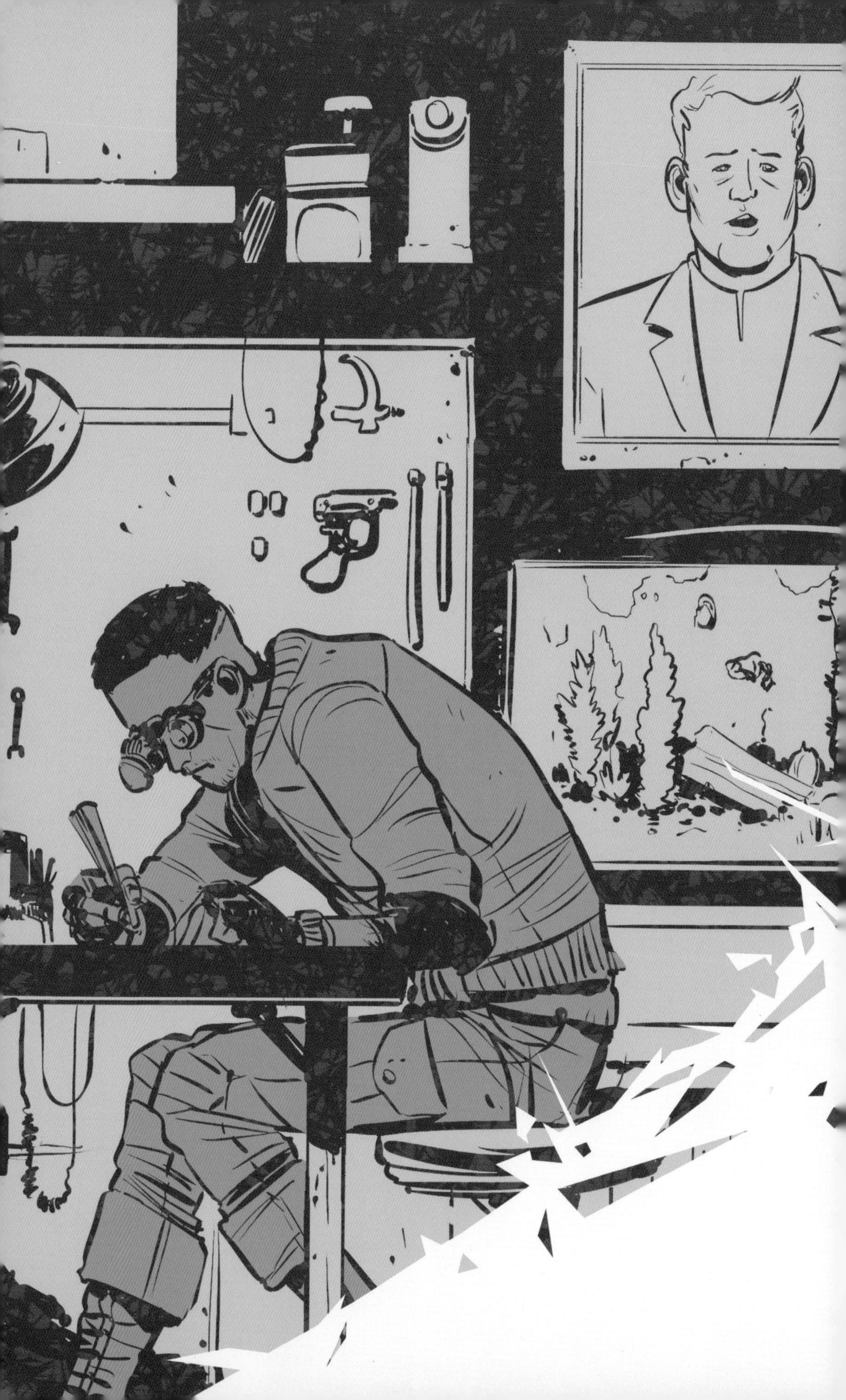

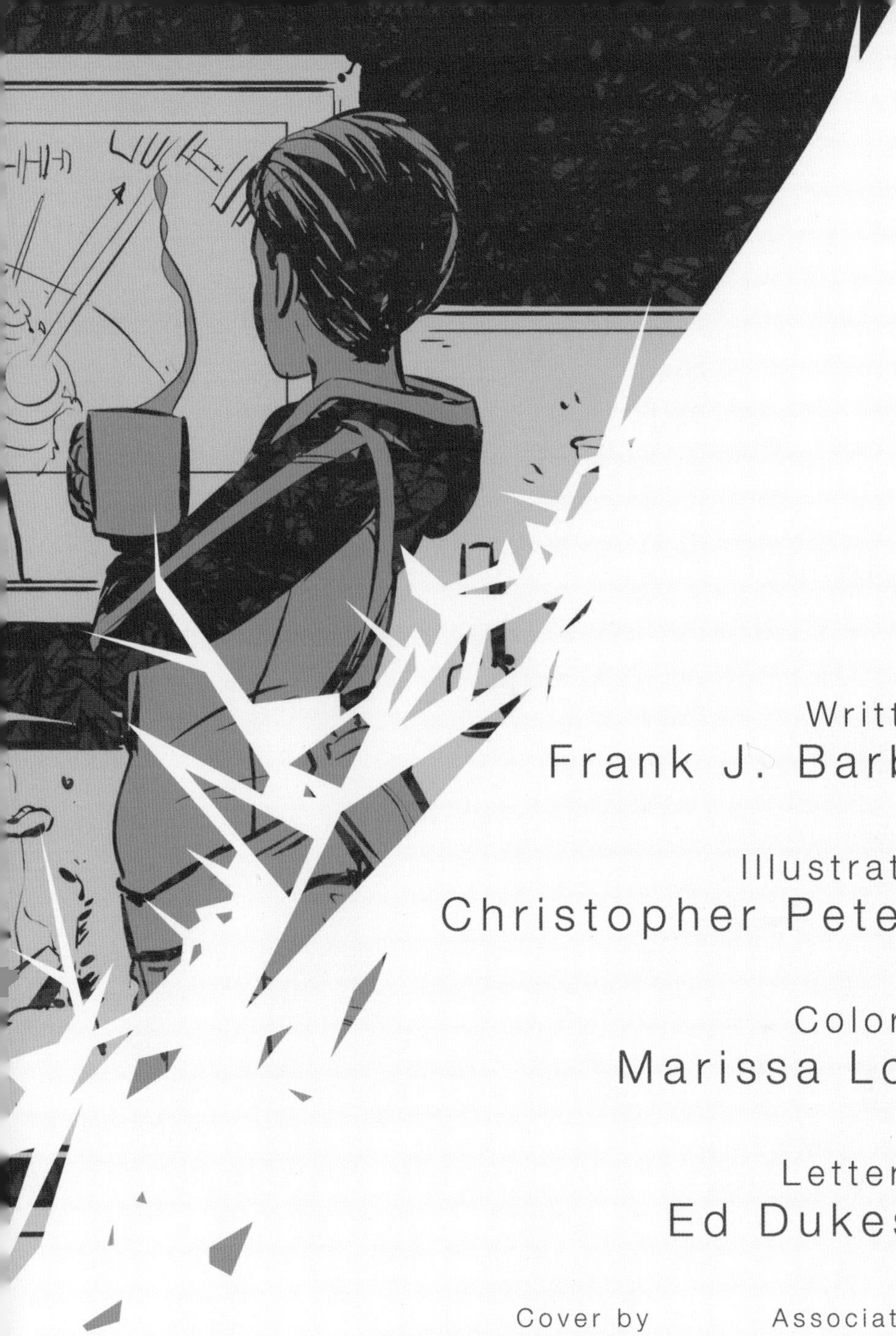

Written by
Frank J. Barbiere

Illustrated by
Christopher Peterson

Colored by
Marissa Louise

Lettered by
Ed Dukeshire

Cover by
Christian Ward

Associate Editor
Chris Rosa

Designer
Scott Newman

Editor
Eric Harburn

BROKEN WORLD™

Created by Frank J. Barbiere & Christopher Peterson

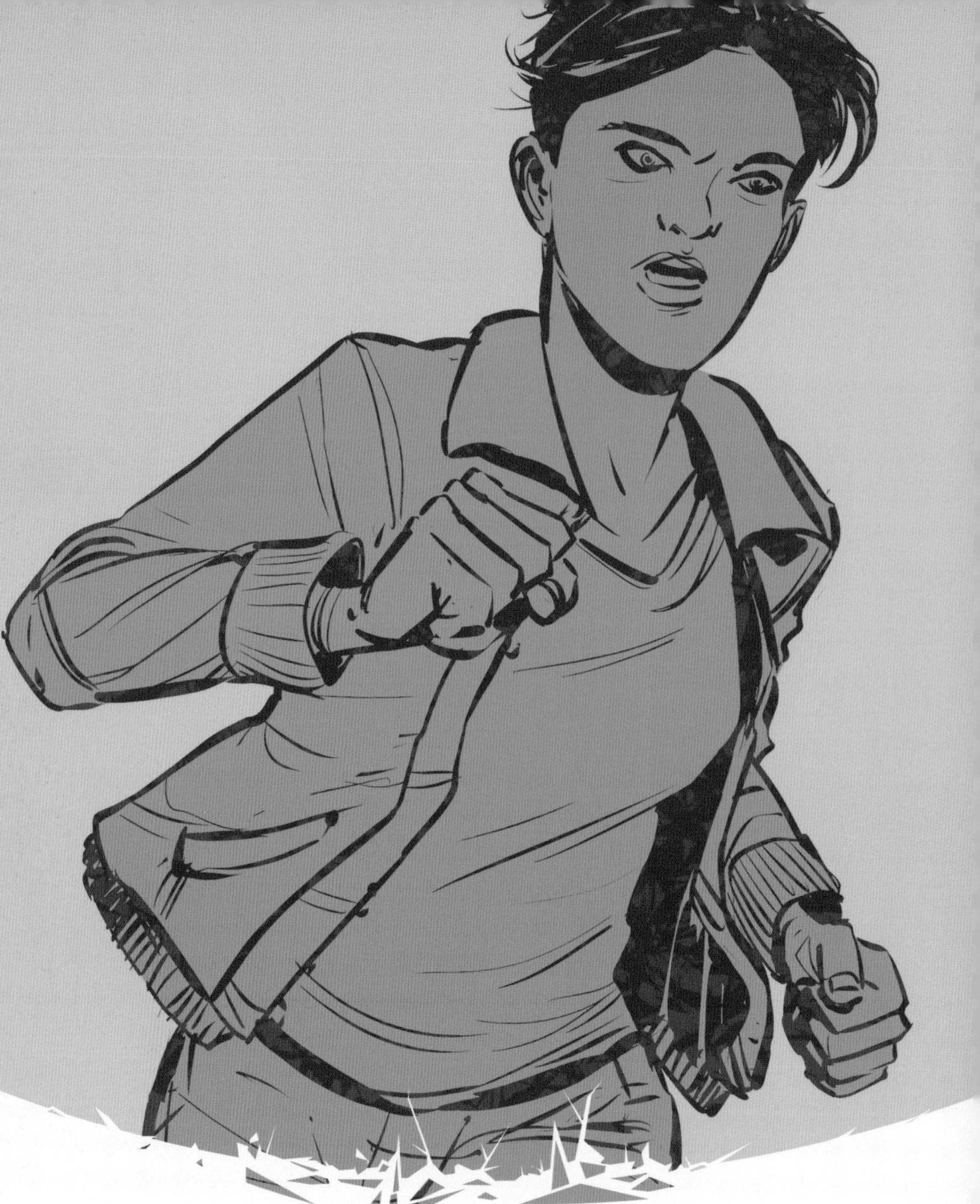

CHAPTER ONE

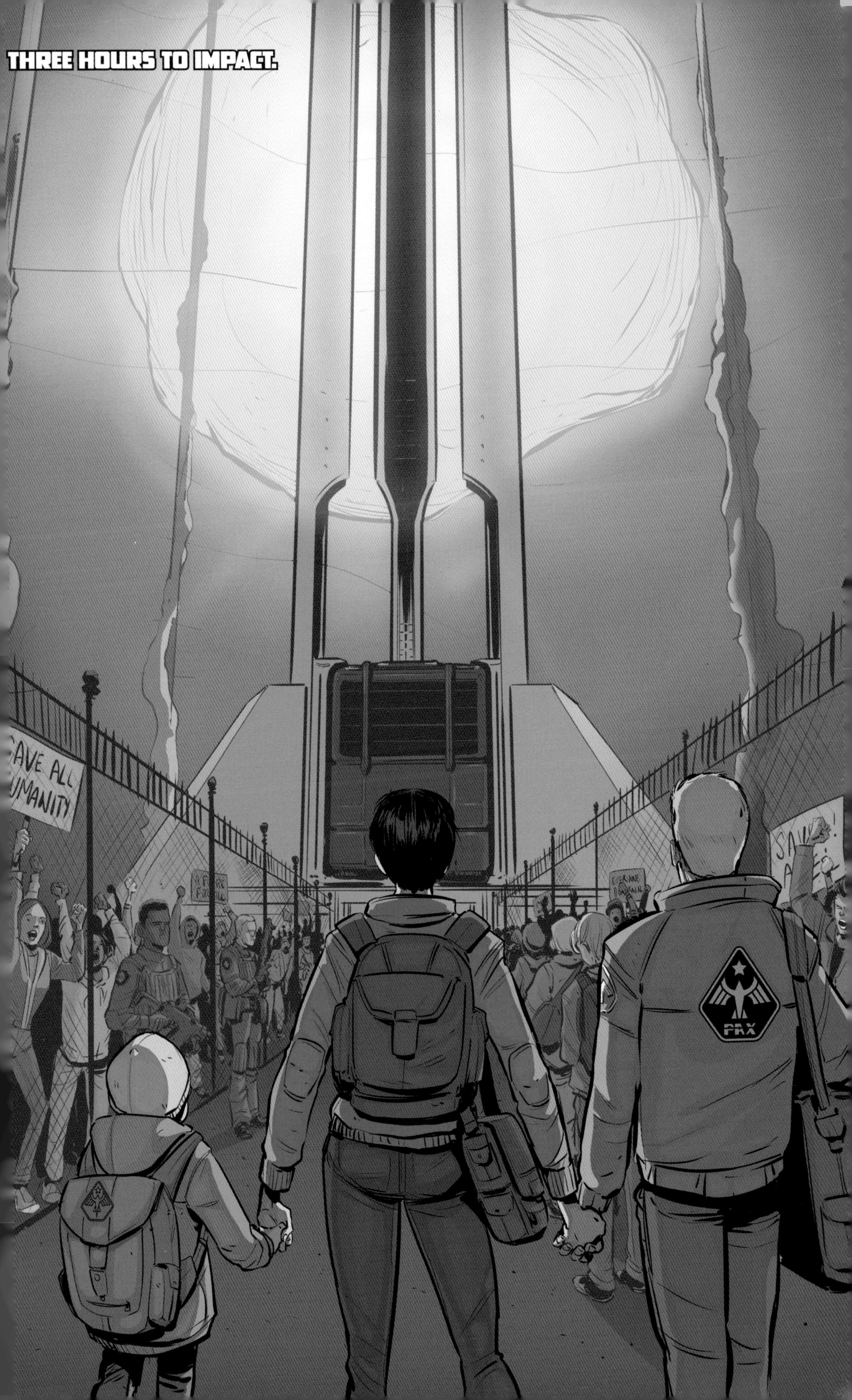
THREE HOURS TO IMPACT.
PRX

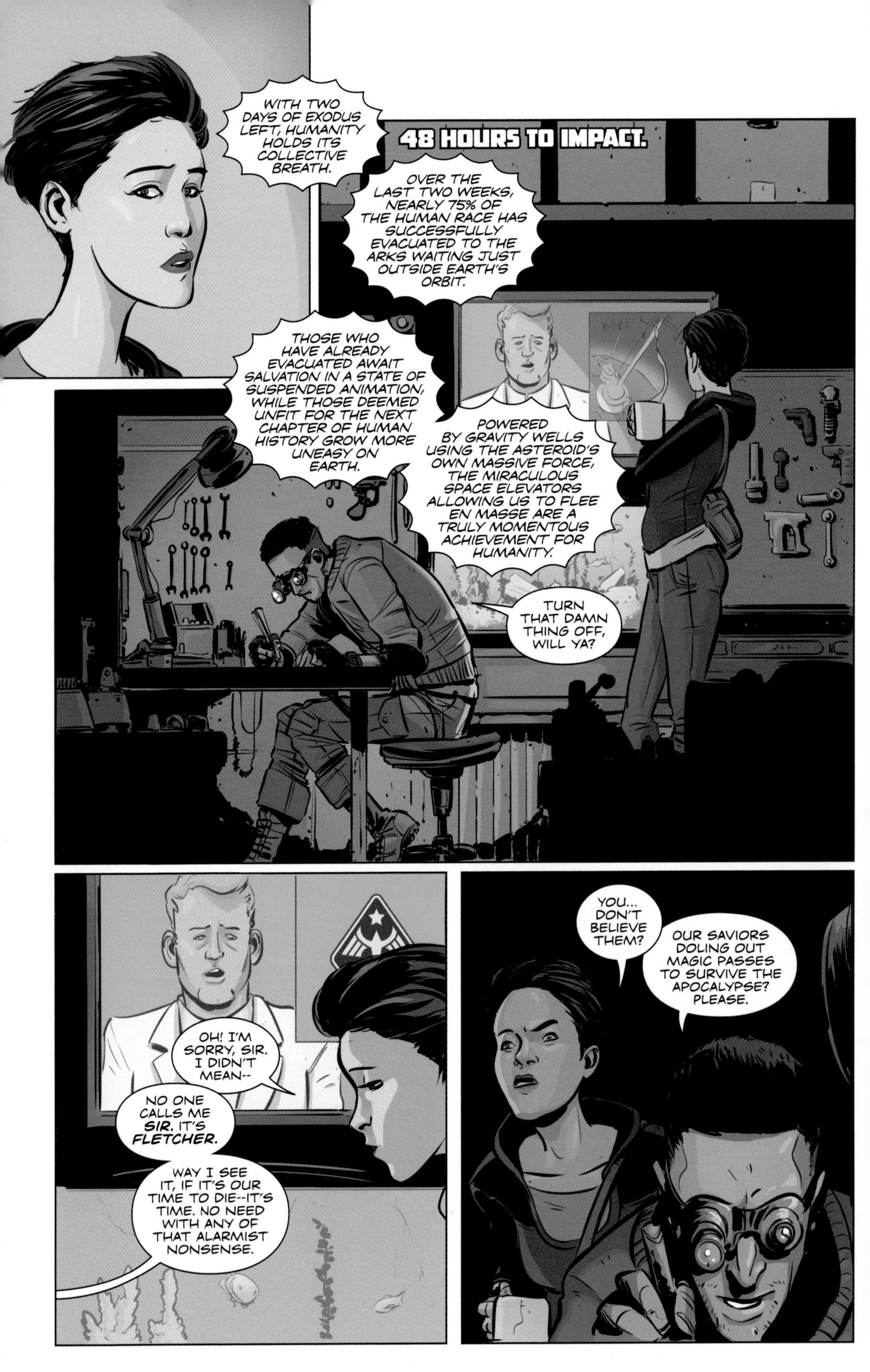

WITH TWO DAYS OF EXODUS LEFT, HUMANITY HOLDS ITS COLLECTIVE BREATH.
48 HOURS TO IMPACT.
OVER THE LAST TWO WEEKS, NEARLY 75% OF THE HUMAN RACE HAS SUCCESSFULLY EVACUATED TO THE ARKS WAITING JUST OUTSIDE EARTH'S ORBIT.
THOSE WHO HAVE ALREADY EVACUATED AWAIT SALVATION IN A STATE OF SUSPENDED ANIMATION, WHILE THOSE DEEMED UNFIT FOR THE NEXT CHAPTER OF HUMAN HISTORY GROW MORE UNEASY ON EARTH.
POWERED BY GRAVITY WELLS USING THE ASTEROID'S OWN MASSIVE FORCE, THE MIRACULOUS SPACE ELEVATORS ALLOWING US TO FLEE EN MASSE ARE A TRULY MOMENTOUS ACHIEVEMENT FOR HUMANITY.
TURN THAT DAMN THING OFF, WILL YA?
OH! I'M SORRY, SIR. I DIDN'T MEAN--
NO ONE CALLS ME SIR. IT'S FLETCHER.
WAY I SEE IT, IF IT'S OUR TIME TO DIE--IT'S TIME. NO NEED WITH ANY OF THAT ALARMIST NONSENSE.
YOU... DON'T BELIEVE THEM?
OUR SAVIORS DOLING OUT MAGIC PASSES TO SURVIVE THE APOCALYPSE? PLEASE.

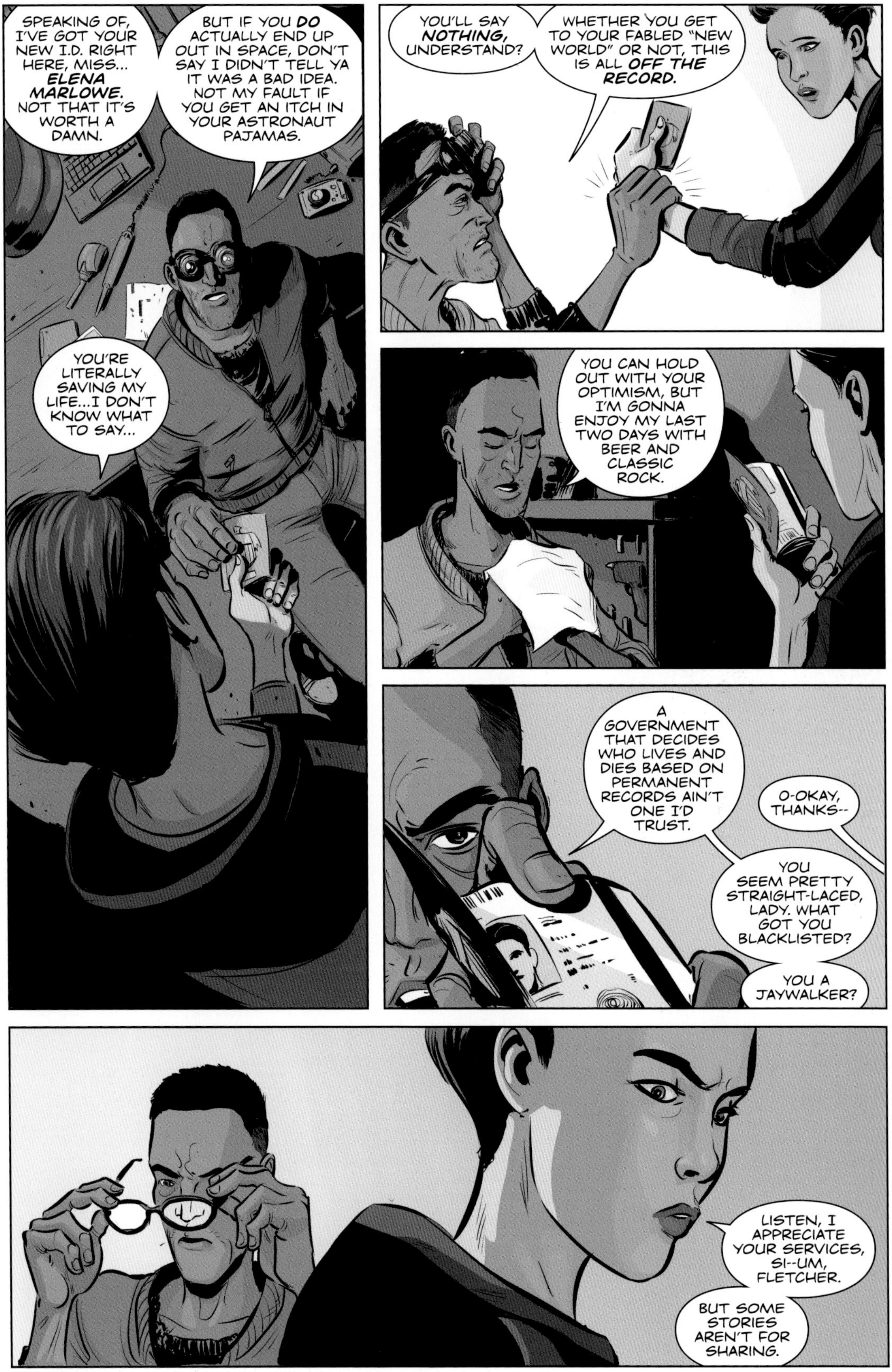
SPEAKING OF, I'VE GOT YOUR NEW I.D. RIGHT HERE, MISS... ELENA MARLOWE. NOT THAT IT'S WORTH A DAMN.
BUT IF YOU DO ACTUALLY END UP OUT IN SPACE, DON'T SAY I DIDN'T TELL YA IT WAS A BAD IDEA. NOT MY FAULT IF YOU GET AN ITCH IN YOUR ASTRONAUT PAJAMAS.
YOU'RE LITERALLY SAVING MY LIFE...I DON'T KNOW WHAT TO SAY...
YOU'LL SAY NOTHING, UNDERSTAND?
WHETHER YOU GET TO YOUR FABLED "NEW WORLD" OR NOT, THIS IS ALL OFF THE RECORD.
YOU CAN HOLD OUT WITH YOUR OPTIMISM, BUT I'M GONNA ENJOY MY LAST TWO DAYS WITH BEER AND CLASSIC ROCK.
A GOVERNMENT THAT DECIDES WHO LIVES AND DIES BASED ON PERMANENT RECORDS AIN'T ONE I'D TRUST.
O-OKAY, THANKS--
YOU SEEM PRETTY STRAIGHT-LACED, LADY. WHAT GOT YOU BLACKLISTED?
YOU A JAYWALKER?
LISTEN, I APPRECIATE YOUR SERVICES, SI--UM, FLETCHER.
BUT SOME STORIES AREN'T FOR SHARING.

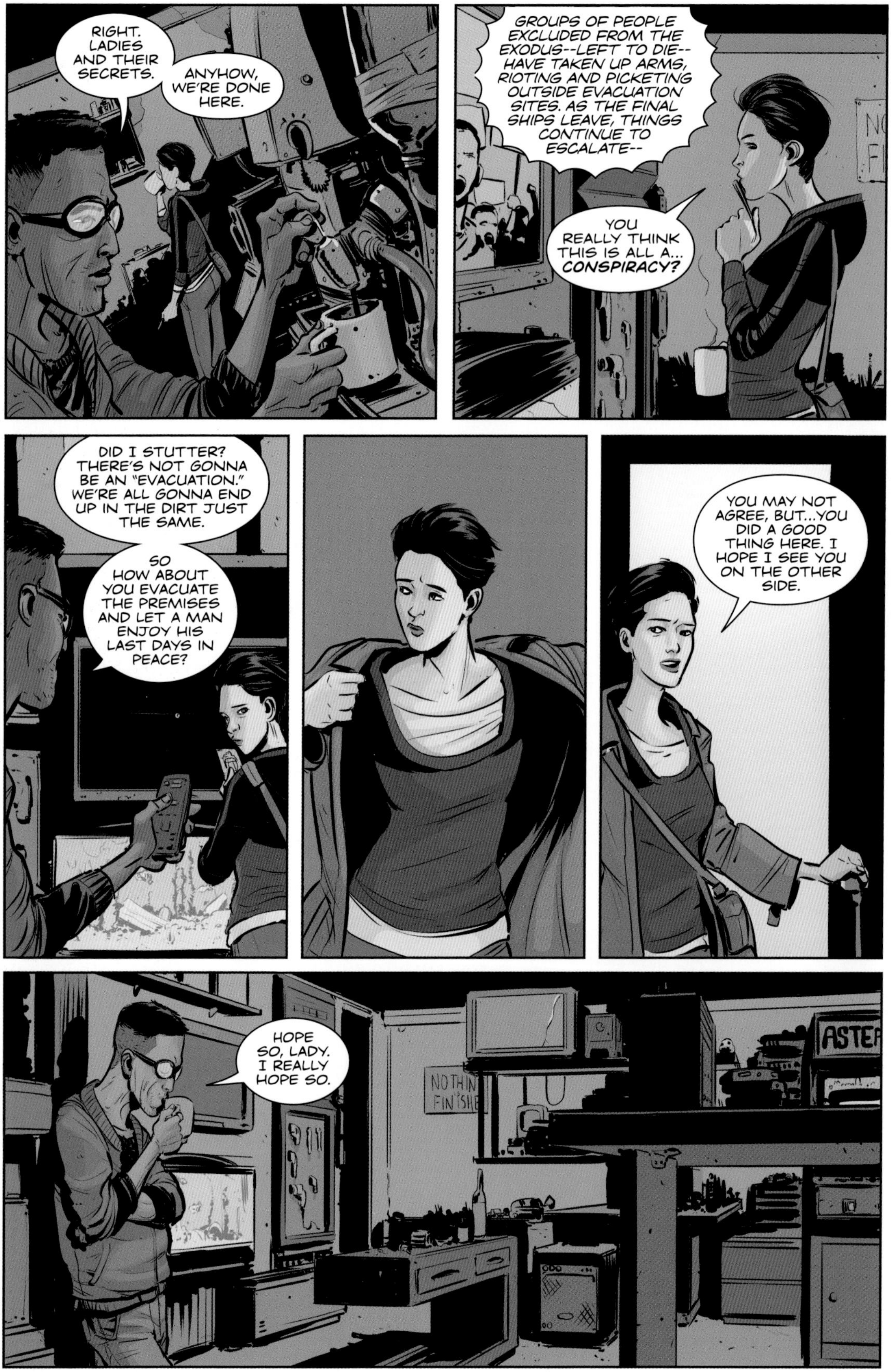
RIGHT. LADIES AND THEIR SECRETS.
ANYHOW, WE'RE DONE HERE.
GROUPS OF PEOPLE EXCLUDED FROM THE EXODUS--LEFT TO DIE--HAVE TAKEN UP ARMS, RIOTING AND PICKETING OUTSIDE EVACUATION SITES. AS THE FINAL SHIPS LEAVE, THINGS CONTINUE TO ESCALATE--
YOU REALLY THINK THIS IS ALL A... CONSPIRACY?
DID I STUTTER? THERE'S NOT GONNA BE AN "EVACUATION." WE'RE ALL GONNA END UP IN THE DIRT JUST THE SAME.
SO HOW ABOUT YOU EVACUATE THE PREMISES AND LET A MAN ENJOY HIS LAST DAYS IN PEACE?
YOU MAY NOT AGREE, BUT...YOU DID A GOOD THING HERE. I HOPE I SEE YOU ON THE OTHER SIDE.
HOPE SO, LADY. I REALLY HOPE SO.
NOTHIN FIN'ISHE
ASTER

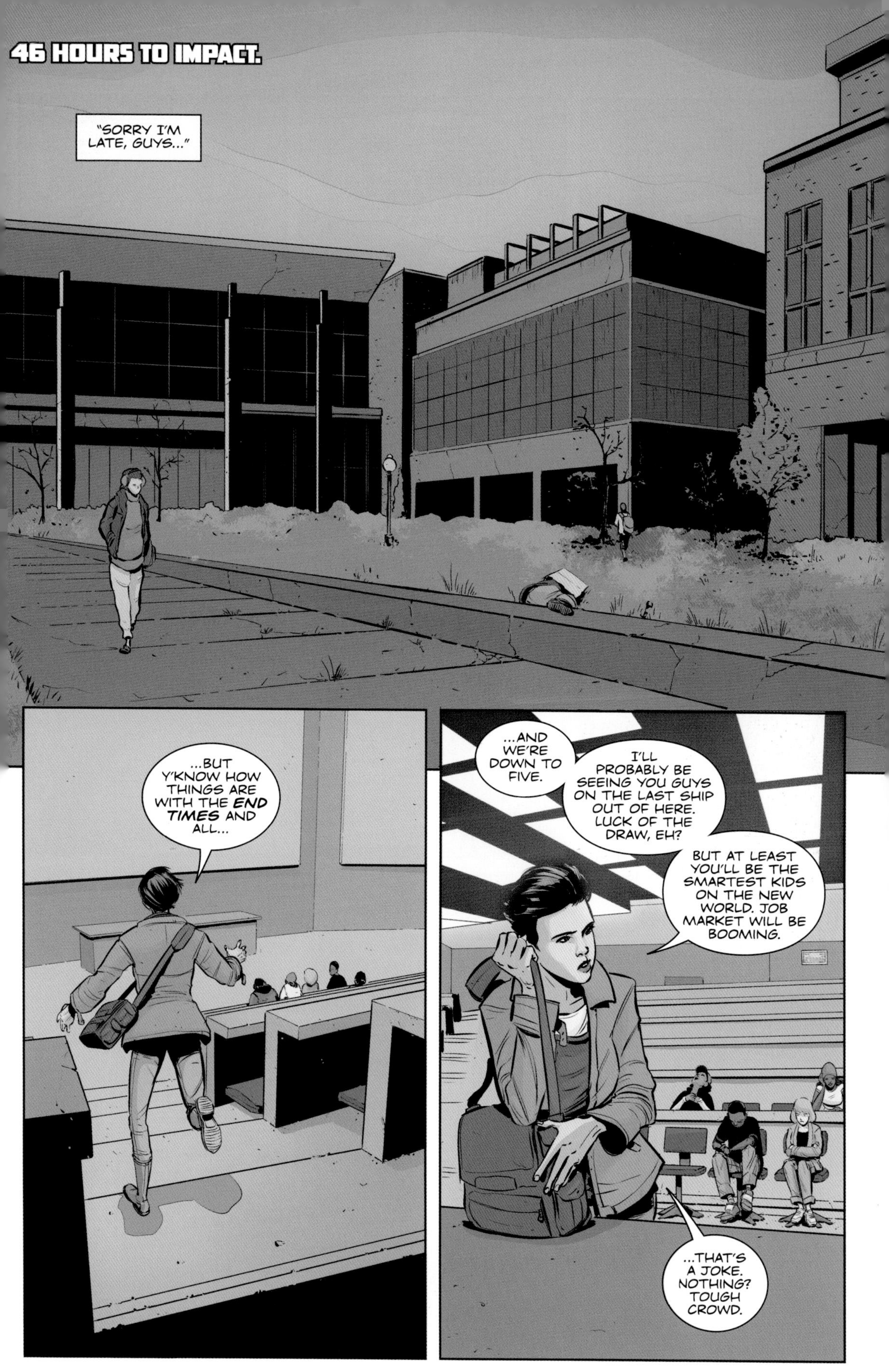
46 HOURS TO IMPACT.
"SORRY I'M LATE, GUYS..."
...BUT Y'KNOW HOW THINGS ARE WITH THE *END TIMES* AND ALL...
...AND WE'RE DOWN TO FIVE.
I'LL PROBABLY BE SEEING YOU GUYS ON THE LAST SHIP OUT OF HERE. LUCK OF THE DRAW, EH?
BUT AT LEAST YOU'LL BE THE SMARTEST KIDS ON THE NEW WORLD. JOB MARKET WILL BE BOOMING.
...THAT'S A JOKE. NOTHING? TOUGH CROWD.

NO OFFENSE, PROFESSOR MARLOWE...BUT A GIANT ASTEROID IS ABOUT TO WIPE OUT MANKIND.

THIS IS THE ONLY PLACE I CAN GO TO HELP GET MY MIND OFF IT.

EMMA'S RIGHT--WE ALL NEED DISTRACTIONS. ANYONE GOT ANYTHING TO PRESENT FOR US? I'VE BEEN LECTURING YOU TO DEATH AND CAN USE A BREATHER.

I'VE GOT SOME STUFF.

PLEASE, ILLUMINATE US.

WHAT'S KICKING AROUND IN YOUR NOGGIN, ROBBY?

WITH THINGS AS CRAZY AS THEY ARE, I'VE BEEN WATCHING AND ANALYZING. WONDERING WHAT'S GOING ON IN PEOPLE'S HEADS.

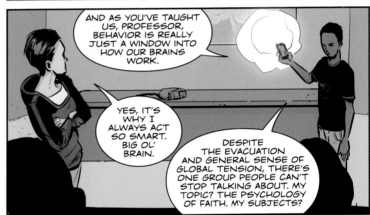

AND AS YOU'VE TAUGHT US, PROFESSOR, BEHAVIOR IS REALLY JUST A WINDOW INTO HOW OUR BRAINS WORK.

YES, IT'S WHY I ALWAYS ACT SO SMART. BIG OL' BRAIN.

DESPITE THE EVACUATION AND GENERAL SENSE OF GLOBAL TENSION, THERE'S ONE GROUP PEOPLE CAN'T STOP TALKING ABOUT. MY TOPIC? THE PSYCHOLOGY OF FAITH. MY SUBJECTS?

THE CHILDREN OF THE REVELATION.

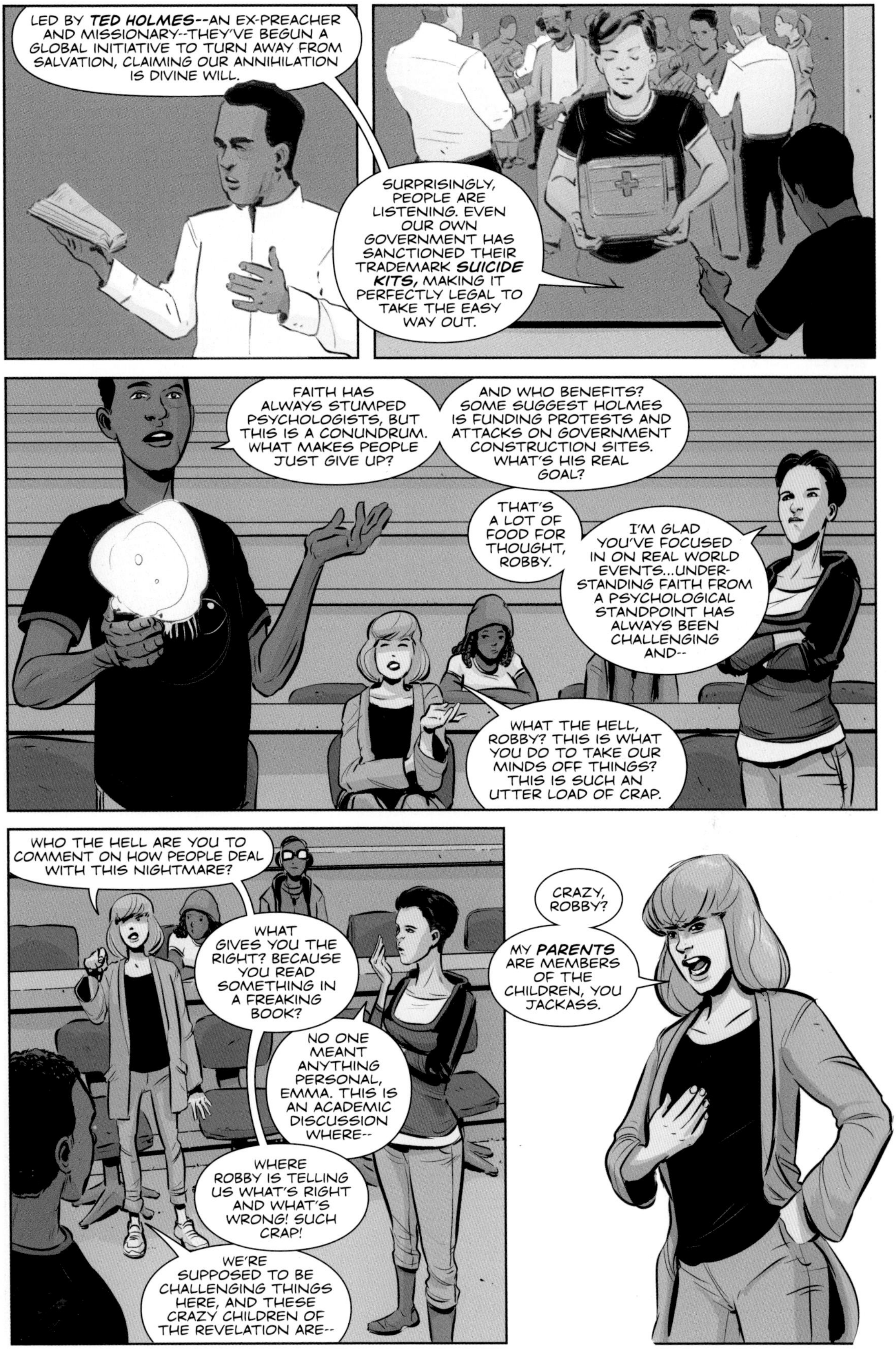
LED BY **TED HOLMES**--AN EX-PREACHER AND MISSIONARY--THEY'VE BEGUN A GLOBAL INITIATIVE TO TURN AWAY FROM SALVATION, CLAIMING OUR ANNIHILATION IS DIVINE WILL.
SURPRISINGLY, PEOPLE ARE LISTENING. EVEN OUR OWN GOVERNMENT HAS SANCTIONED THEIR TRADEMARK **SUICIDE KITS,** MAKING IT PERFECTLY LEGAL TO TAKE THE EASY WAY OUT.
FAITH HAS ALWAYS STUMPED PSYCHOLOGISTS, BUT THIS IS A CONUNDRUM. WHAT MAKES PEOPLE JUST GIVE UP?
AND WHO BENEFITS? SOME SUGGEST HOLMES IS FUNDING PROTESTS AND ATTACKS ON GOVERNMENT CONSTRUCTION SITES. WHAT'S HIS REAL GOAL?
THAT'S A LOT OF FOOD FOR THOUGHT, ROBBY.
I'M GLAD YOU'VE FOCUSED IN ON REAL WORLD EVENTS...UNDER-STANDING FAITH FROM A PSYCHOLOGICAL STANDPOINT HAS ALWAYS BEEN CHALLENGING AND--
WHAT THE HELL, ROBBY? THIS IS WHAT YOU DO TO TAKE OUR MINDS OFF THINGS? THIS IS SUCH AN UTTER LOAD OF CRAP.
WHO THE HELL ARE YOU TO COMMENT ON HOW PEOPLE DEAL WITH THIS NIGHTMARE?
WHAT GIVES YOU THE RIGHT? BECAUSE YOU READ SOMETHING IN A FREAKING BOOK?
NO ONE MEANT ANYTHING PERSONAL, EMMA. THIS IS AN ACADEMIC DISCUSSION WHERE--
WHERE ROBBY IS TELLING US WHAT'S RIGHT AND WHAT'S WRONG! SUCH CRAP!
WE'RE SUPPOSED TO BE CHALLENGING THINGS HERE, AND THESE CRAZY CHILDREN OF THE REVELATION ARE--
CRAZY, ROBBY?
MY **PARENTS** ARE MEMBERS OF THE CHILDREN, YOU JACKASS.

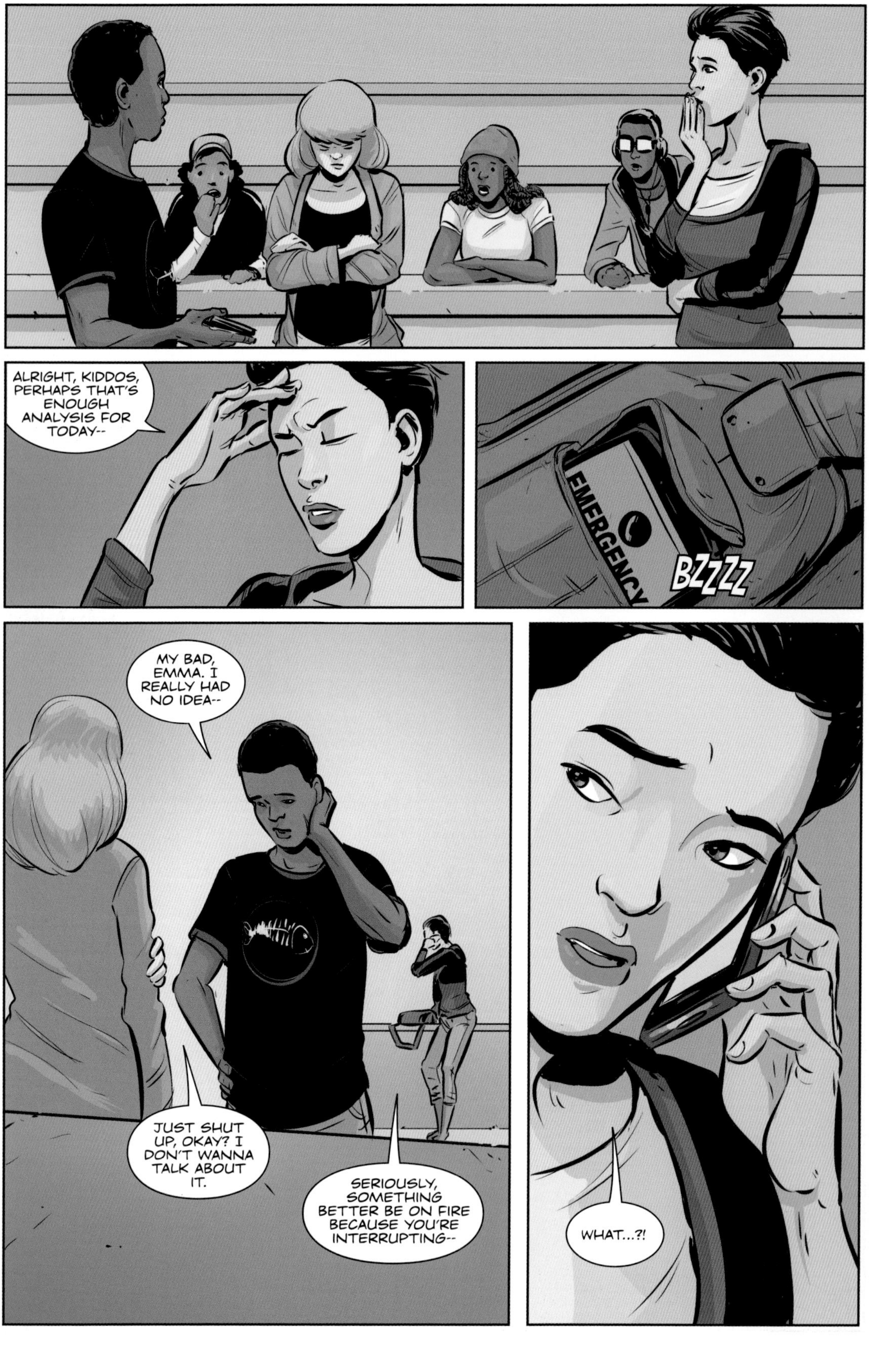

ALRIGHT, KIDDOS, PERHAPS THAT'S ENOUGH ANALYSIS FOR TODAY--
EMERGENCY
BZZZZ
MY BAD, EMMA. I REALLY HAD NO IDEA--
JUST SHUT UP, OKAY? I DON'T WANNA TALK ABOUT IT.
SERIOUSLY, SOMETHING BETTER BE ON FIRE BECAUSE YOU'RE INTERRUPTING--
WHAT...?!

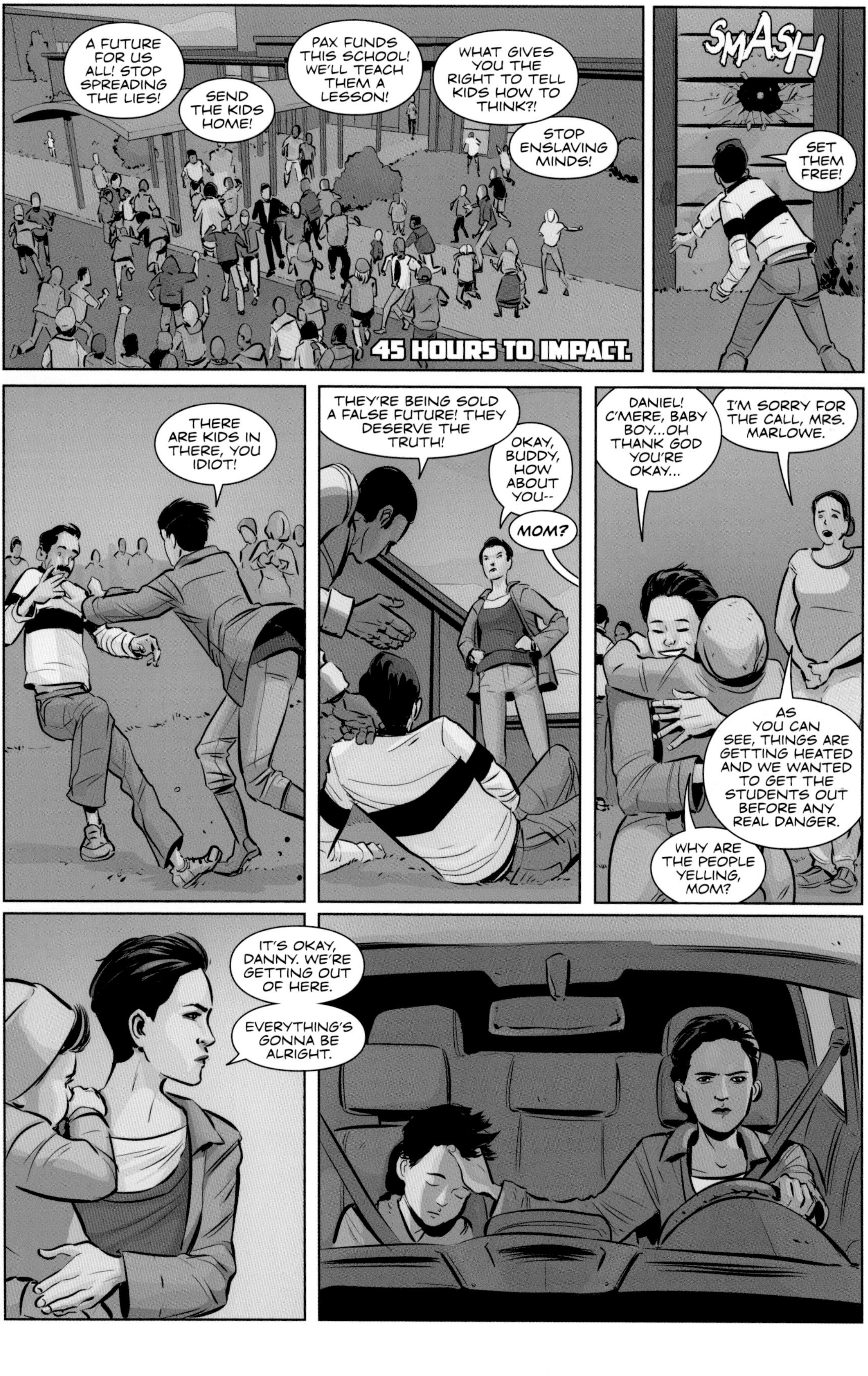
A FUTURE FOR US ALL! STOP SPREADING THE LIES!
SEND THE KIDS HOME!
PAX FUNDS THIS SCHOOL! WE'LL TEACH THEM A LESSON!
WHAT GIVES YOU THE RIGHT TO TELL KIDS HOW TO THINK?!
STOP ENSLAVING MINDS!
45 HOURS TO IMPACT.
SMASH
SET THEM FREE!
THERE ARE KIDS IN THERE, YOU IDIOT!
THEY'RE BEING SOLD A FALSE FUTURE! THEY DESERVE THE TRUTH!
OKAY, BUDDY, HOW ABOUT YOU--
MOM?
DANIEL! C'MERE, BABY BOY...OH THANK GOD YOU'RE OKAY...
I'M SORRY FOR THE CALL, MRS. MARLOWE.
AS YOU CAN SEE, THINGS ARE GETTING HEATED AND WE WANTED TO GET THE STUDENTS OUT BEFORE ANY REAL DANGER.
WHY ARE THE PEOPLE YELLING, MOM?
IT'S OKAY, DANNY. WE'RE GETTING OUT OF HERE.
EVERYTHING'S GONNA BE ALRIGHT.

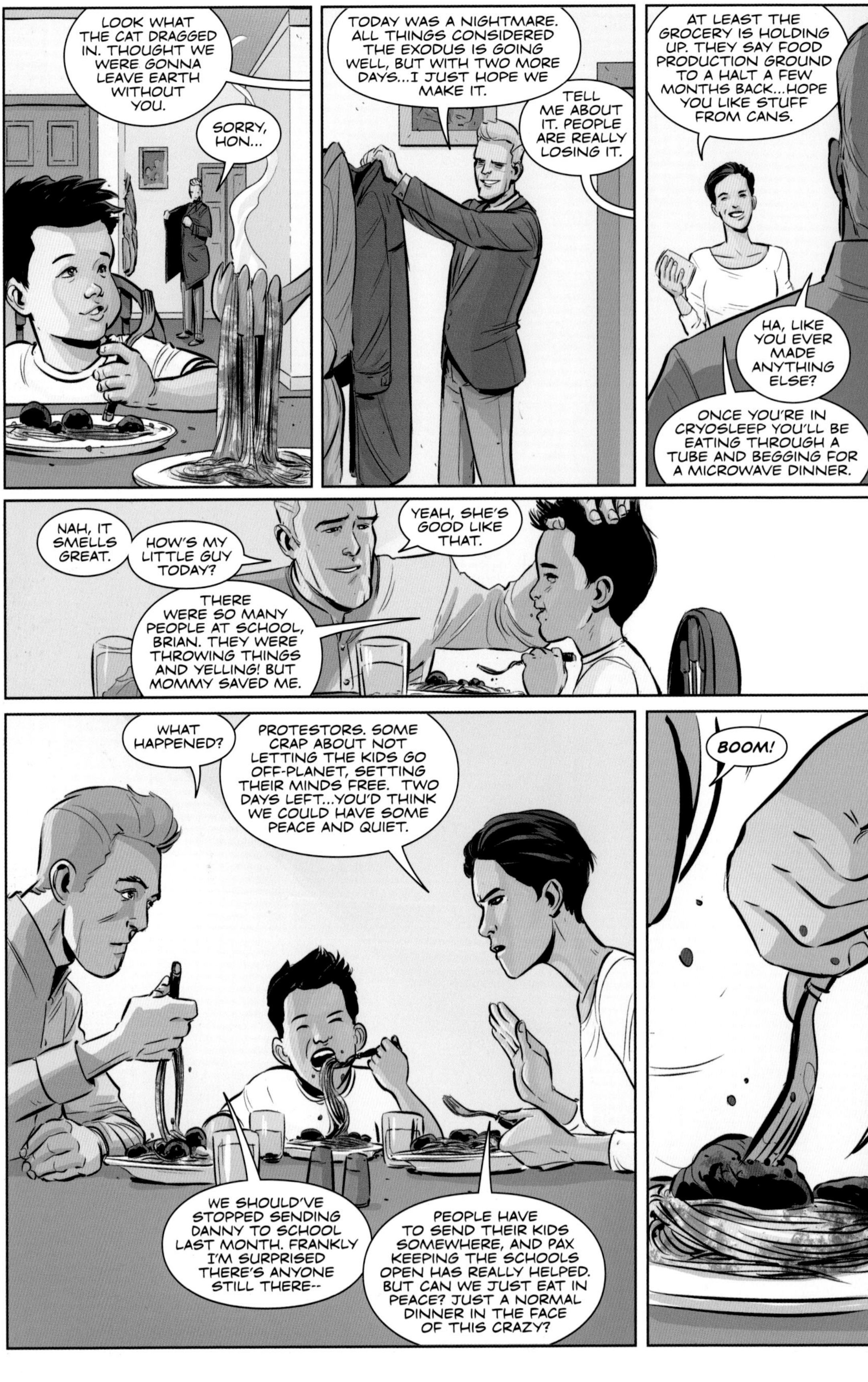
LOOK WHAT THE CAT DRAGGED IN. THOUGHT WE WERE GONNA LEAVE EARTH WITHOUT YOU.
SORRY, HON...
TODAY WAS A NIGHTMARE. ALL THINGS CONSIDERED THE EXODUS IS GOING WELL, BUT WITH TWO MORE DAYS...I JUST HOPE WE MAKE IT.
TELL ME ABOUT IT. PEOPLE ARE REALLY LOSING IT.
AT LEAST THE GROCERY IS HOLDING UP. THEY SAY FOOD PRODUCTION GROUND TO A HALT A FEW MONTHS BACK...HOPE YOU LIKE STUFF FROM CANS.
HA, LIKE YOU EVER MADE ANYTHING ELSE?
ONCE YOU'RE IN CRYOSLEEP YOU'LL BE EATING THROUGH A TUBE AND BEGGING FOR A MICROWAVE DINNER.
NAH, IT SMELLS GREAT.
HOW'S MY LITTLE GUY TODAY?
YEAH, SHE'S GOOD LIKE THAT.
THERE WERE SO MANY PEOPLE AT SCHOOL, BRIAN. THEY WERE THROWING THINGS AND YELLING! BUT MOMMY SAVED ME.
WHAT HAPPENED?
PROTESTORS. SOME CRAP ABOUT NOT LETTING THE KIDS GO OFF-PLANET, SETTING THEIR MINDS FREE. TWO DAYS LEFT...YOU'D THINK WE COULD HAVE SOME PEACE AND QUIET.
WE SHOULD'VE STOPPED SENDING DANNY TO SCHOOL LAST MONTH. FRANKLY I'M SURPRISED THERE'S ANYONE STILL THERE--
PEOPLE HAVE TO SEND THEIR KIDS SOMEWHERE, AND PAX KEEPING THE SCHOOLS OPEN HAS REALLY HELPED. BUT CAN WE JUST EAT IN PEACE? JUST A NORMAL DINNER IN THE FACE OF THIS CRAZY?
BOOM!

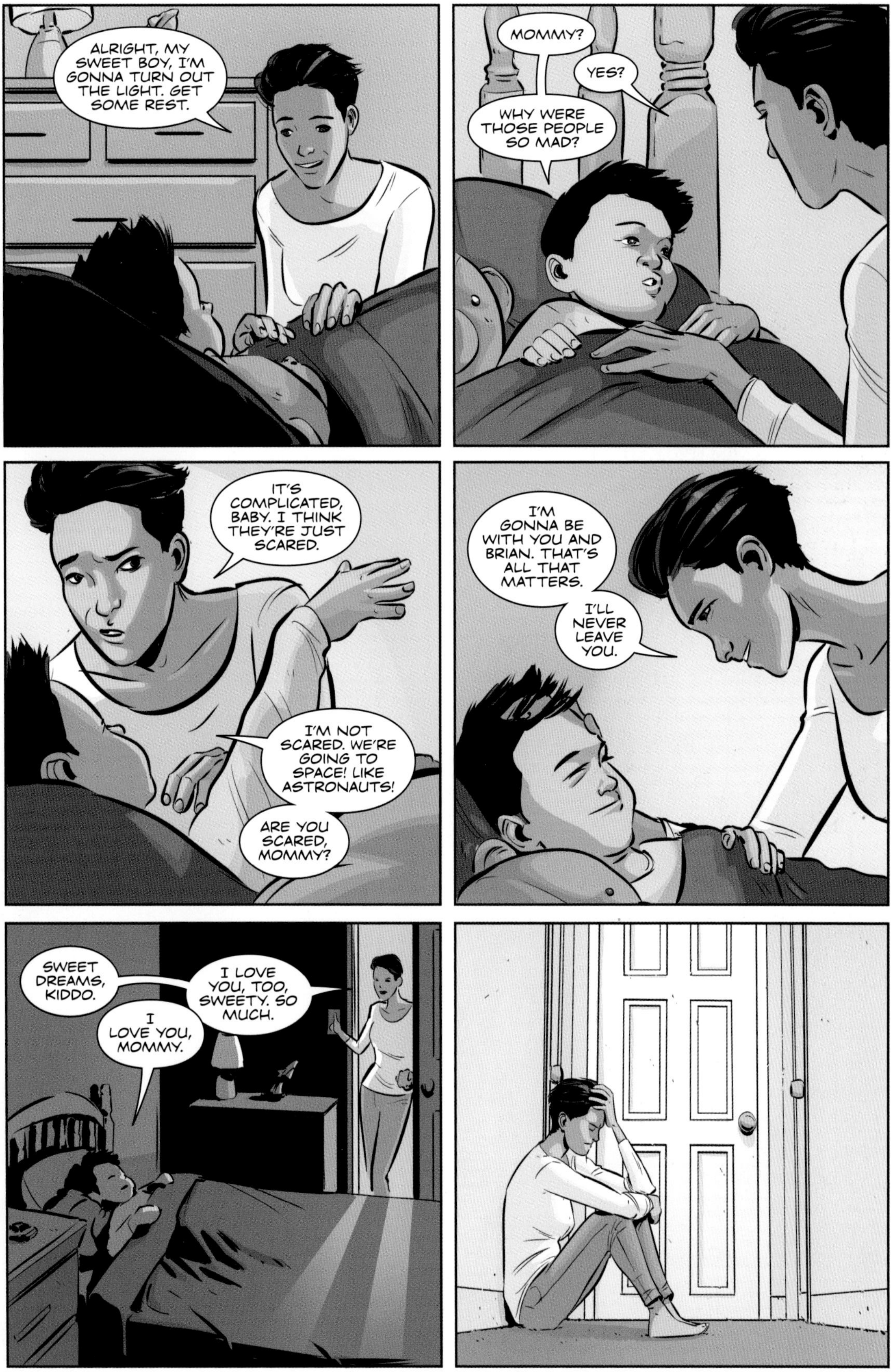

ALRIGHT, MY SWEET BOY, I'M GONNA TURN OUT THE LIGHT. GET SOME REST.
MOMMY?
YES?
WHY WERE THOSE PEOPLE SO MAD?
IT'S COMPLICATED, BABY. I THINK THEY'RE JUST SCARED.
I'M NOT SCARED. WE'RE GOING TO SPACE! LIKE ASTRONAUTS!
ARE YOU SCARED, MOMMY?
I'M GONNA BE WITH YOU AND BRIAN. THAT'S ALL THAT MATTERS.
I'LL NEVER LEAVE YOU.
SWEET DREAMS, KIDDO.
I LOVE YOU, MOMMY.
I LOVE YOU, TOO, SWEETY. SO MUCH.

FINAL STRETCH. CAN'T BELIEVE WE'RE SAYING GOODBYE TO THE EARTH...

I KNOW IT'S RISKY LEAVING SO LATE IN THE EVACUATION, BUT I HAD TO SEE THIS THROUGH.

YOU'RE A GOOD MAN, BRIAN. PAX NEEDS PEOPLE LIKE YOU, AND THERE'S NO WAY I'D LEAVE WITHOUT YOU BY MY SIDE.

AND HERE WE ARE. HEY, YOU FINALLY GET THAT PAPERWORK SORTED?

OH, YEAH. YEAH, IT'S ALL FINE.

GLAD YOU CAUGHT THE I.D. CHIP **MALFUNCTIONING.** WOULDN'T WANT THEM THINKING YOU WERE SOME KIND OF **CRIMINAL** AT THE EVAC SITE.

HEH...

YOU AND DANNY COMING INTO MY LIFE HAVE MADE ME A BETTER MAN. WE'LL GET THROUGH THIS.

BRIAN...

IT'S BEEN DIFFICULT, BUT I COULDN'T ABANDON MY GUYS BEFORE THE CIVILIANS EVACUATED. THANKS FOR STANDING BY ME.

ALWAYS. YOU AND DANNY ARE EVERYTHING TO ME. BUT...I'M SCARED.

I KNOW, IT'LL ALL BE OKAY--

NOT FOR ME--FOR THE PEOPLE **LEFT BEHIND.** WHAT'S GOING TO HAPPEN--

EVERYONE HAD A CHANCE, BABE. WE ALL GOT THROUGH THE **LOTTERY** FAIR AND SQUARE...

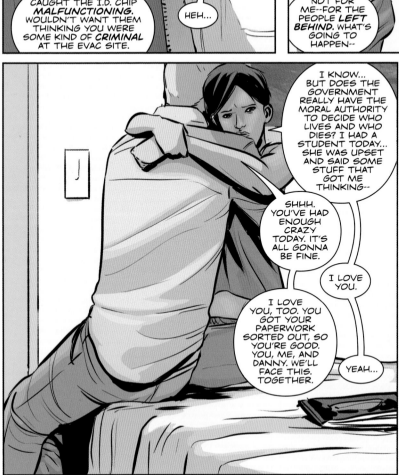

I KNOW... BUT DOES THE GOVERNMENT REALLY HAVE THE MORAL AUTHORITY TO DECIDE WHO LIVES AND WHO DIES? I HAD A STUDENT TODAY... SHE WAS UPSET AND SAID SOME STUFF THAT GOT ME THINKING--

SHHH. YOU'VE HAD ENOUGH CRAZY TODAY. IT'S ALL GONNA BE FINE.

I LOVE YOU.

I LOVE YOU, TOO. YOU GOT YOUR PAPERWORK SORTED OUT, SO YOU'RE GOOD. YOU, ME, AND DANNY. WE'LL FACE THIS. TOGETHER.

YEAH...

PASSPORT

...TOGETHER.

36 HOURS TO IMPACT.

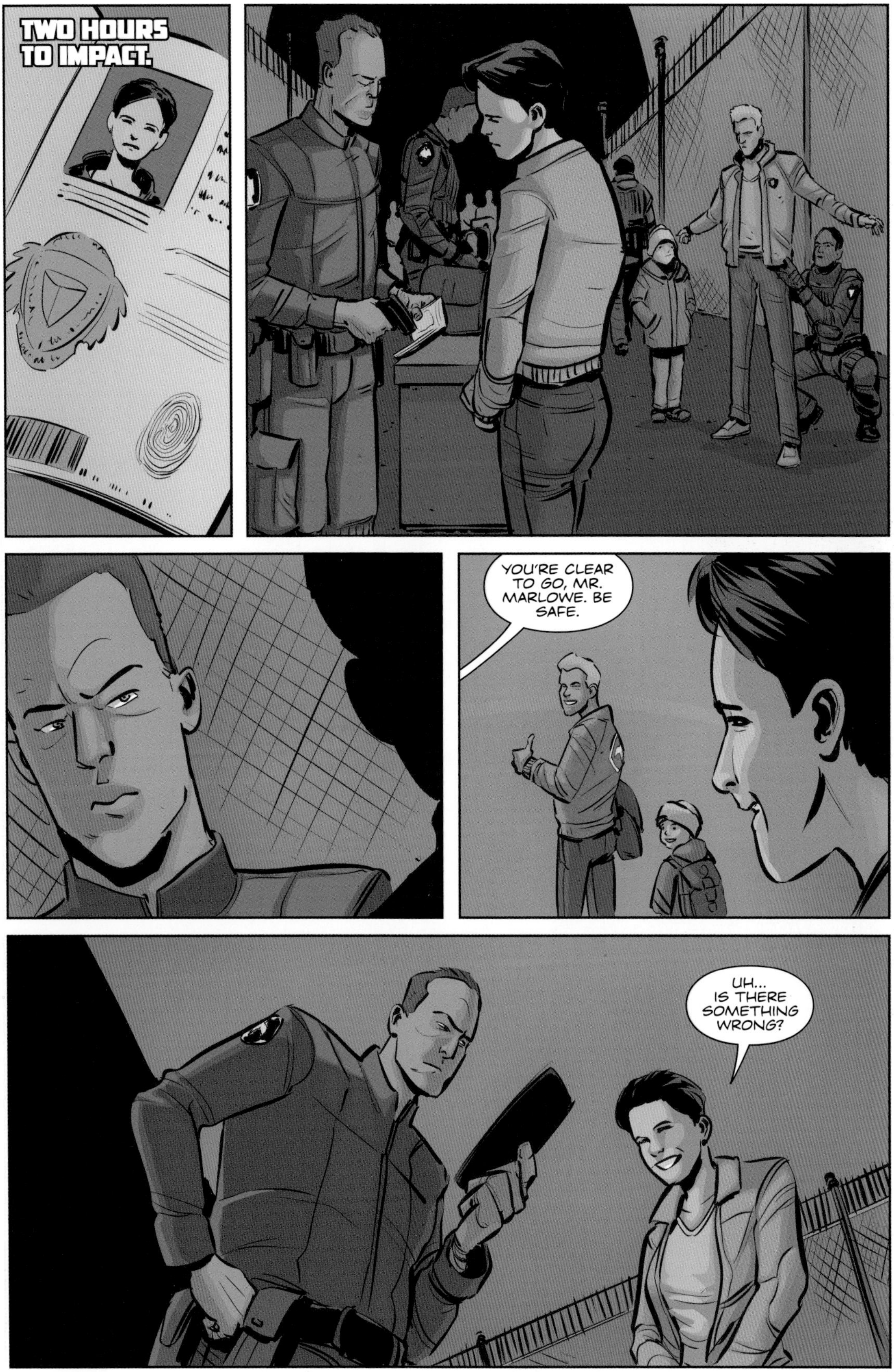
TWO HOURS TO IMPACT.
YOU'RE CLEAR TO GO, MR. MARLOWE. BE SAFE.
UH... IS THERE SOMETHING WRONG?

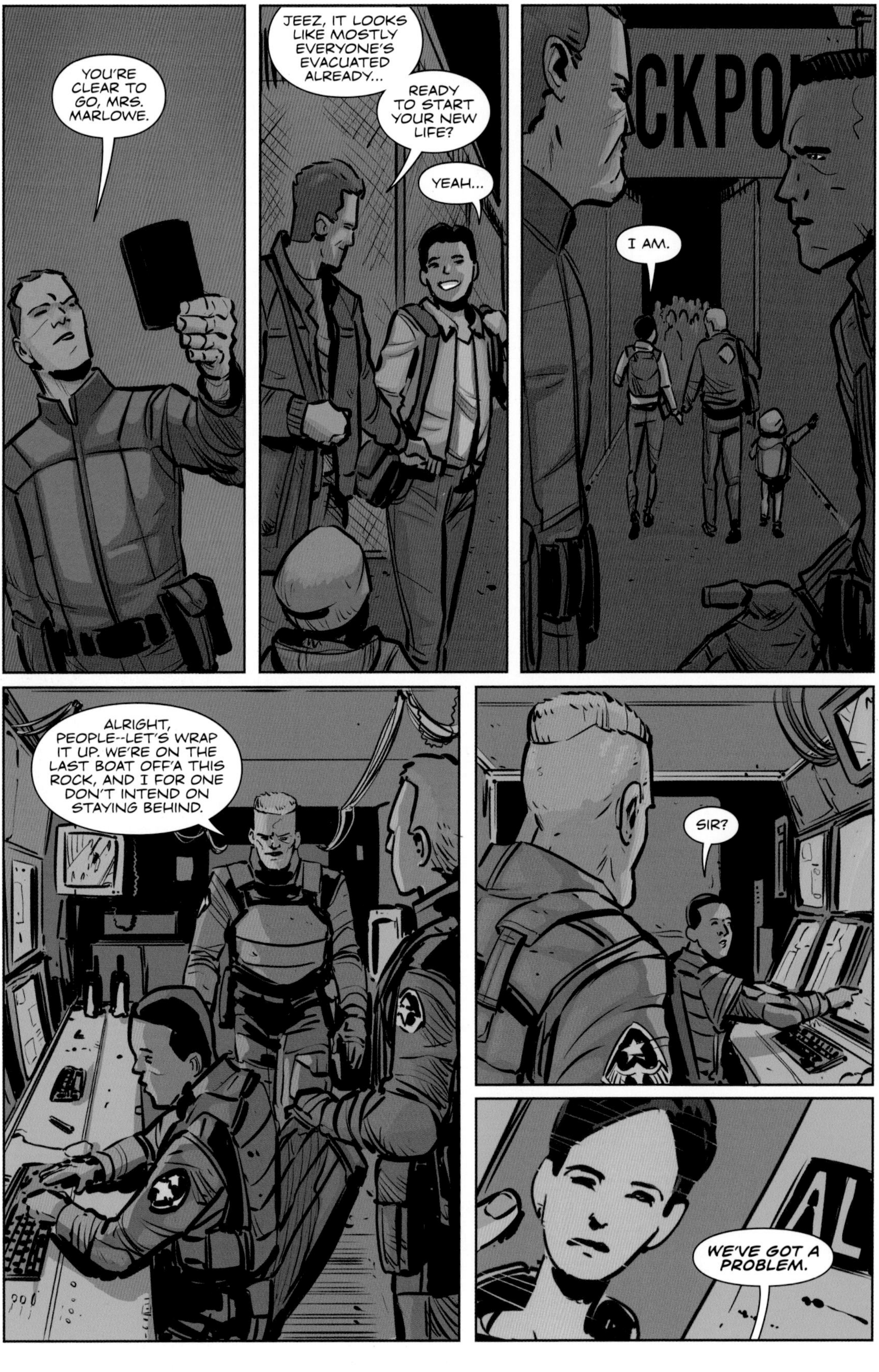
YOU'RE CLEAR TO GO, MRS. MARLOWE.
JEEZ, IT LOOKS LIKE MOSTLY EVERYONE'S EVACUATED ALREADY...
READY TO START YOUR NEW LIFE?
YEAH...
CKPO
I AM.
ALRIGHT, PEOPLE--LET'S WRAP IT UP. WE'RE ON THE LAST BOAT OFF'A THIS ROCK, AND I FOR ONE DON'T INTEND ON STAYING BEHIND.
SIR?
WE'VE GOT A PROBLEM.

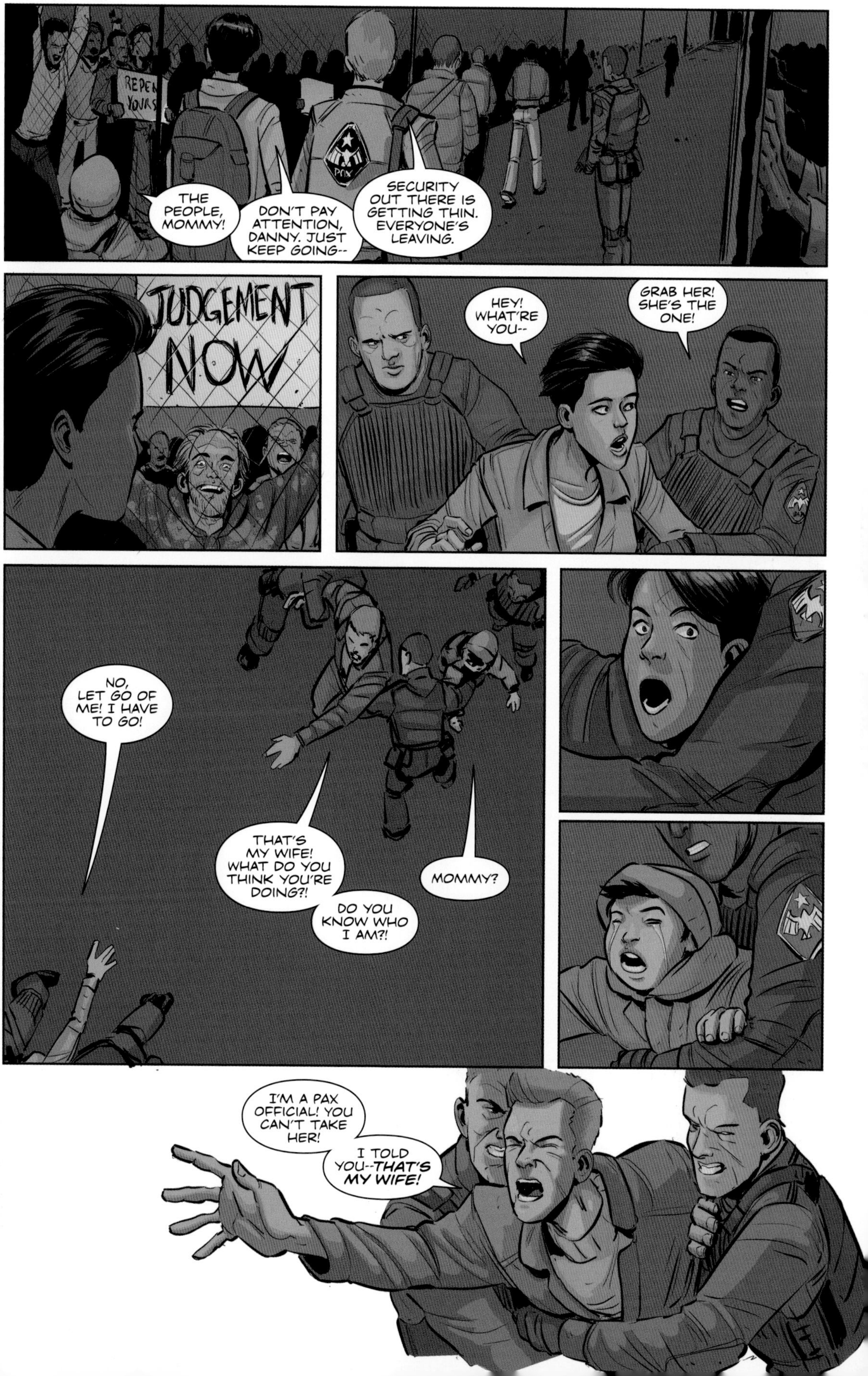
REPEN
YOURS
THE PEOPLE, MOMMY!
DON'T PAY ATTENTION, DANNY. JUST KEEP GOING--
SECURITY OUT THERE IS GETTING THIN. EVERYONE'S LEAVING.
JUDGEMENT NOW
HEY! WHAT'RE YOU--
GRAB HER! SHE'S THE ONE!
NO, LET GO OF ME! I HAVE TO GO!
THAT'S MY WIFE! WHAT DO YOU THINK YOU'RE DOING?!
DO YOU KNOW WHO I AM?!
MOMMY?
I'M A PAX OFFICIAL! YOU CAN'T TAKE HER!
I TOLD YOU--*THAT'S MY WIFE!*

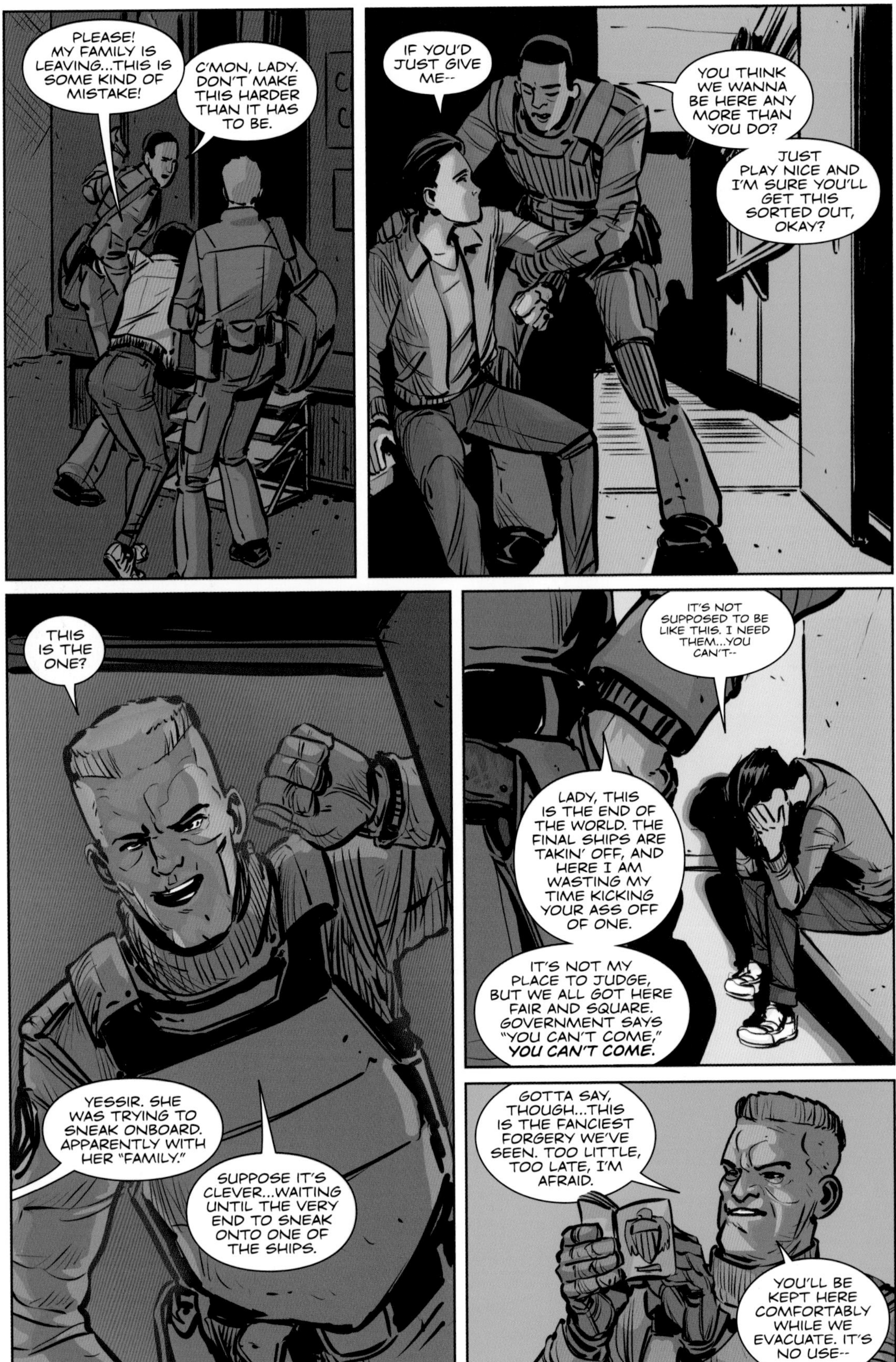
PLEASE! MY FAMILY IS LEAVING...THIS IS SOME KIND OF MISTAKE!
C'MON, LADY. DON'T MAKE THIS HARDER THAN IT HAS TO BE.
IF YOU'D JUST GIVE ME--
YOU THINK WE WANNA BE HERE ANY MORE THAN YOU DO?
JUST PLAY NICE AND I'M SURE YOU'LL GET THIS SORTED OUT, OKAY?
THIS IS THE ONE?
YESSIR. SHE WAS TRYING TO SNEAK ONBOARD. APPARENTLY WITH HER "FAMILY."
SUPPOSE IT'S CLEVER...WAITING UNTIL THE VERY END TO SNEAK ONTO ONE OF THE SHIPS.
IT'S NOT SUPPOSED TO BE LIKE THIS. I NEED THEM...YOU CAN'T--
LADY, THIS IS THE END OF THE WORLD. THE FINAL SHIPS ARE TAKIN' OFF, AND HERE I AM WASTING MY TIME KICKING YOUR ASS OFF OF ONE.
IT'S NOT MY PLACE TO JUDGE, BUT WE ALL GOT HERE FAIR AND SQUARE. GOVERNMENT SAYS "YOU CAN'T COME," ***YOU CAN'T COME.***
GOTTA SAY, THOUGH...THIS IS THE FANCIEST FORGERY WE'VE SEEN. TOO LITTLE, TOO LATE, I'M AFRAID.
YOU'LL BE KEPT HERE COMFORTABLY WHILE WE EVACUATE. IT'S NO USE--

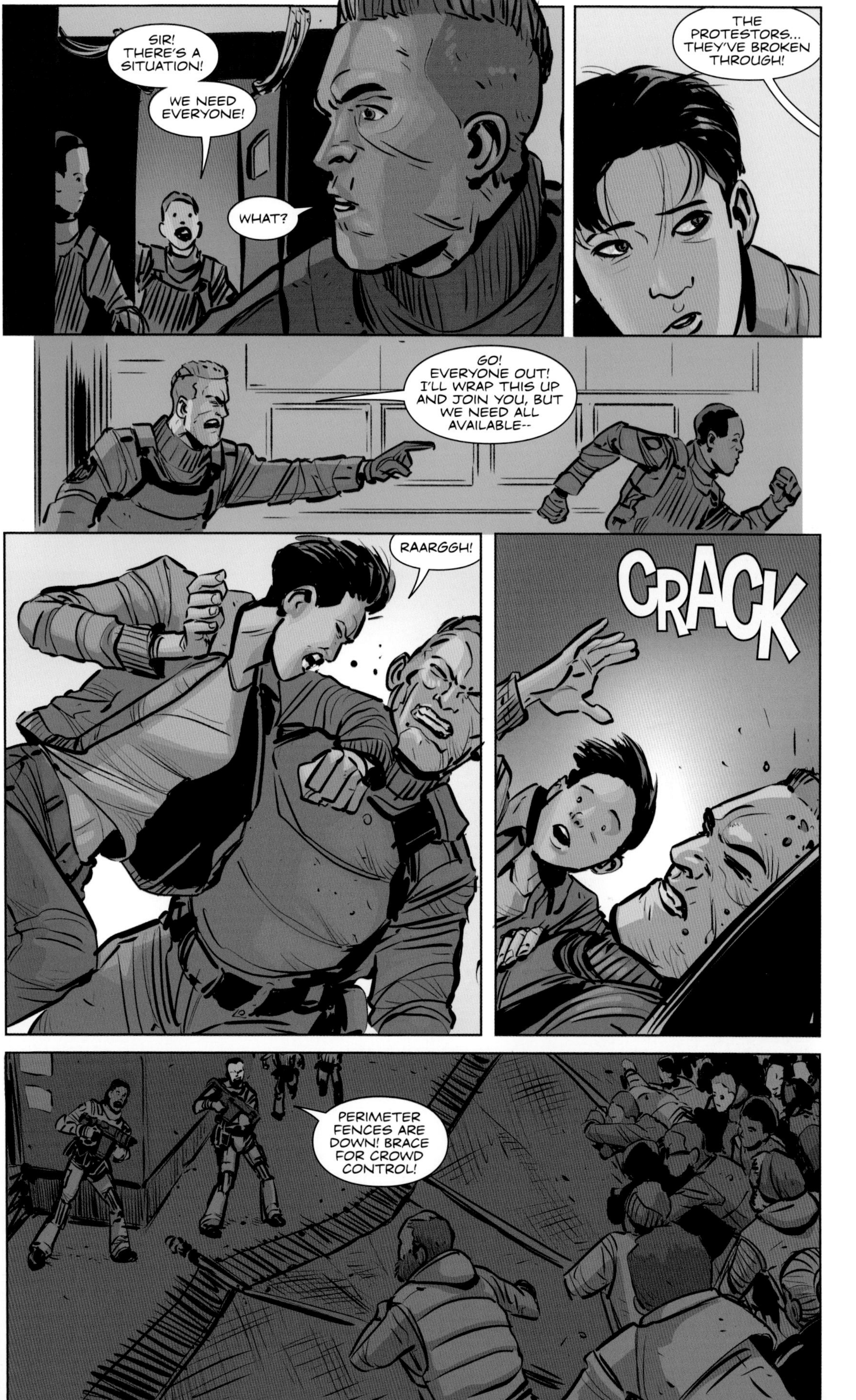
SIR! THERE'S A SITUATION!
WE NEED EVERYONE!
WHAT?
THE PROTESTORS... THEY'VE BROKEN THROUGH!
GO! EVERYONE OUT! I'LL WRAP THIS UP AND JOIN YOU, BUT WE NEED ALL AVAILABLE--
RAARGGH!
CRACK
PERIMETER FENCES ARE DOWN! BRACE FOR CROWD CONTROL!

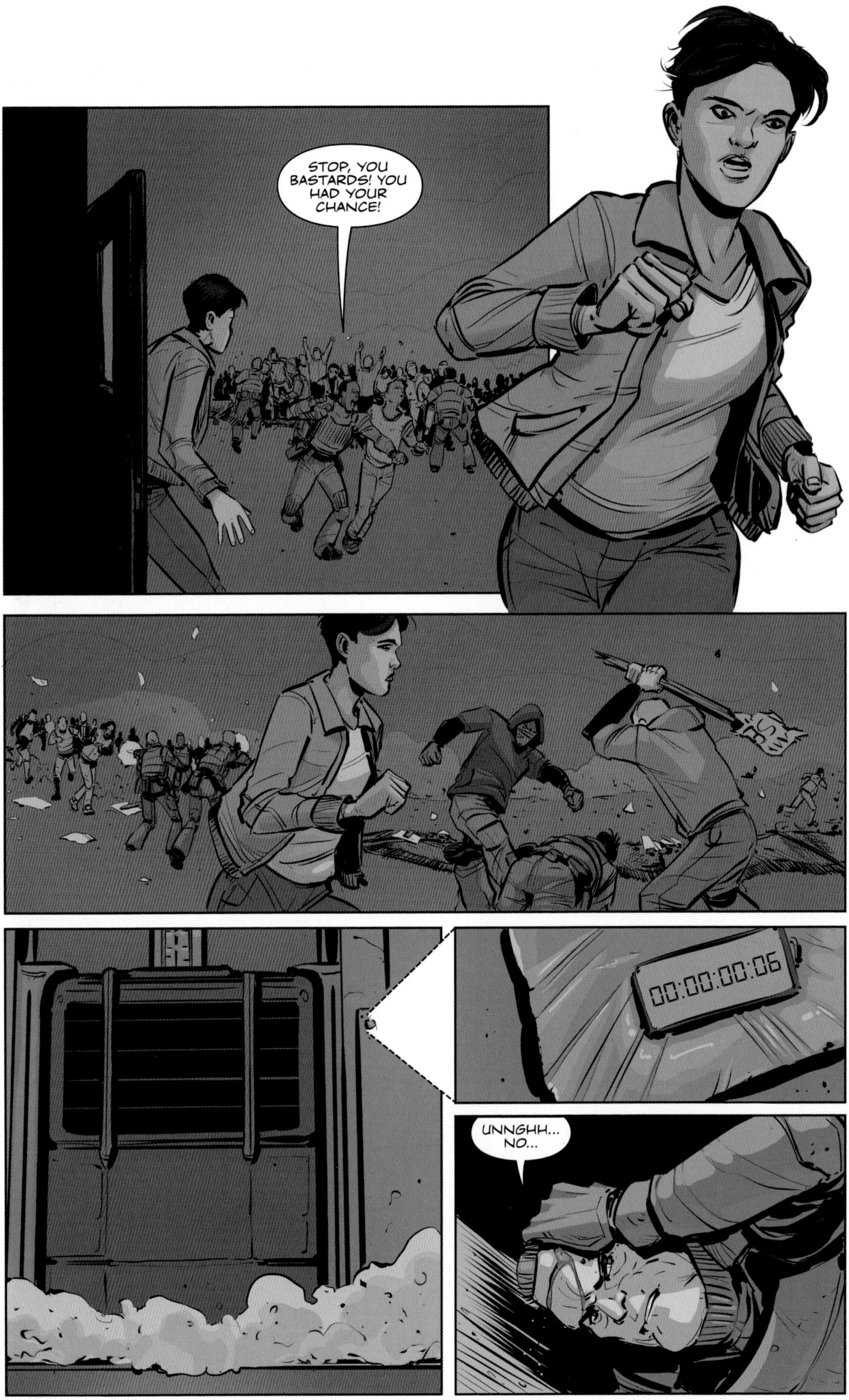
STOP, YOU BASTARDS! YOU HAD YOUR CHANCE!
00:00:00:06
UNNGHH... NO...

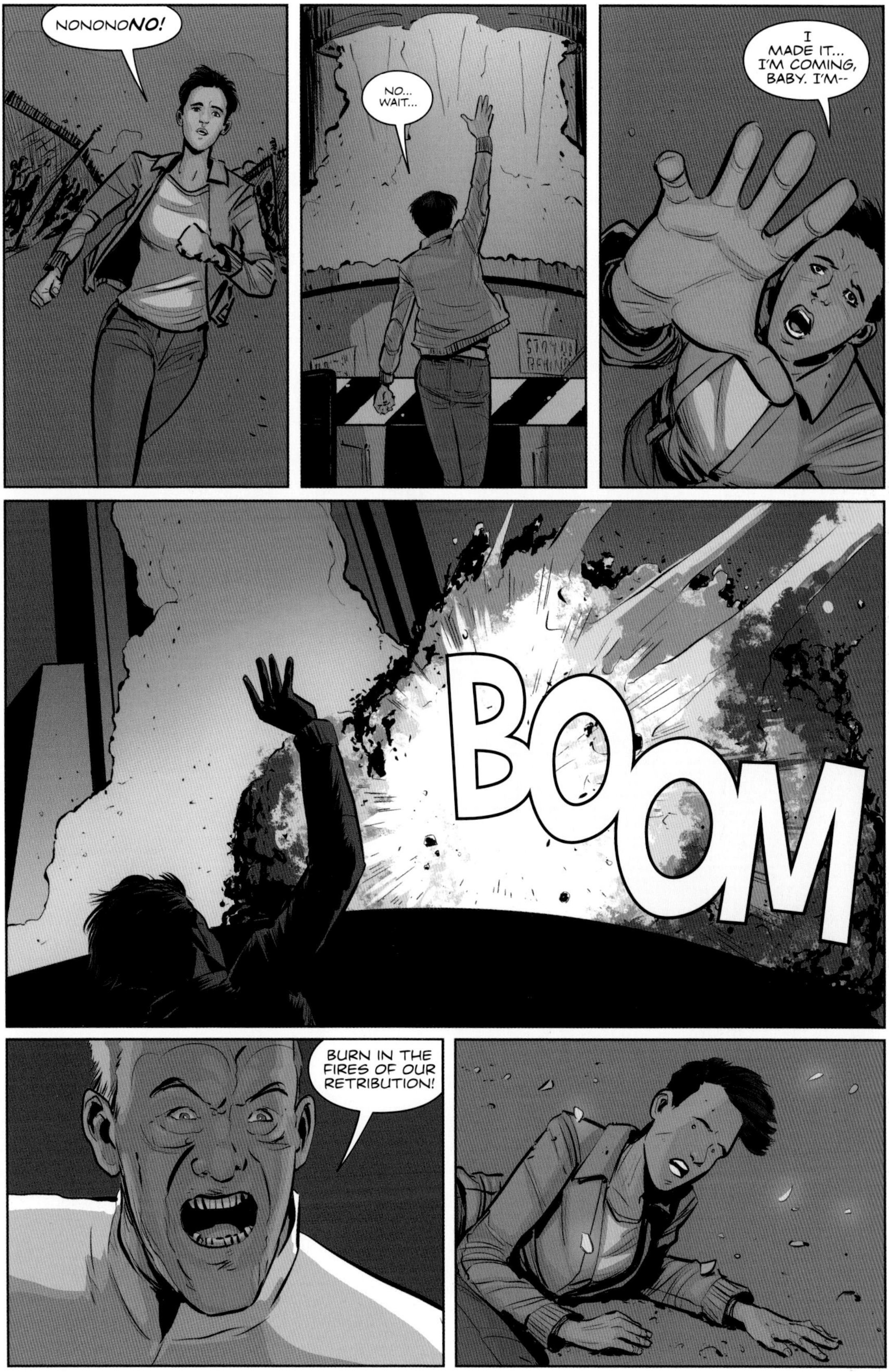
NONONONO!
NO... WAIT...
I MADE IT... I'M COMING, BABY. I'M--
BOOM
BURN IN THE FIRES OF OUR RETRIBUTION!

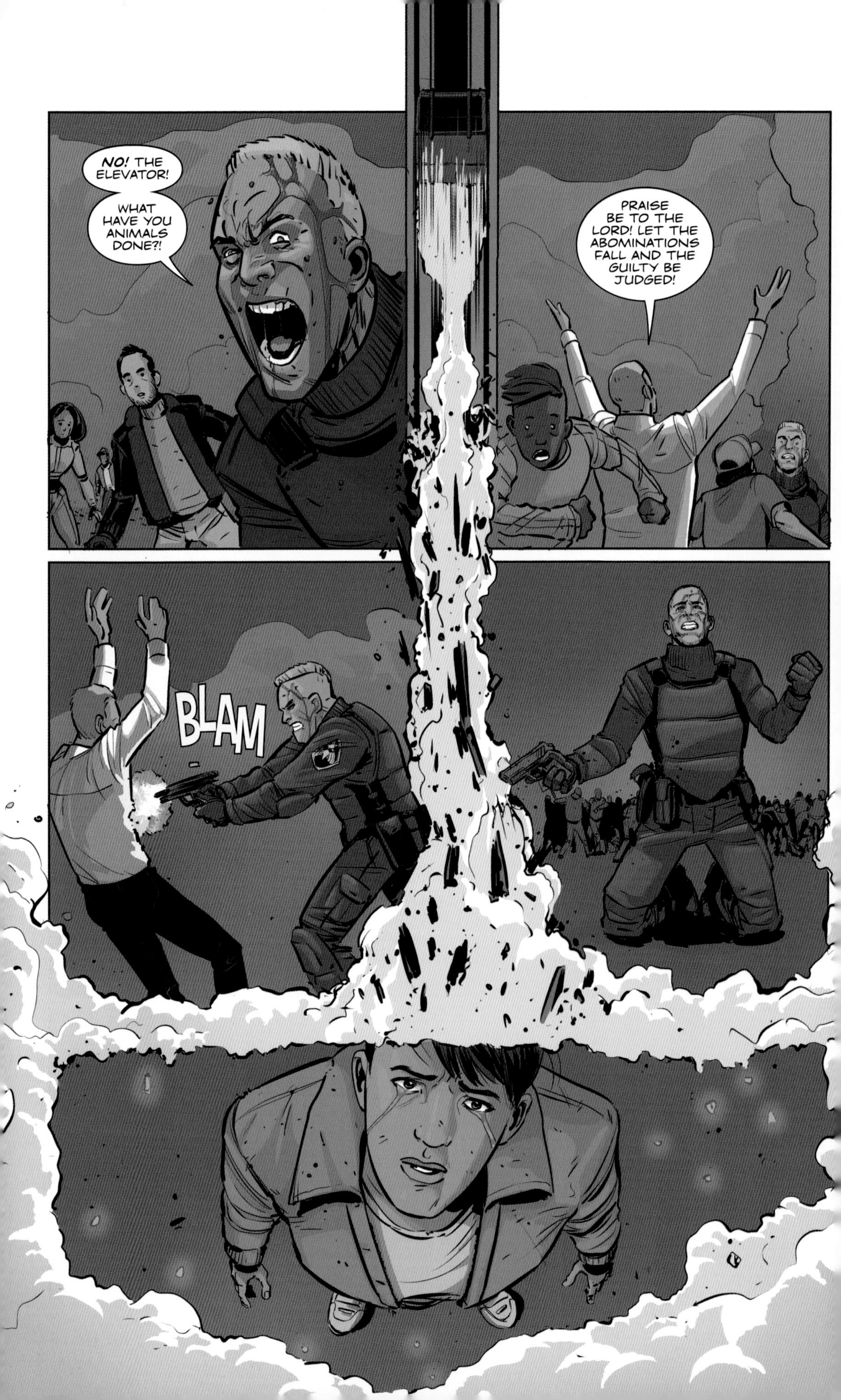
NO! THE ELEVATOR!
WHAT HAVE YOU ANIMALS DONE?!
PRAISE BE TO THE LORD! LET THE ABOMINATIONS FALL AND THE GUILTY BE JUDGED!
BLAM

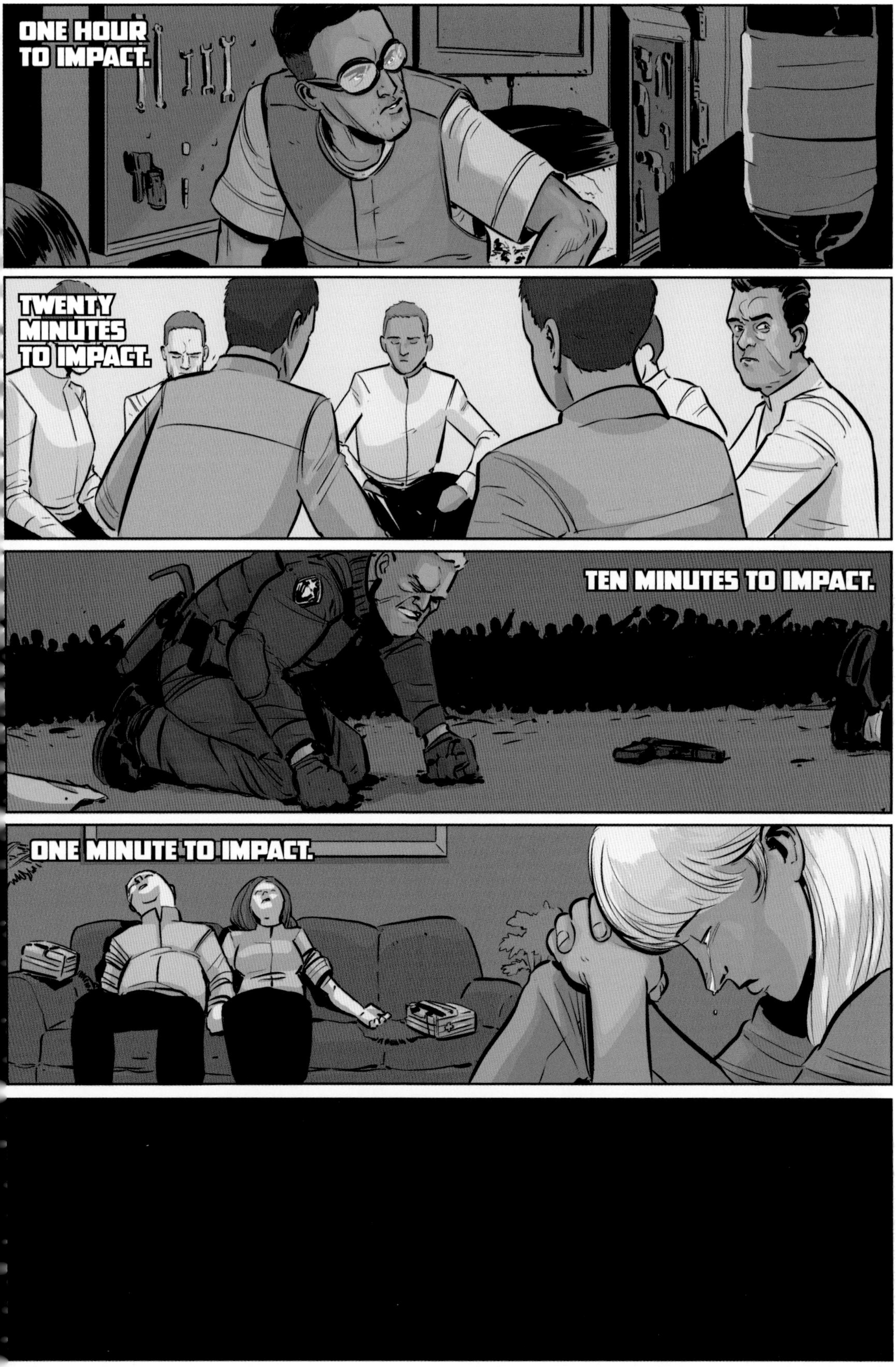
ONE HOUR TO IMPACT.
TWENTY MINUTES TO IMPACT.
TEN MINUTES TO IMPACT.
ONE MINUTE TO IMPACT.

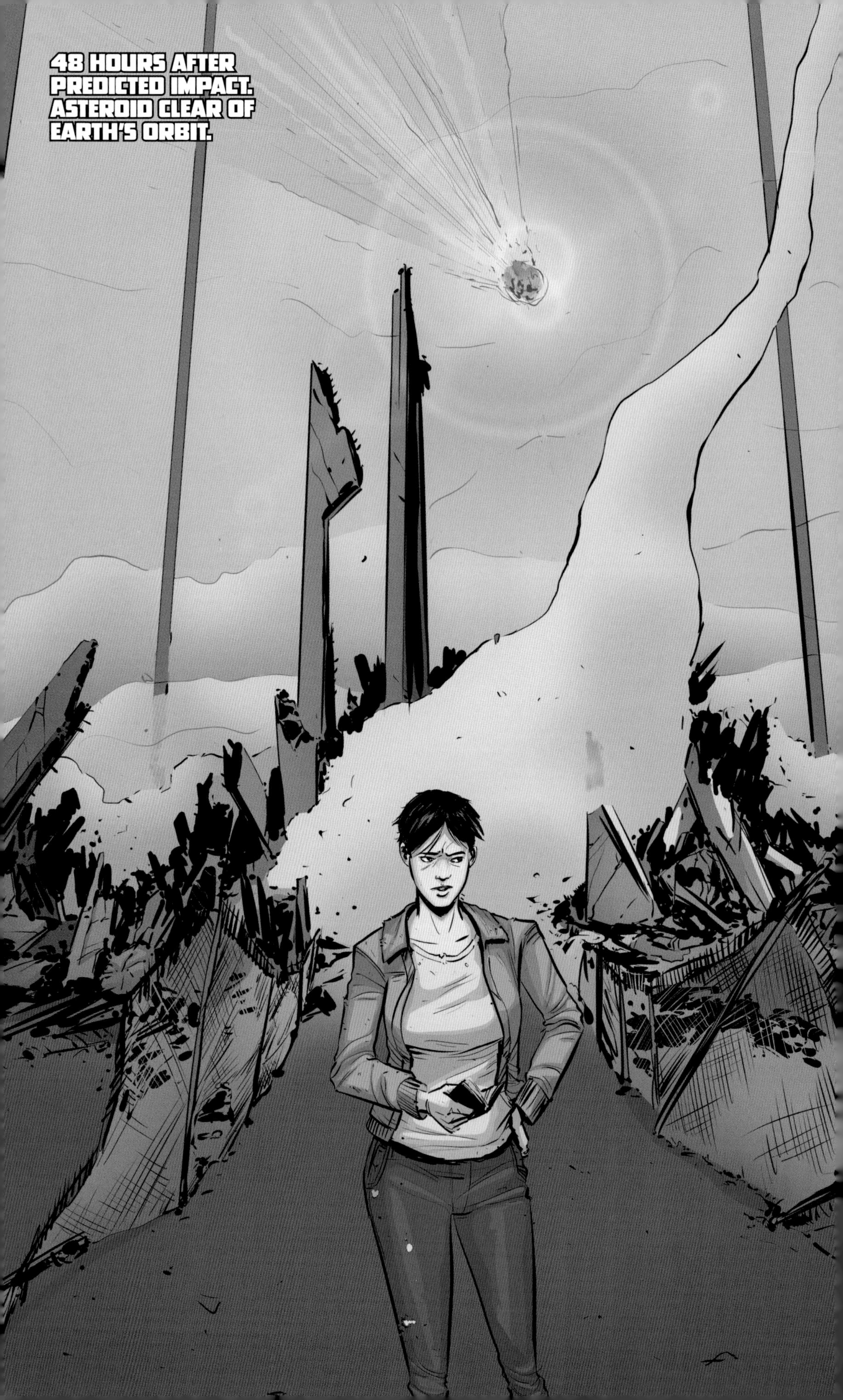
48 HOURS AFTER PREDICTED IMPACT. ASTEROID CLEAR OF EARTH'S ORBIT.

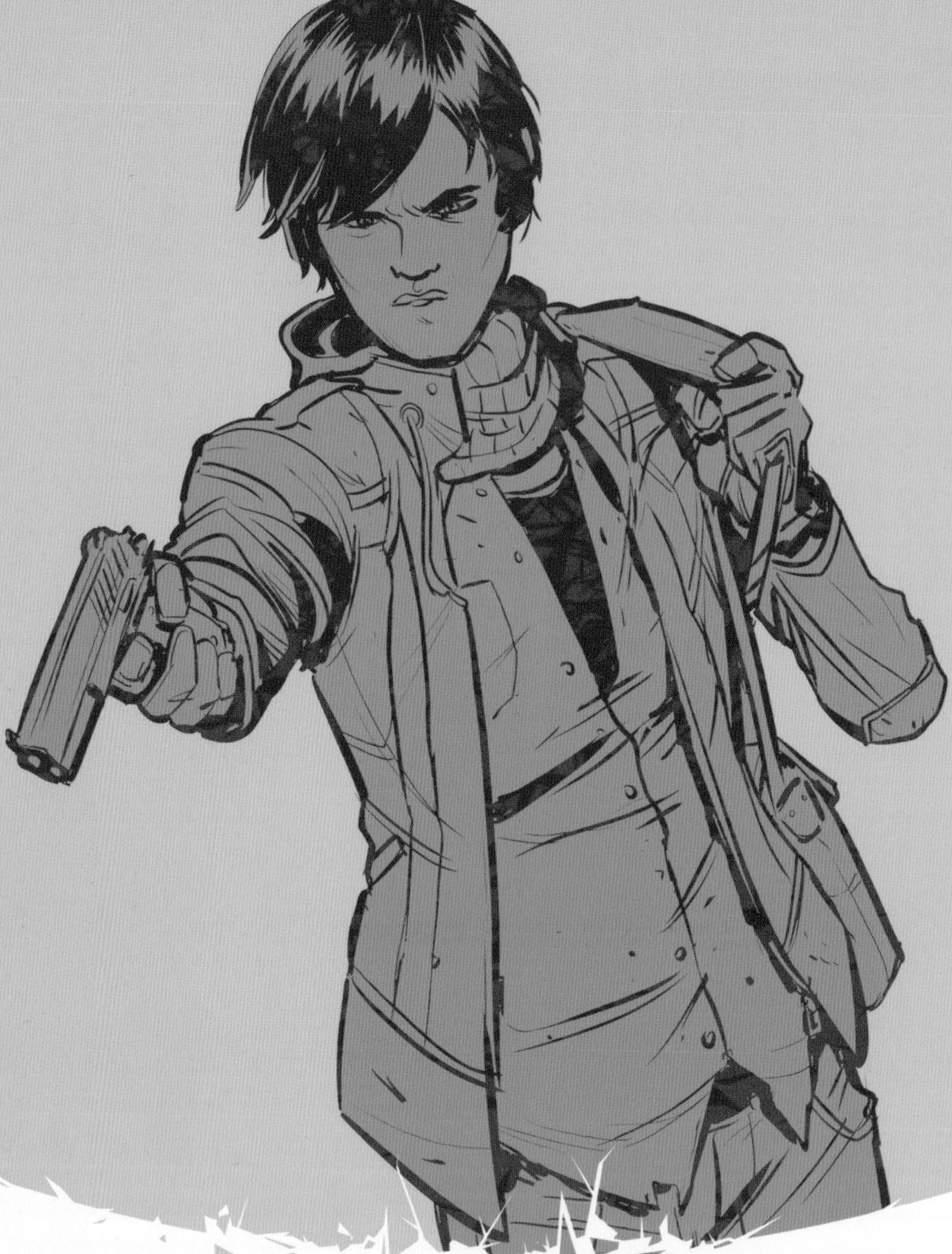

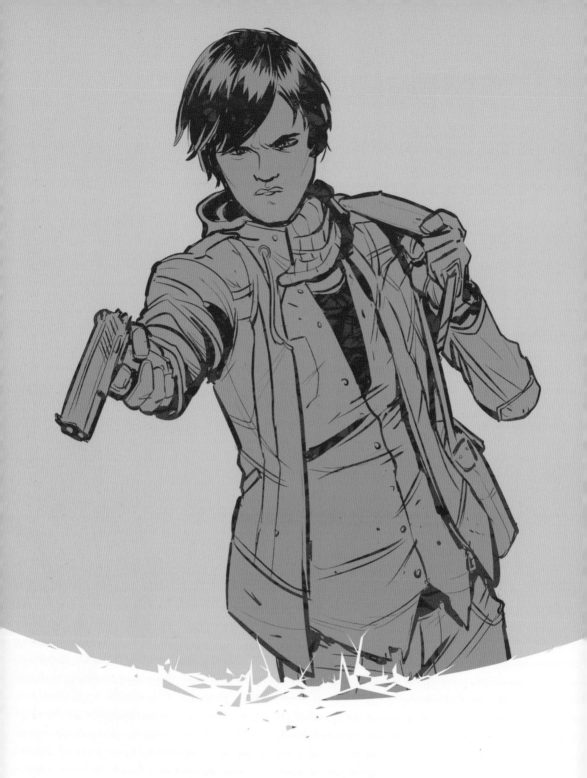

CHAPTER TWO

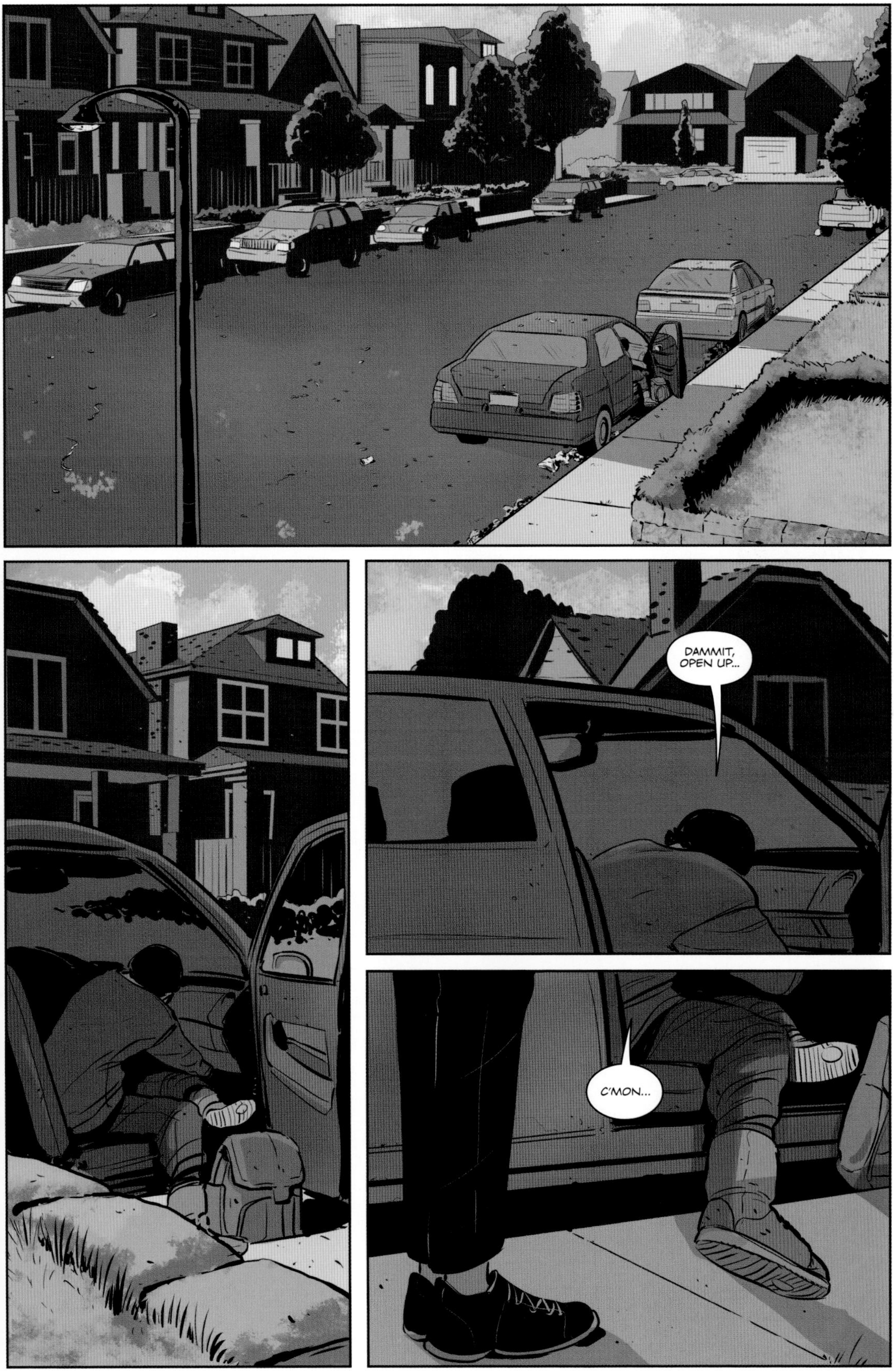
DAMMIT, OPEN UP...
C'MON...

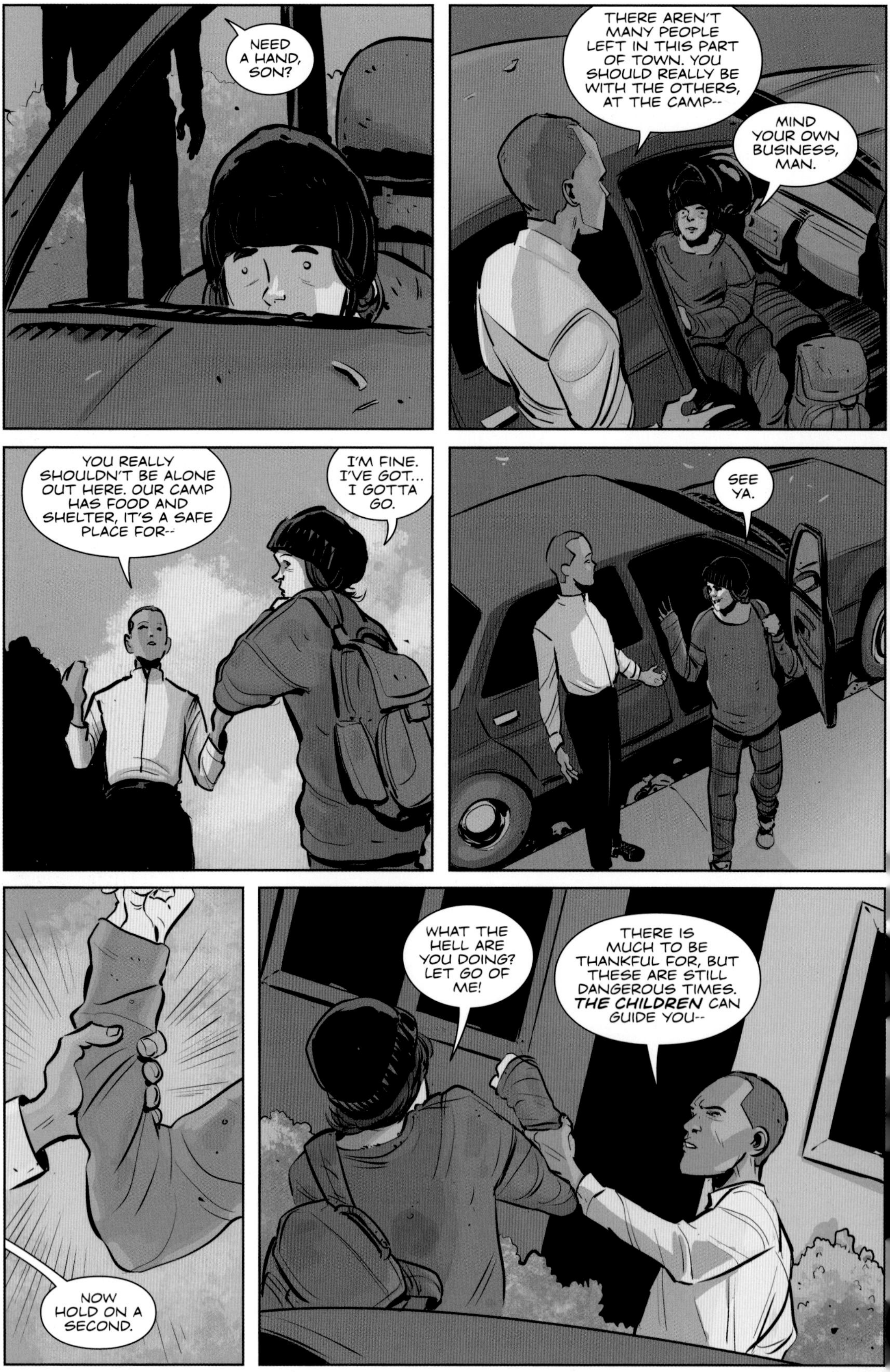
NEED A HAND, SON?
THERE AREN'T MANY PEOPLE LEFT IN THIS PART OF TOWN. YOU SHOULD REALLY BE WITH THE OTHERS, AT THE CAMP--
MIND YOUR OWN BUSINESS, MAN.
YOU REALLY SHOULDN'T BE ALONE OUT HERE. OUR CAMP HAS FOOD AND SHELTER, IT'S A SAFE PLACE FOR--
I'M FINE. I'VE GOT... I GOTTA GO.
SEE YA.
NOW HOLD ON A SECOND.
WHAT THE HELL ARE YOU DOING? LET GO OF ME!
THERE IS MUCH TO BE THANKFUL FOR, BUT THESE ARE STILL DANGEROUS TIMES. THE CHILDREN CAN GUIDE YOU--

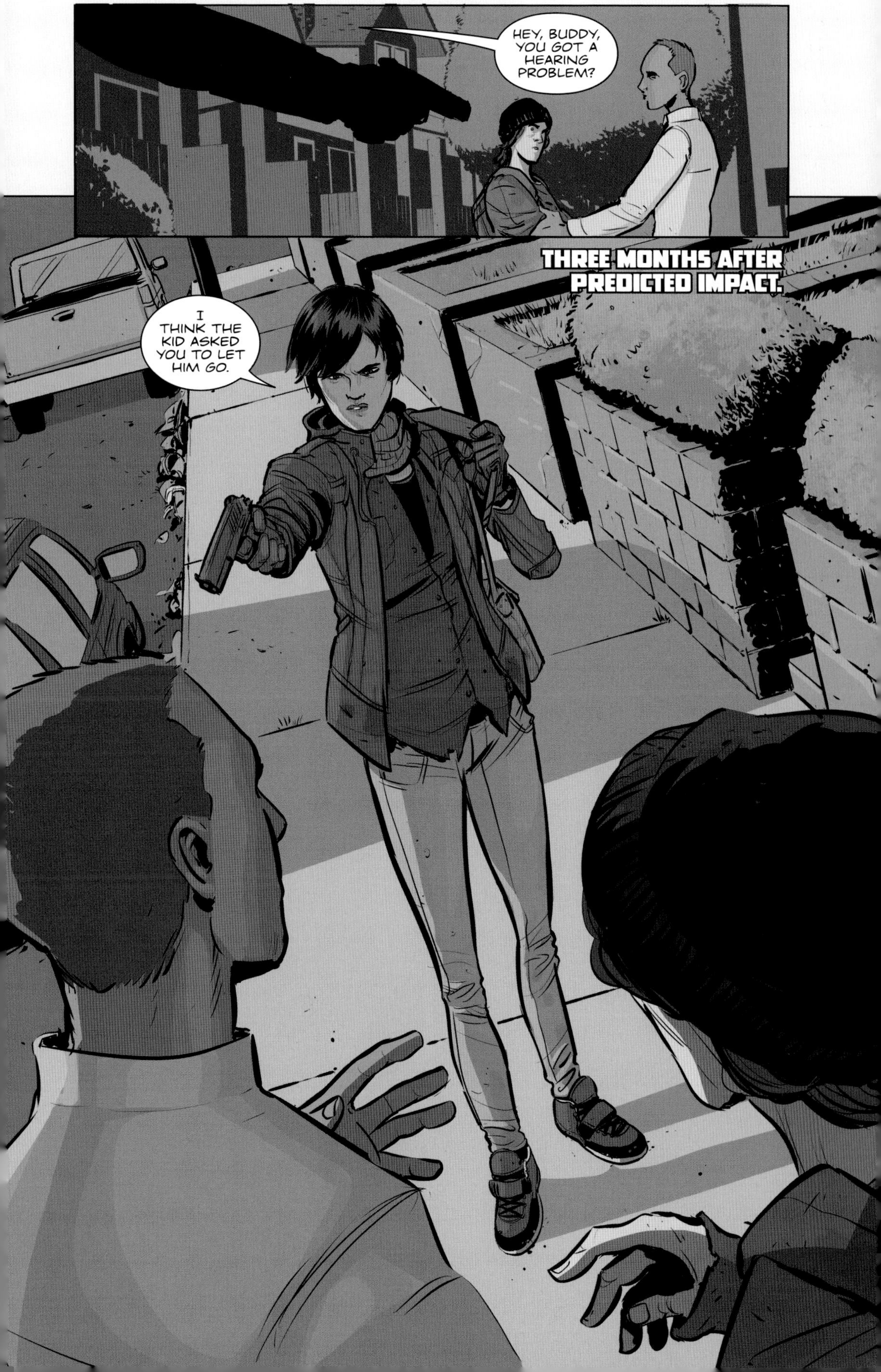
HEY, BUDDY, YOU GOT A HEARING PROBLEM?
THREE MONTHS AFTER PREDICTED IMPACT.
I THINK THE KID ASKED YOU TO LET HIM GO.

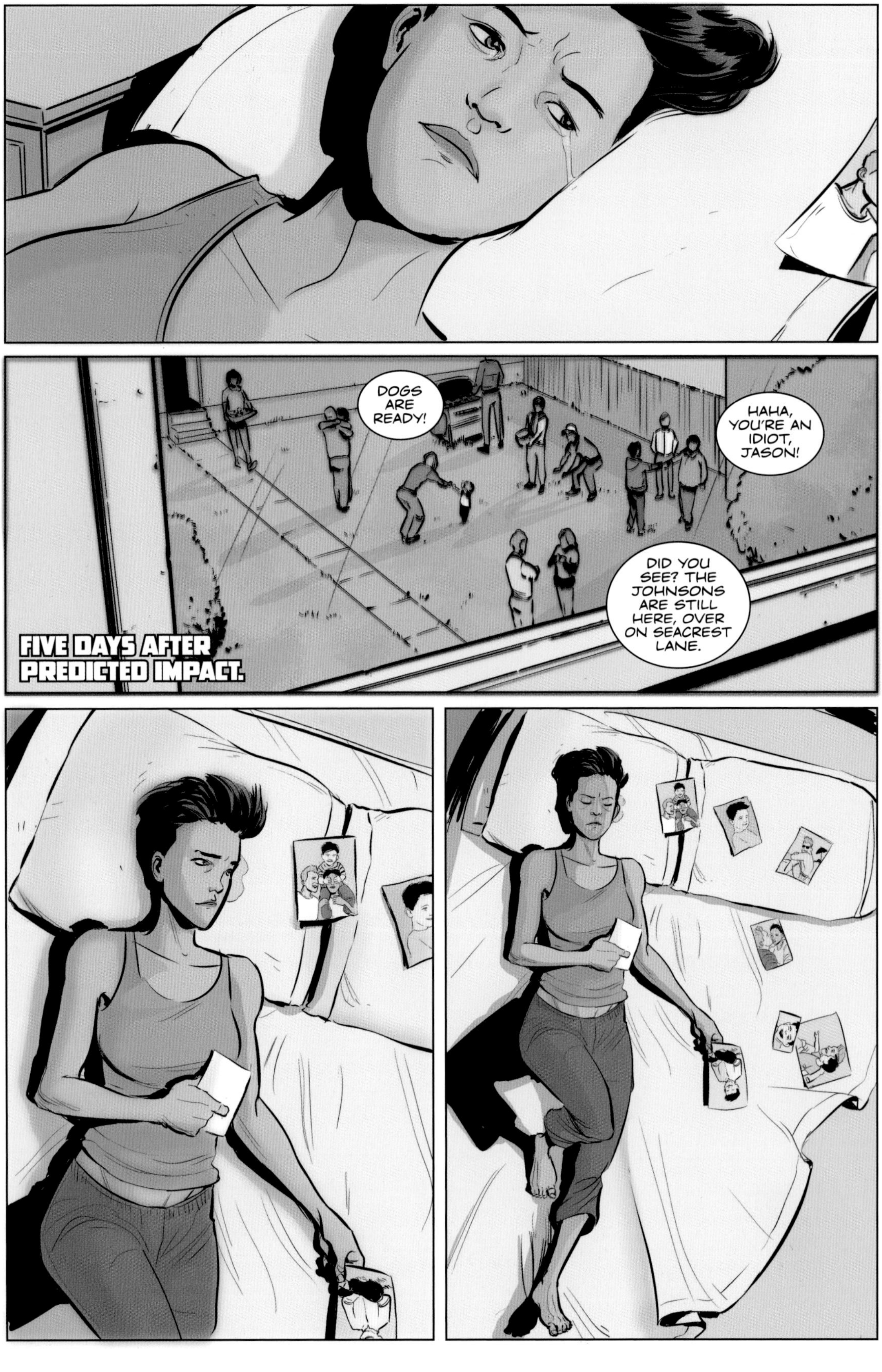

DOGS ARE READY!
HAHA, YOU'RE AN IDIOT, JASON!
DID YOU SEE? THE JOHNSONS ARE STILL HERE, OVER ON SEACREST LANE.
FIVE DAYS AFTER PREDICTED IMPACT.

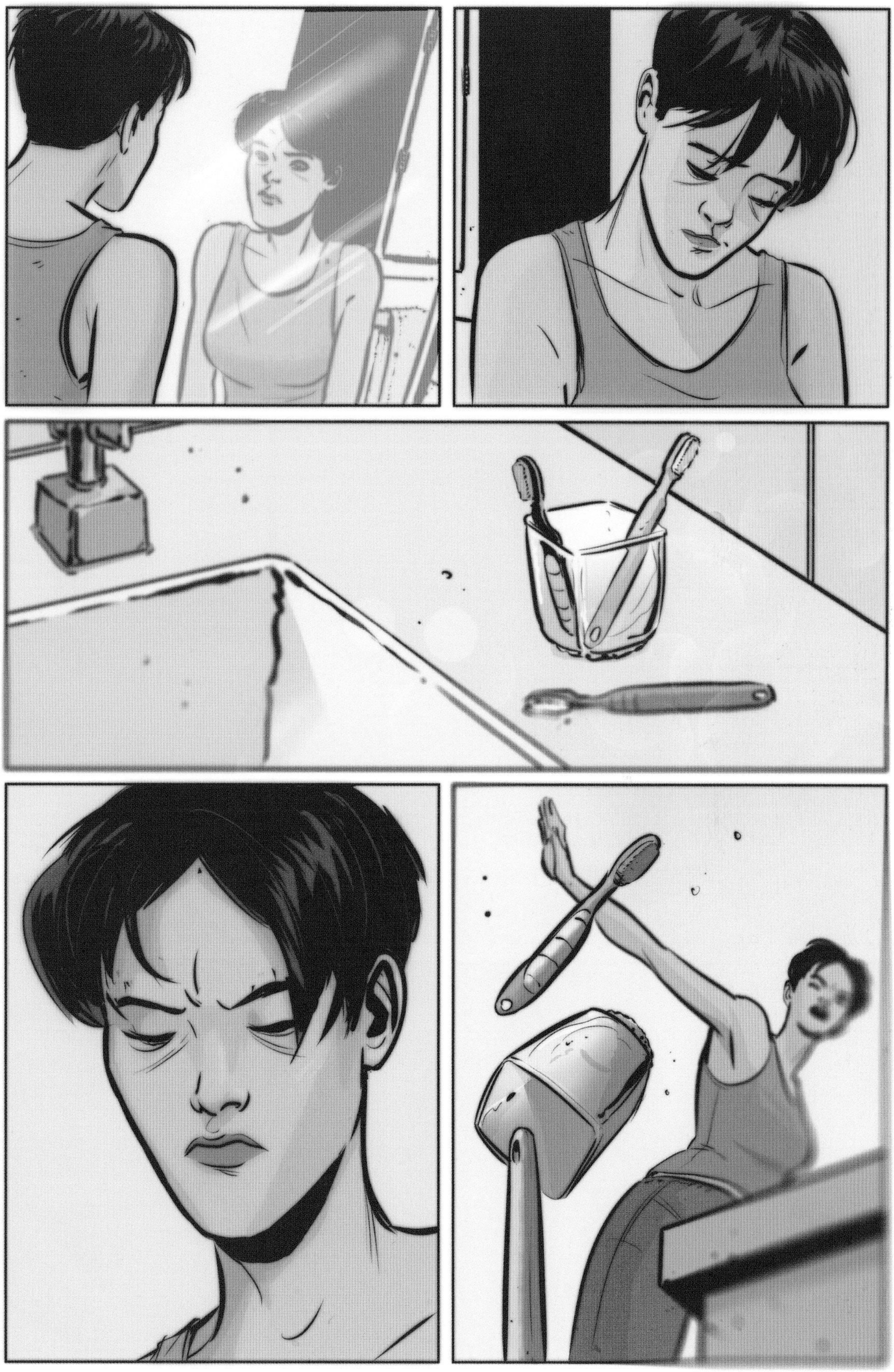

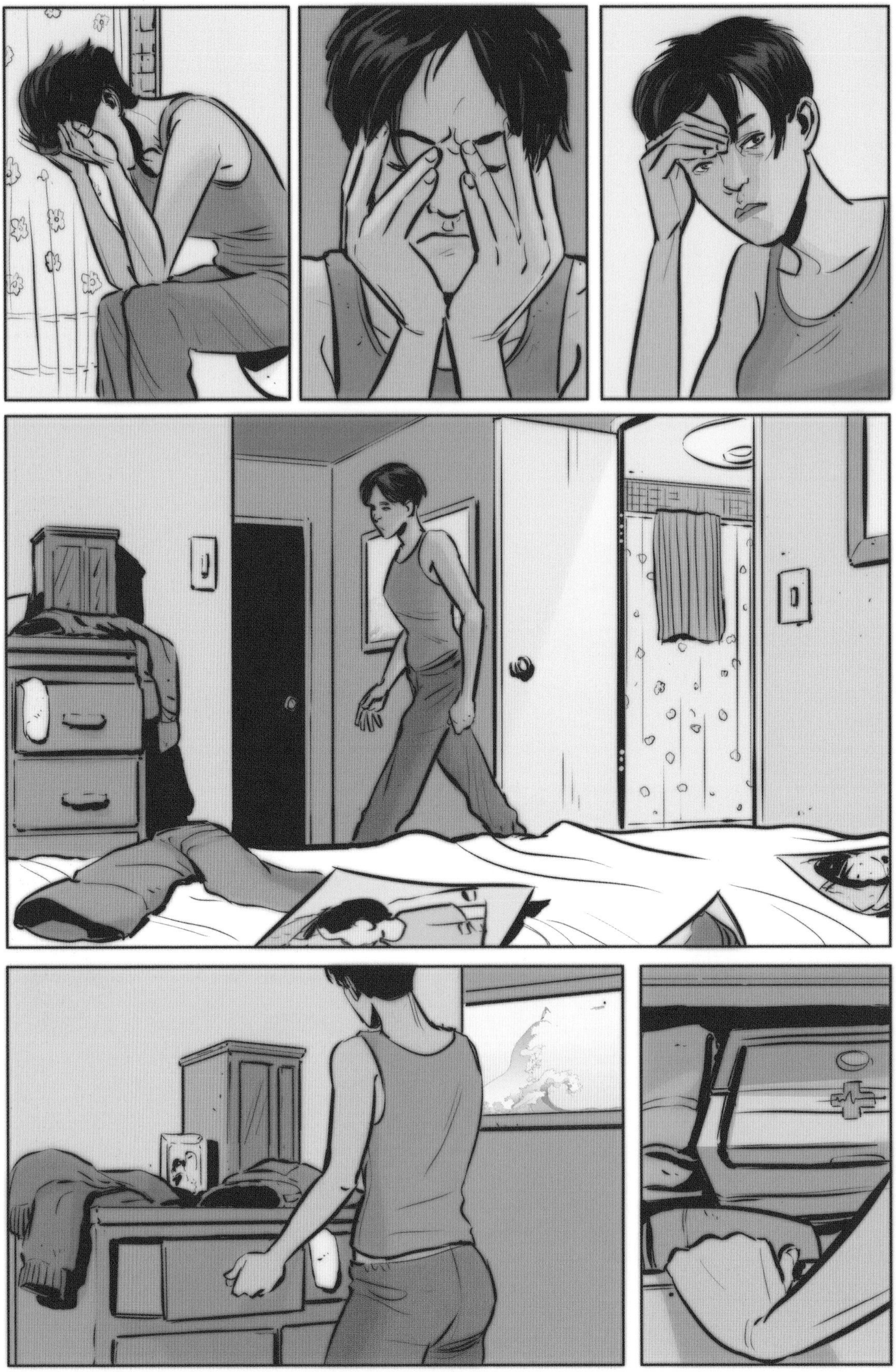

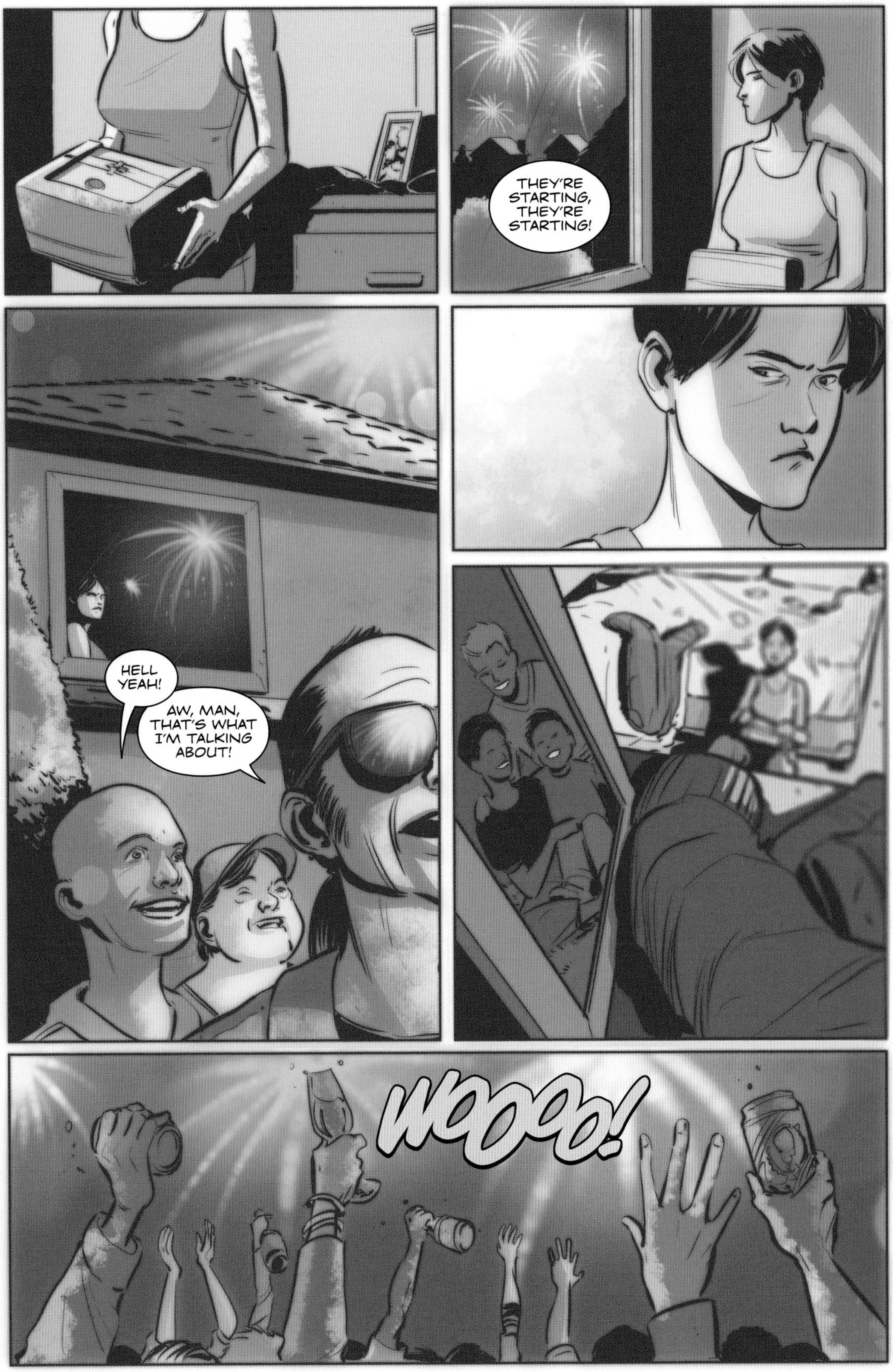
THEY'RE STARTING, THEY'RE STARTING!
HELL YEAH!
AW, MAN, THAT'S WHAT I'M TALKING ABOUT!
WOOOO!

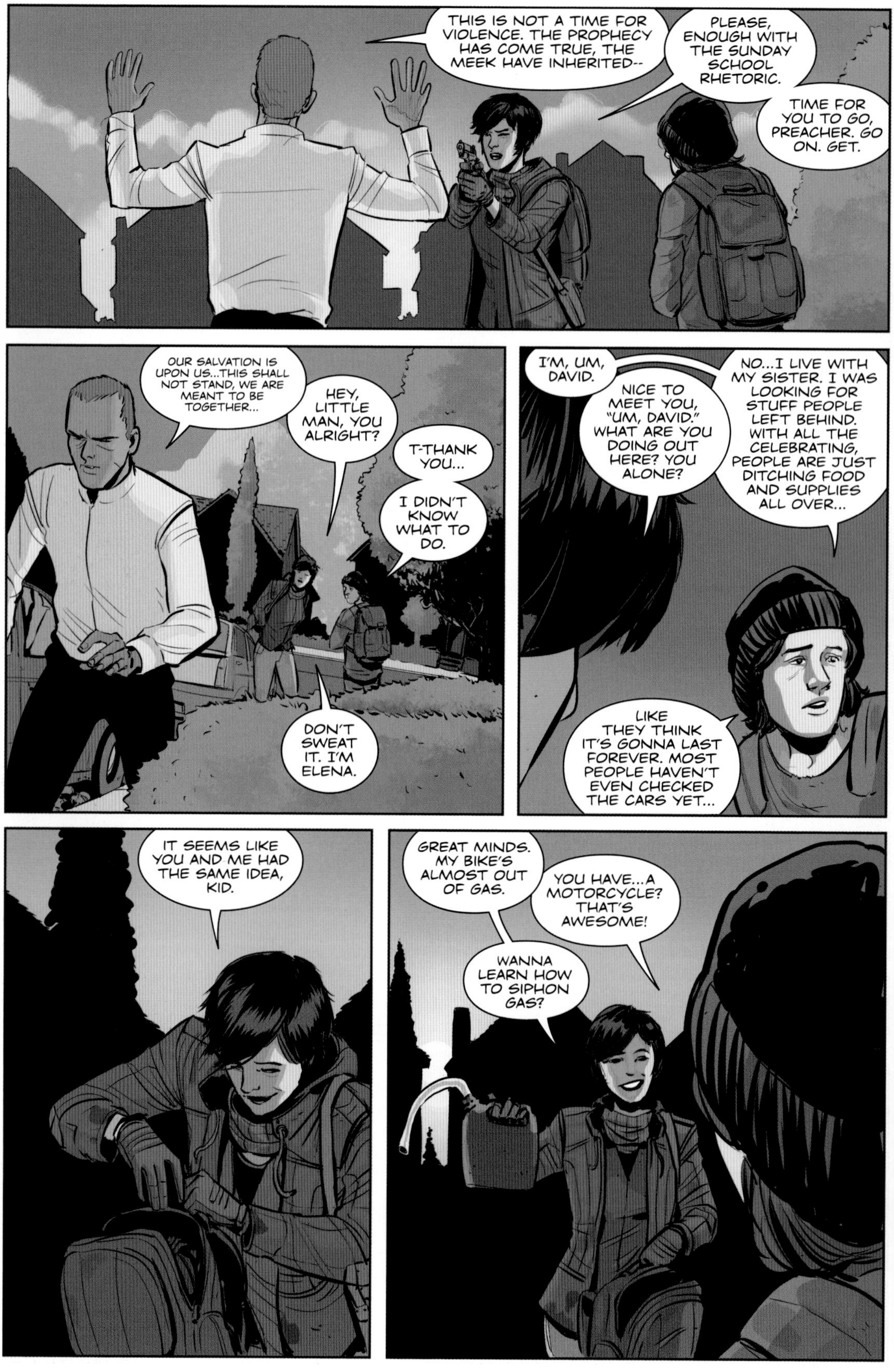
THIS IS NOT A TIME FOR VIOLENCE. THE PROPHECY HAS COME TRUE, THE MEEK HAVE INHERITED--
PLEASE, ENOUGH WITH THE SUNDAY SCHOOL RHETORIC.
TIME FOR YOU TO GO, PREACHER. GO ON. GET.
OUR SALVATION IS UPON US...THIS SHALL NOT STAND, WE ARE MEANT TO BE TOGETHER...
HEY, LITTLE MAN, YOU ALRIGHT?
T-THANK YOU...
I DIDN'T KNOW WHAT TO DO.
DON'T SWEAT IT. I'M ELENA.
I'M, UM, DAVID.
NICE TO MEET YOU, "UM, DAVID." WHAT ARE YOU DOING OUT HERE? YOU ALONE?
NO...I LIVE WITH MY SISTER. I WAS LOOKING FOR STUFF PEOPLE LEFT BEHIND. WITH ALL THE CELEBRATING, PEOPLE ARE JUST DITCHING FOOD AND SUPPLIES ALL OVER...
LIKE THEY THINK IT'S GONNA LAST FOREVER. MOST PEOPLE HAVEN'T EVEN CHECKED THE CARS YET...
IT SEEMS LIKE YOU AND ME HAD THE SAME IDEA, KID.
GREAT MINDS. MY BIKE'S ALMOST OUT OF GAS.
YOU HAVE...A MOTORCYCLE? THAT'S AWESOME!
WANNA LEARN HOW TO SIPHON GAS?

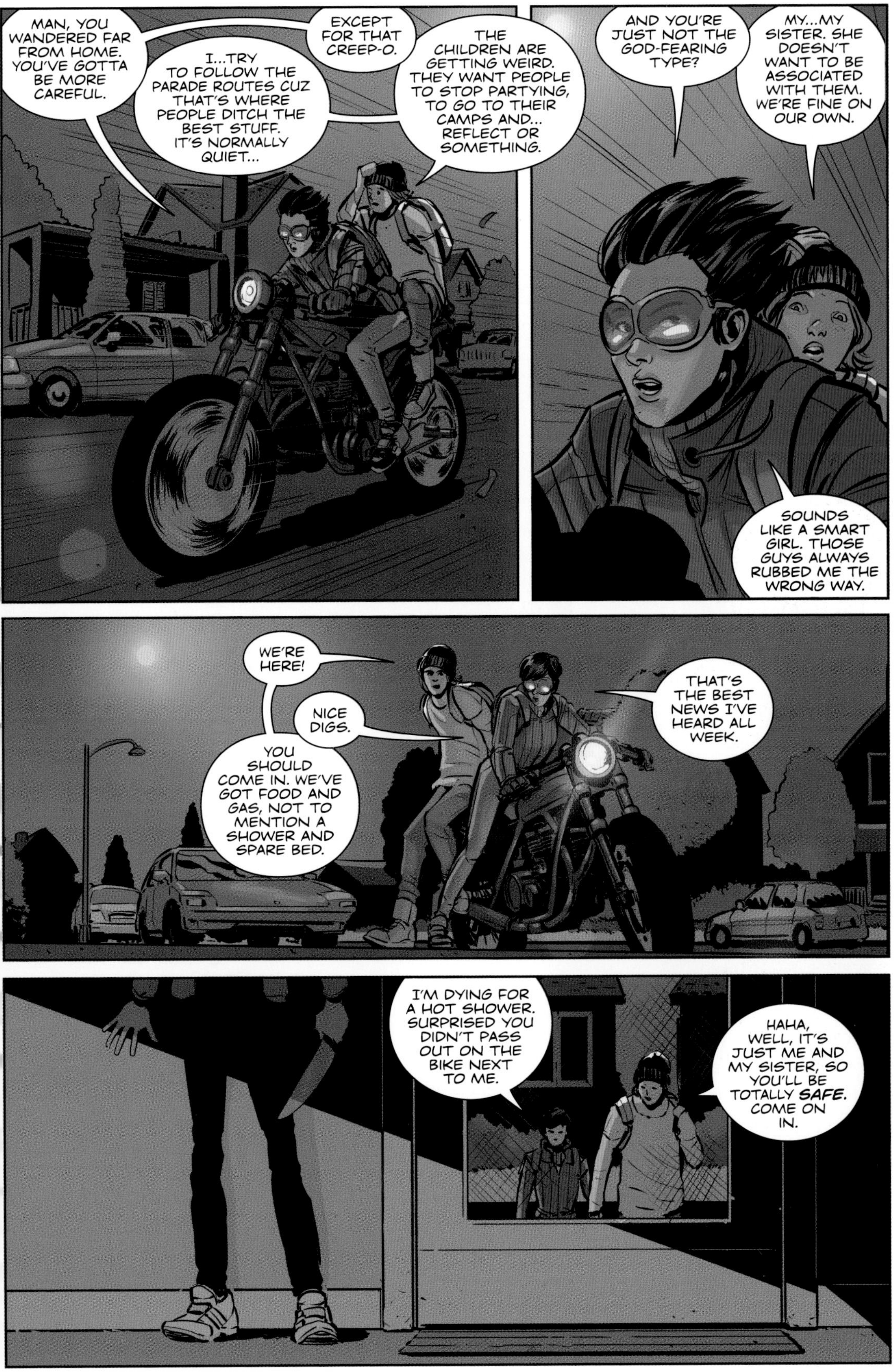
MAN, YOU WANDERED FAR FROM HOME. YOU'VE GOTTA BE MORE CAREFUL.
EXCEPT FOR THAT CREEP-O.
I...TRY TO FOLLOW THE PARADE ROUTES CUZ THAT'S WHERE PEOPLE DITCH THE BEST STUFF. IT'S NORMALLY QUIET...
THE CHILDREN ARE GETTING WEIRD. THEY WANT PEOPLE TO STOP PARTYING, TO GO TO THEIR CAMPS AND... REFLECT OR SOMETHING.
AND YOU'RE JUST NOT THE GOD-FEARING TYPE?
MY...MY SISTER. SHE DOESN'T WANT TO BE ASSOCIATED WITH THEM. WE'RE FINE ON OUR OWN.
SOUNDS LIKE A SMART GIRL. THOSE GUYS ALWAYS RUBBED ME THE WRONG WAY.
WE'RE HERE!
NICE DIGS.
YOU SHOULD COME IN. WE'VE GOT FOOD AND GAS, NOT TO MENTION A SHOWER AND SPARE BED.
THAT'S THE BEST NEWS I'VE HEARD ALL WEEK.
I'M DYING FOR A HOT SHOWER. SURPRISED YOU DIDN'T PASS OUT ON THE BIKE NEXT TO ME.
HAHA, WELL, IT'S JUST ME AND MY SISTER, SO YOU'LL BE TOTALLY **SAFE.** COME ON IN.

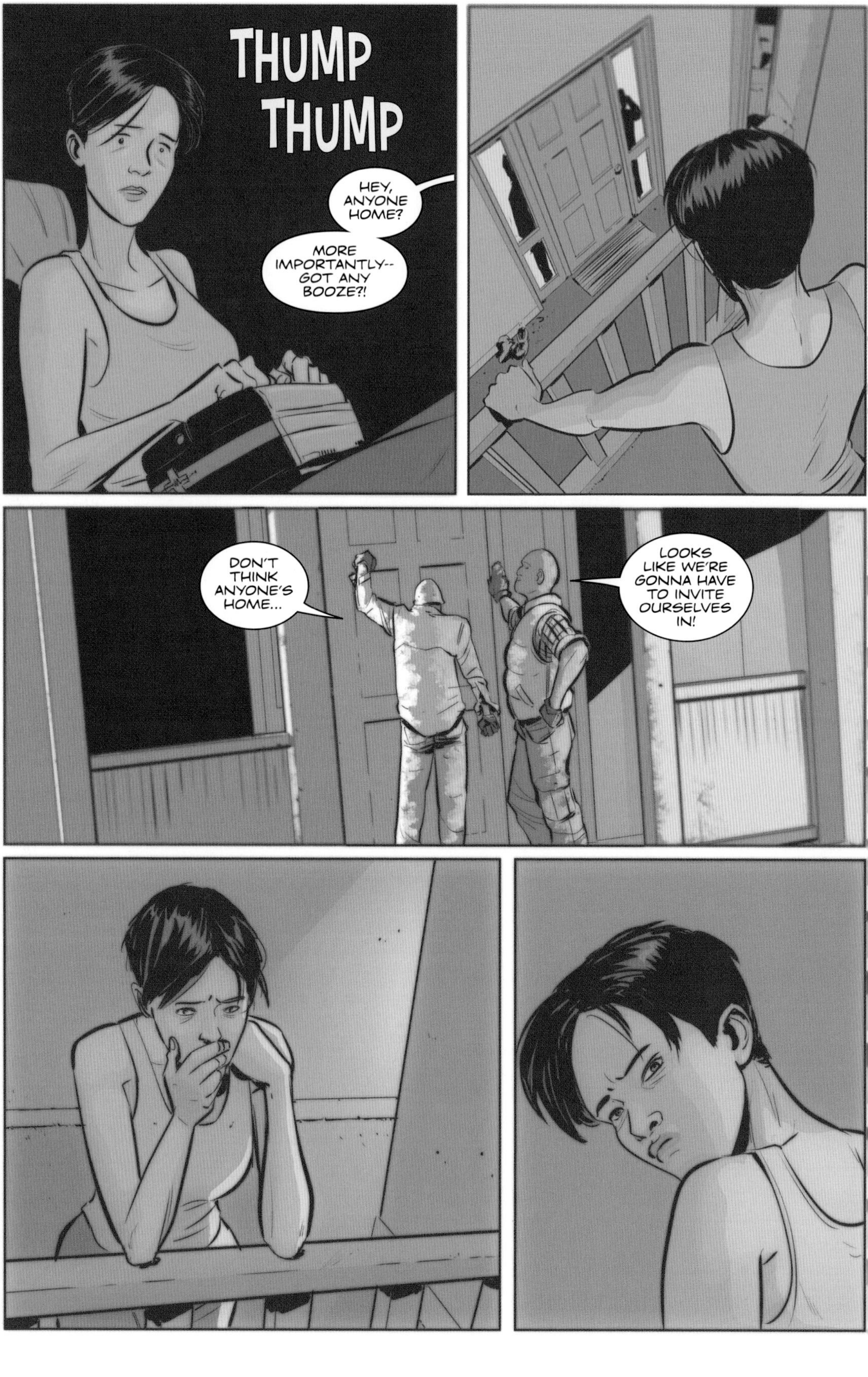
THUMP
THUMP
HEY, ANYONE HOME?
MORE IMPORTANTLY--GOT ANY BOOZE?!
DON'T THINK ANYONE'S HOME...
LOOKS LIKE WE'RE GONNA HAVE TO INVITE OURSELVES IN!

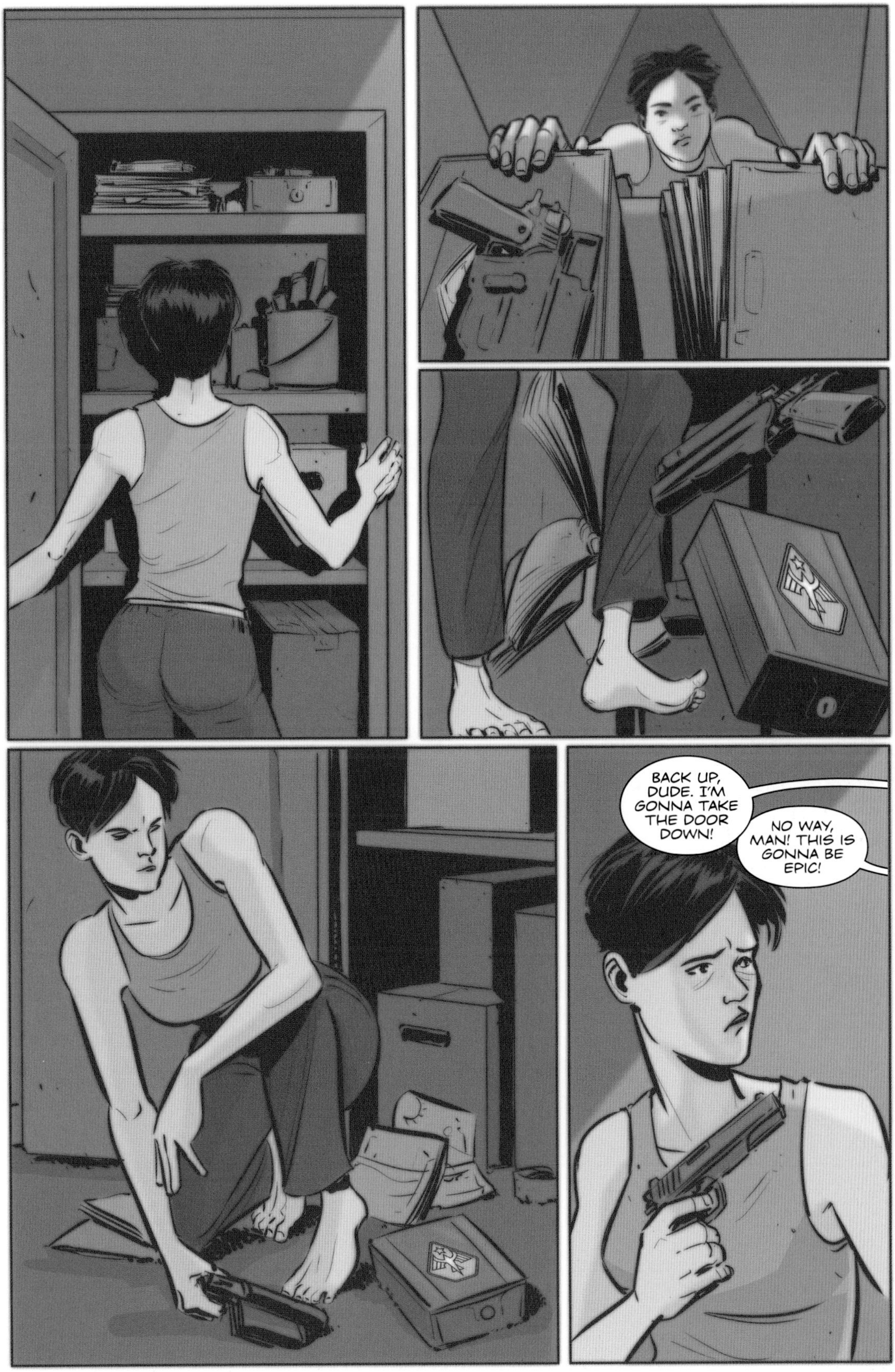
BACK UP, DUDE. I'M GONNA TAKE THE DOOR DOWN!
NO WAY, MAN! THIS IS GONNA BE EPIC!

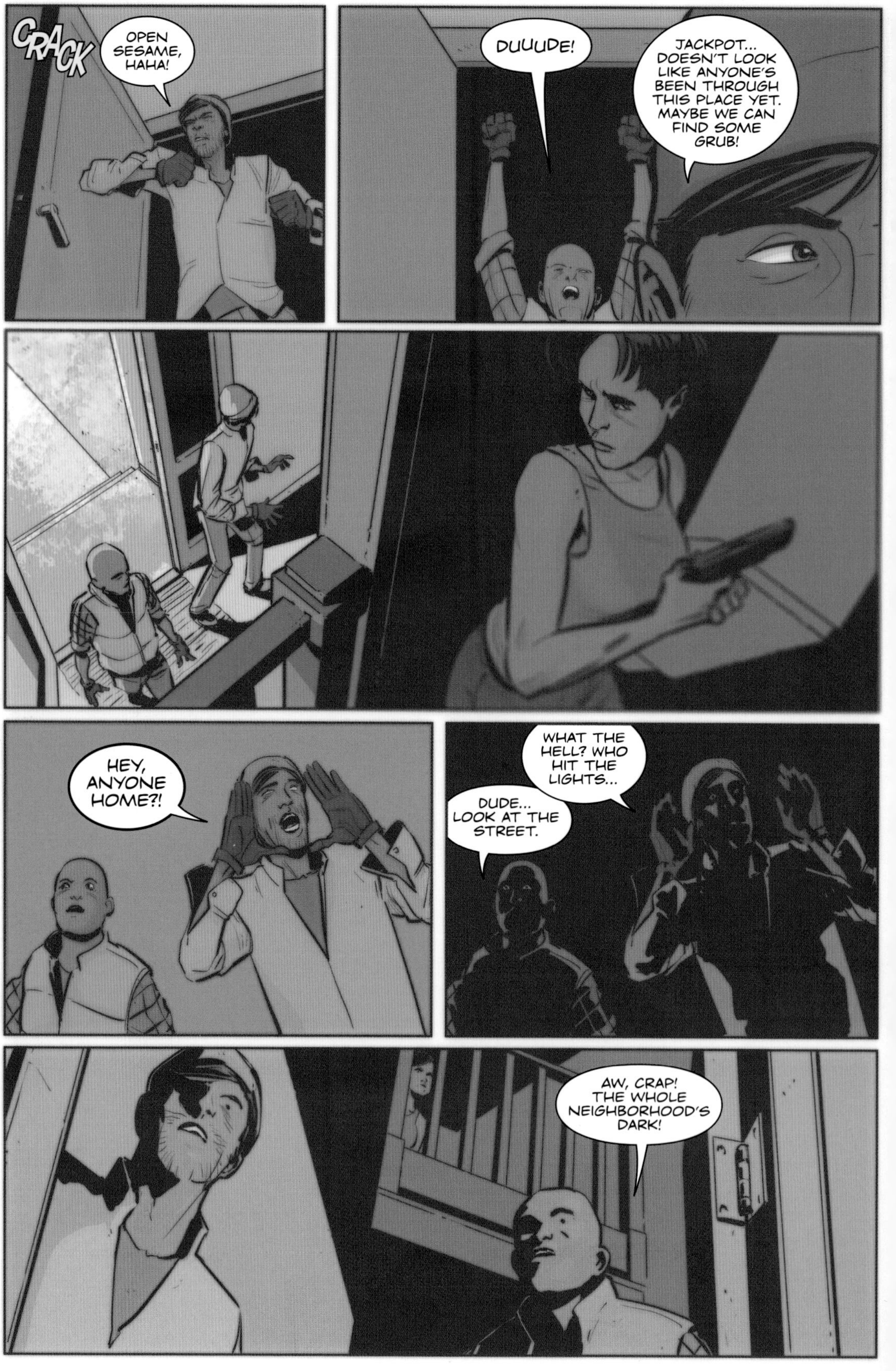
CRACK
OPEN SESAME, HAHA!
DUUUDE!
JACKPOT... DOESN'T LOOK LIKE ANYONE'S BEEN THROUGH THIS PLACE YET. MAYBE WE CAN FIND SOME GRUB!
HEY, ANYONE HOME?!
WHAT THE HELL? WHO HIT THE LIGHTS...
DUDE... LOOK AT THE STREET.
AW, CRAP! THE WHOLE NEIGHBORHOOD'S DARK!

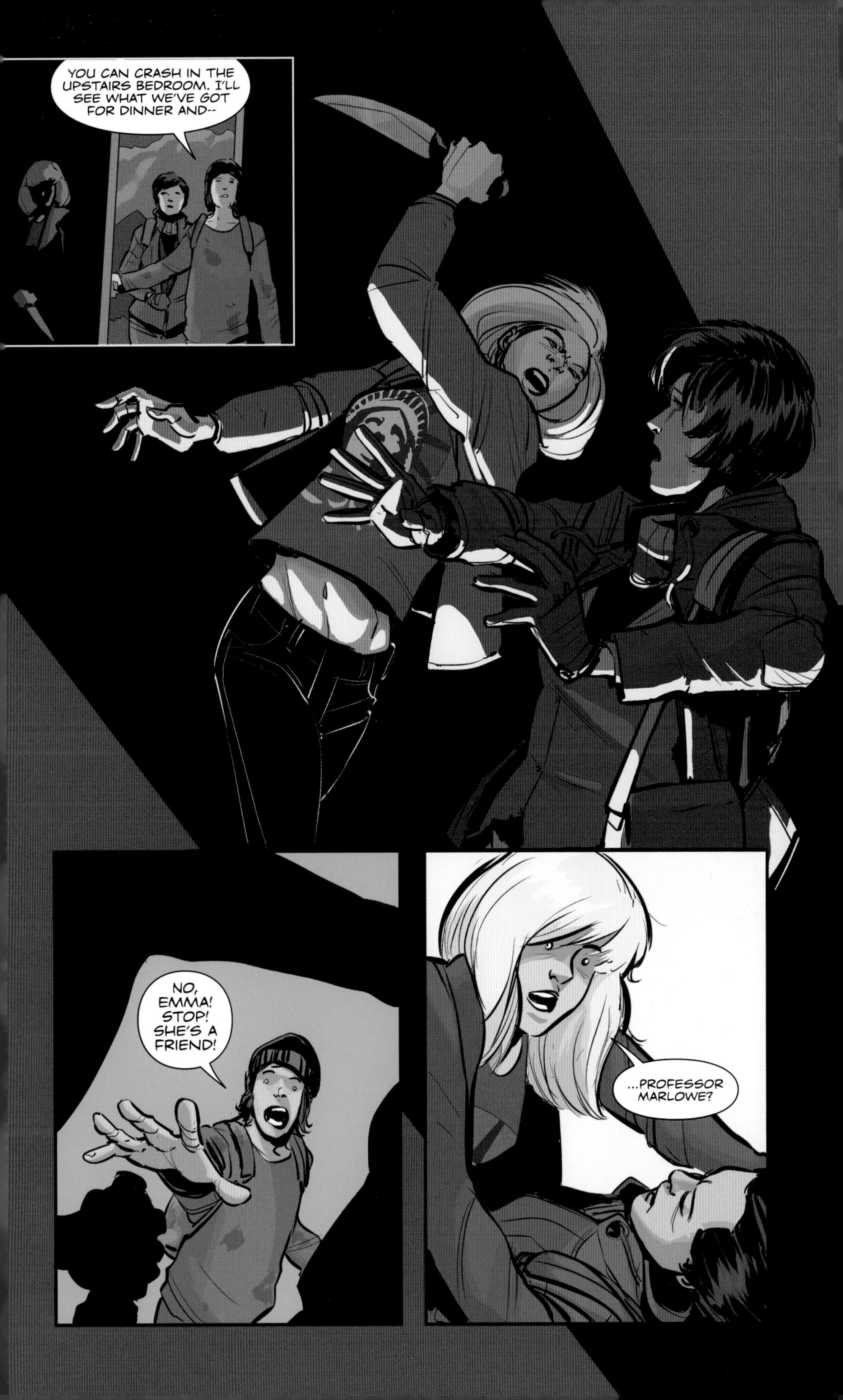
YOU CAN CRASH IN THE UPSTAIRS BEDROOM. I'LL SEE WHAT WE'VE GOT FOR DINNER AND--
NO, EMMA! STOP! SHE'S A FRIEND!
...PROFESSOR MARLOWE?

SORRY FOR COMING AT YOU LIKE THAT, PROFESSOR, BUT THINGS HAVE BEEN KINDA... TENSE LATELY.

PEOPLE ARE GETTING CRAZY. LOOTING, BREAKING INTO HOUSES DRUNK... AND THEN THERE'S THE CHILDREN.

THEY'RE BECOMING RELENTLESS, TRYING TO STOP THE PARTYING AND GET PEOPLE TOGETHER TO... I DUNNO, REPENT?

YOU'VE GOTTA PROTECT YOURSELVES, I GET IT.

YOUR... PARENTS WERE MEMBERS OF THE CHILDREN, YEAH?

YEAH... THEY WERE.

I'VE SPENT WAY TOO LONG LISTENING TO THEIR PSYCHOTIC INDOCTRINATION CRAP TO GO LIVE ON A DAMN COMMUNE.

WE'VE ALL BEEN GIVEN A SECOND CHANCE, AND WE SHOULD DO SOMETHING WITH IT. I'M NOT EXACTLY SURE WHAT THAT MEANS YET, BUT I'D DIE BEFORE JOINING THE CHILDREN.

ARE THEY TARGETING YOU GUYS SPECIFICALLY?

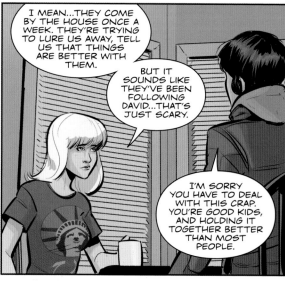

I MEAN...THEY COME BY THE HOUSE ONCE A WEEK. THEY'RE TRYING TO LURE US AWAY, TELL US THAT THINGS ARE BETTER WITH THEM.

BUT IT SOUNDS LIKE THEY'VE BEEN FOLLOWING DAVID...THAT'S JUST SCARY.

I'M SORRY YOU HAVE TO DEAL WITH THIS CRAP. YOU'RE GOOD KIDS, AND HOLDING IT TOGETHER BETTER THAN MOST PEOPLE.

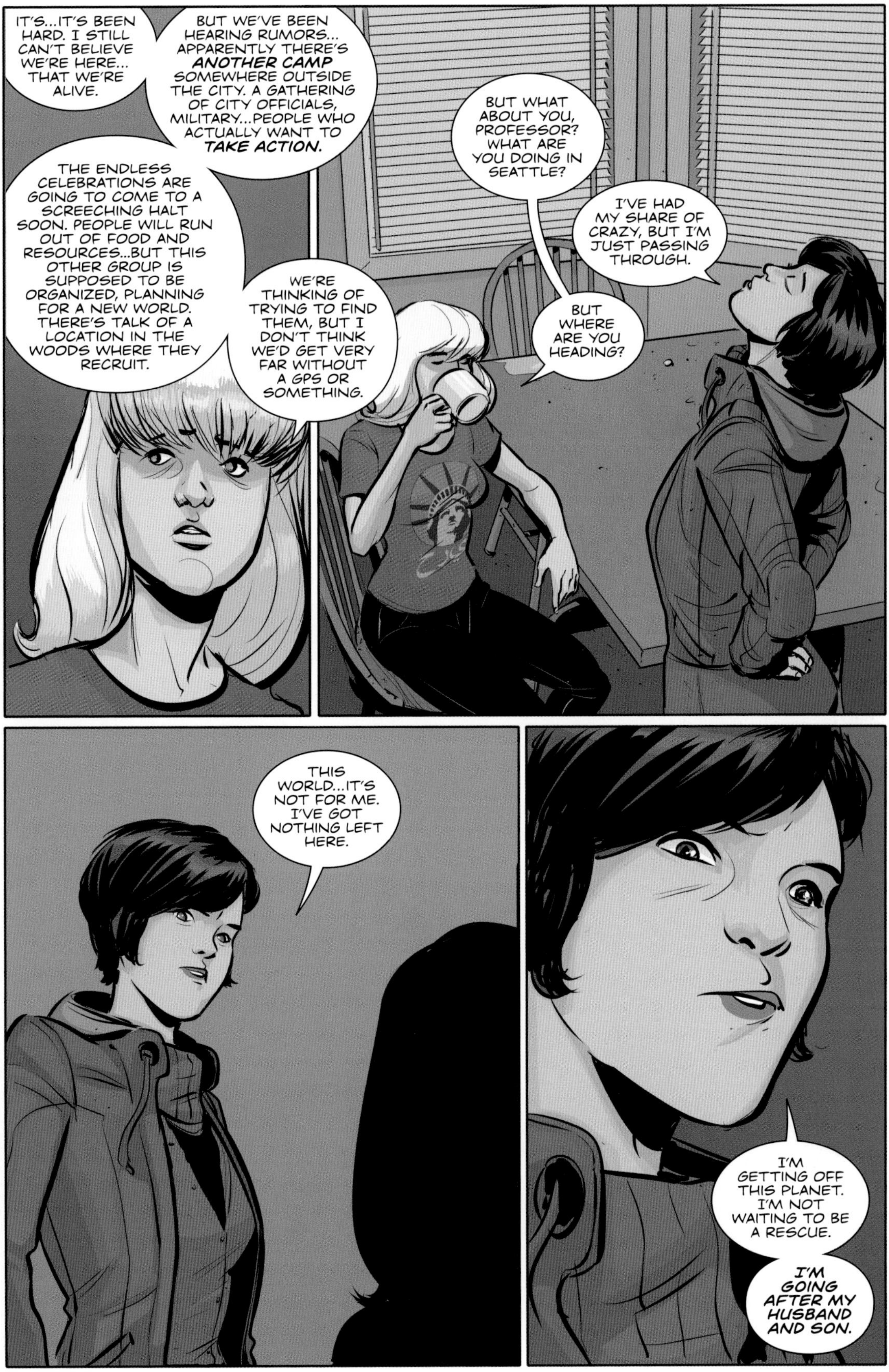

IT'S...IT'S BEEN HARD. I STILL CAN'T BELIEVE WE'RE HERE... THAT WE'RE ALIVE.
BUT WE'VE BEEN HEARING RUMORS... APPARENTLY THERE'S **ANOTHER CAMP** SOMEWHERE OUTSIDE THE CITY. A GATHERING OF CITY OFFICIALS, MILITARY...PEOPLE WHO ACTUALLY WANT TO ***TAKE ACTION.***
THE ENDLESS CELEBRATIONS ARE GOING TO COME TO A SCREECHING HALT SOON. PEOPLE WILL RUN OUT OF FOOD AND RESOURCES...BUT THIS OTHER GROUP IS SUPPOSED TO BE ORGANIZED, PLANNING FOR A NEW WORLD. THERE'S TALK OF A LOCATION IN THE WOODS WHERE THEY RECRUIT.
WE'RE THINKING OF TRYING TO FIND THEM, BUT I DON'T THINK WE'D GET VERY FAR WITHOUT A GPS OR SOMETHING.
BUT WHAT ABOUT YOU, PROFESSOR? WHAT ARE YOU DOING IN SEATTLE?
I'VE HAD MY SHARE OF CRAZY, BUT I'M JUST PASSING THROUGH.
BUT WHERE ARE YOU HEADING?
THIS WORLD...IT'S NOT FOR ME. I'VE GOT NOTHING LEFT HERE.
I'M GETTING OFF THIS PLANET. I'M NOT WAITING TO BE A RESCUE.
I'M GOING AFTER MY HUSBAND AND SON.

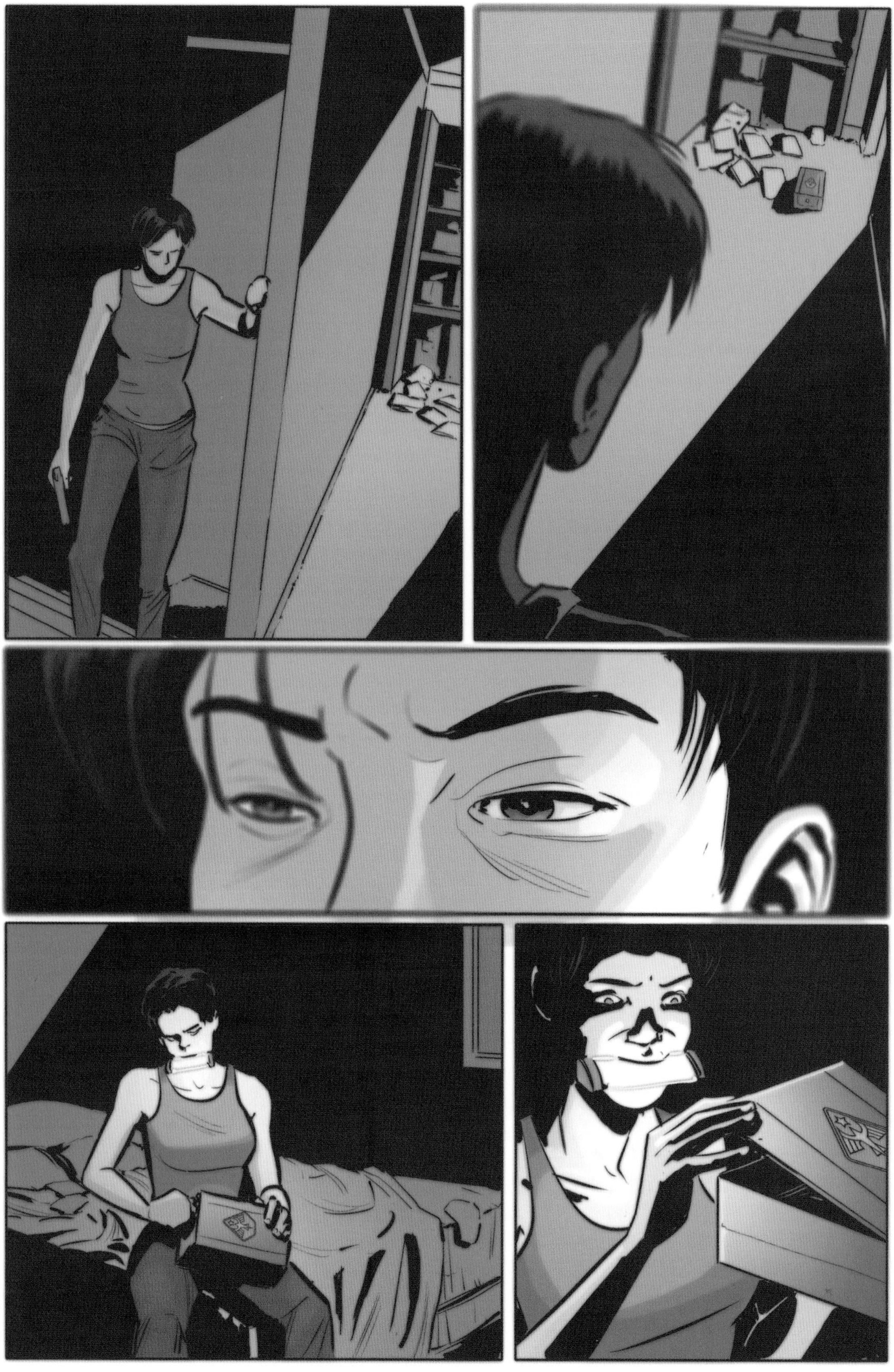

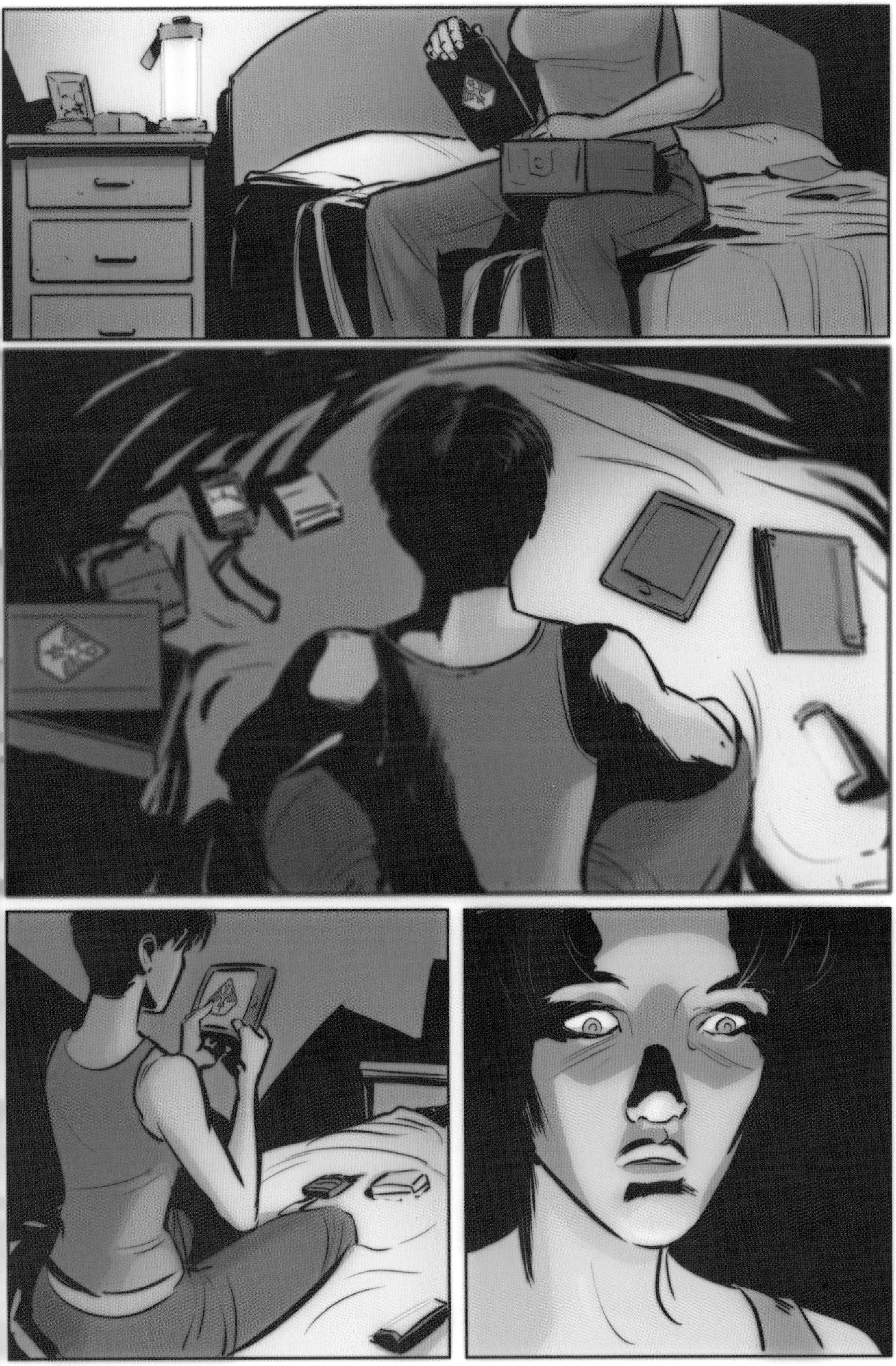

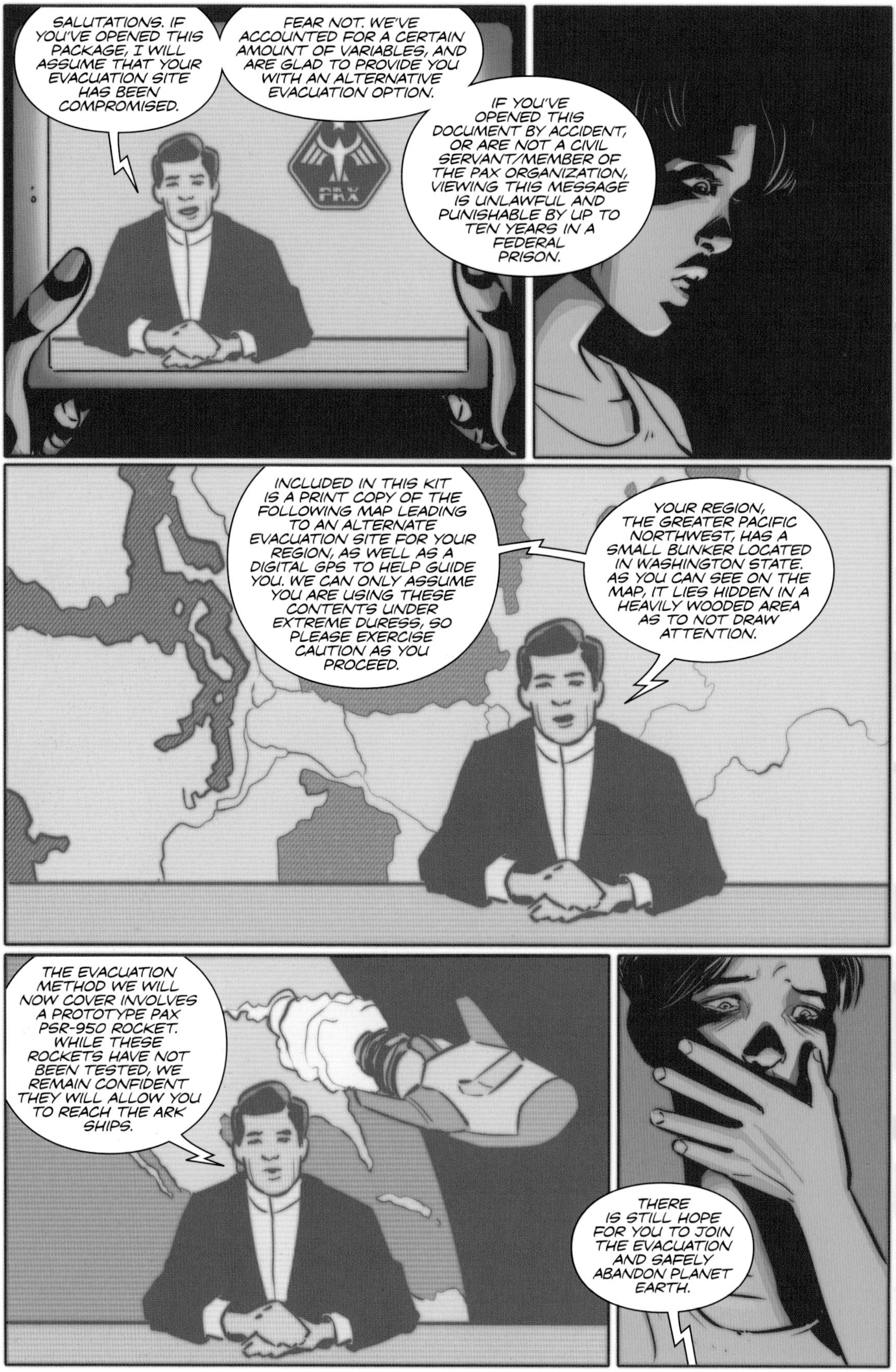
SALUTATIONS. IF YOU'VE OPENED THIS PACKAGE, I WILL ASSUME THAT YOUR EVACUATION SITE HAS BEEN COMPROMISED.
FEAR NOT. WE'VE ACCOUNTED FOR A CERTAIN AMOUNT OF VARIABLES, AND ARE GLAD TO PROVIDE YOU WITH AN ALTERNATIVE EVACUATION OPTION.
PAX
IF YOU'VE OPENED THIS DOCUMENT BY ACCIDENT, OR ARE NOT A CIVIL SERVANT/MEMBER OF THE PAX ORGANIZATION, VIEWING THIS MESSAGE IS UNLAWFUL AND PUNISHABLE BY UP TO TEN YEARS IN A FEDERAL PRISON.
INCLUDED IN THIS KIT IS A PRINT COPY OF THE FOLLOWING MAP LEADING TO AN ALTERNATE EVACUATION SITE FOR YOUR REGION, AS WELL AS A DIGITAL GPS TO HELP GUIDE YOU. WE CAN ONLY ASSUME YOU ARE USING THESE CONTENTS UNDER EXTREME DURESS, SO PLEASE EXERCISE CAUTION AS YOU PROCEED.
YOUR REGION, THE GREATER PACIFIC NORTHWEST, HAS A SMALL BUNKER LOCATED IN WASHINGTON STATE. AS YOU CAN SEE ON THE MAP, IT LIES HIDDEN IN A HEAVILY WOODED AREA AS TO NOT DRAW ATTENTION.
THE EVACUATION METHOD WE WILL NOW COVER INVOLVES A PROTOTYPE PAX PSR-950 ROCKET. WHILE THESE ROCKETS HAVE NOT BEEN TESTED, WE REMAIN CONFIDENT THEY WILL ALLOW YOU TO REACH THE ARK SHIPS.
THERE IS STILL HOPE FOR YOU TO JOIN THE EVACUATION AND SAFELY ABANDON PLANET EARTH.

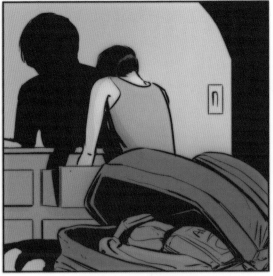

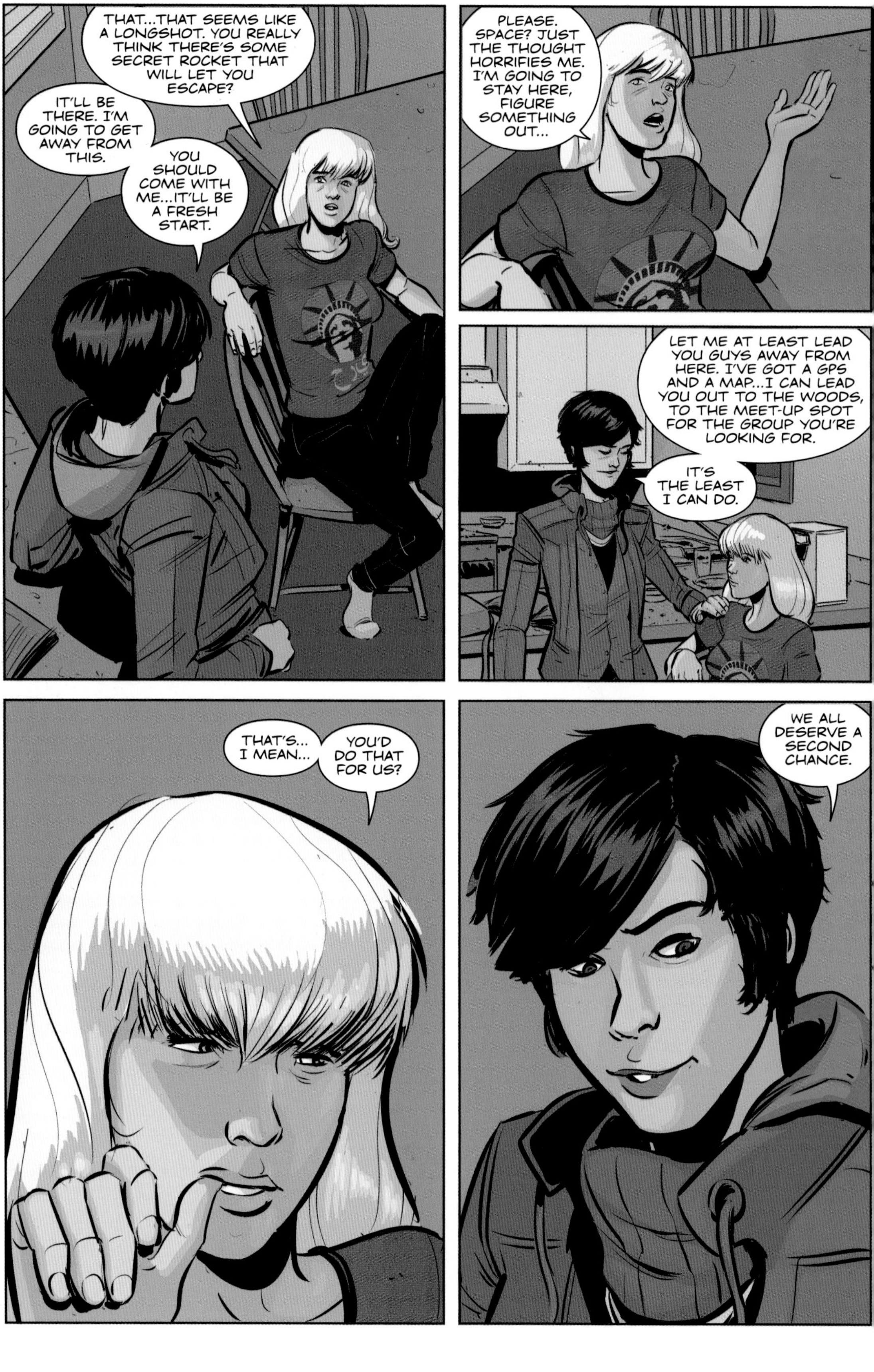
THAT...THAT SEEMS LIKE A LONGSHOT. YOU REALLY THINK THERE'S SOME SECRET ROCKET THAT WILL LET YOU ESCAPE?
IT'LL BE THERE. I'M GOING TO GET AWAY FROM THIS.
YOU SHOULD COME WITH ME...IT'LL BE A FRESH START.
PLEASE. SPACE? JUST THE THOUGHT HORRIFIES ME. I'M GOING TO STAY HERE, FIGURE SOMETHING OUT...
LET ME AT LEAST LEAD YOU GUYS AWAY FROM HERE. I'VE GOT A GPS AND A MAP...I CAN LEAD YOU OUT TO THE WOODS, TO THE MEET-UP SPOT FOR THE GROUP YOU'RE LOOKING FOR.
IT'S THE LEAST I CAN DO.
THAT'S... I MEAN...
YOU'D DO THAT FOR US?
WE ALL DESERVE A SECOND CHANCE.

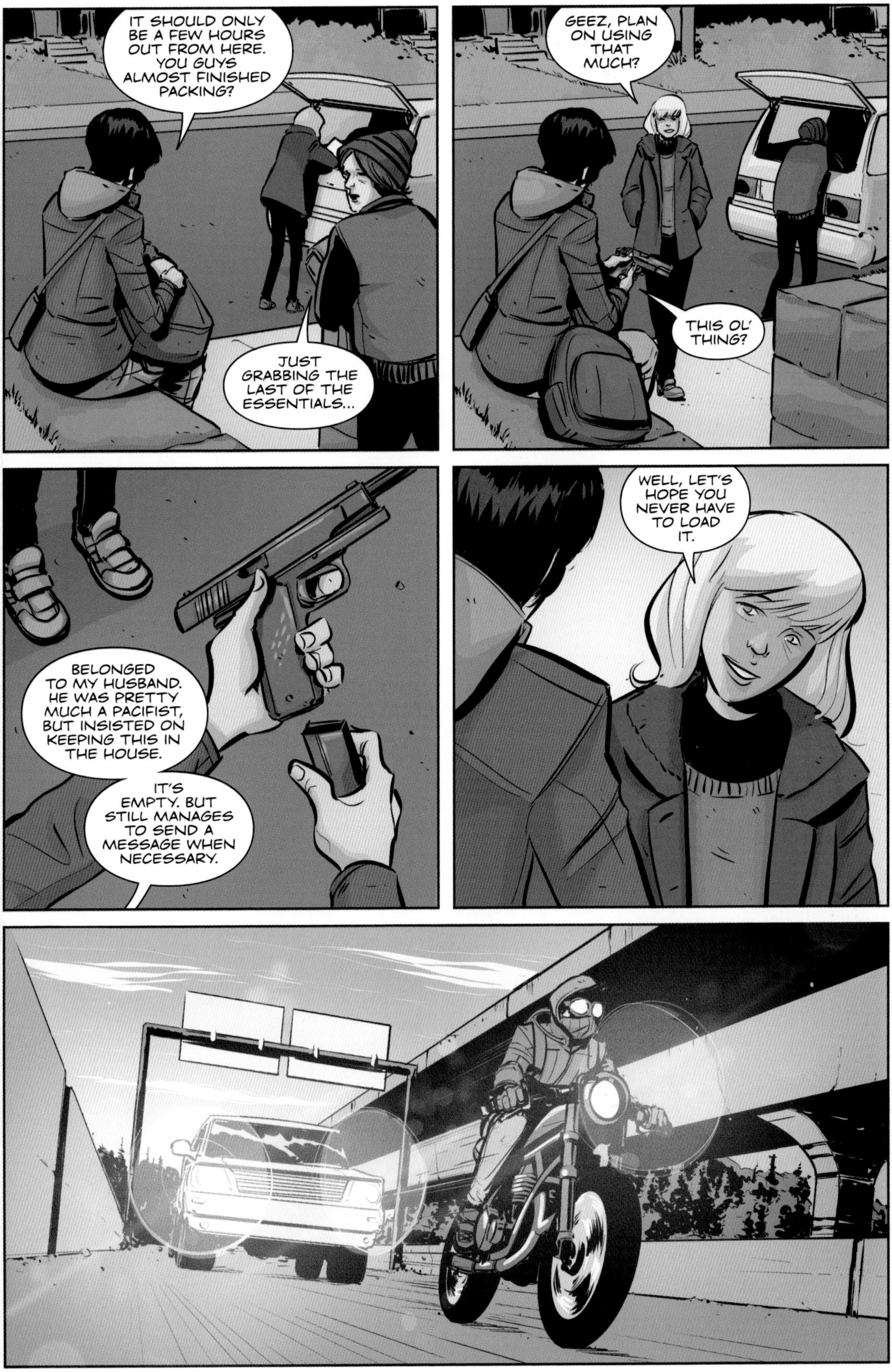

IT SHOULD ONLY BE A FEW HOURS OUT FROM HERE. YOU GUYS ALMOST FINISHED PACKING?
JUST GRABBING THE LAST OF THE ESSENTIALS...
GEEZ, PLAN ON USING THAT MUCH?
THIS OL' THING?
BELONGED TO MY HUSBAND. HE WAS PRETTY MUCH A PACIFIST, BUT INSISTED ON KEEPING THIS IN THE HOUSE.
IT'S EMPTY. BUT STILL MANAGES TO SEND A MESSAGE WHEN NECESSARY.
WELL, LET'S HOPE YOU NEVER HAVE TO LOAD IT.

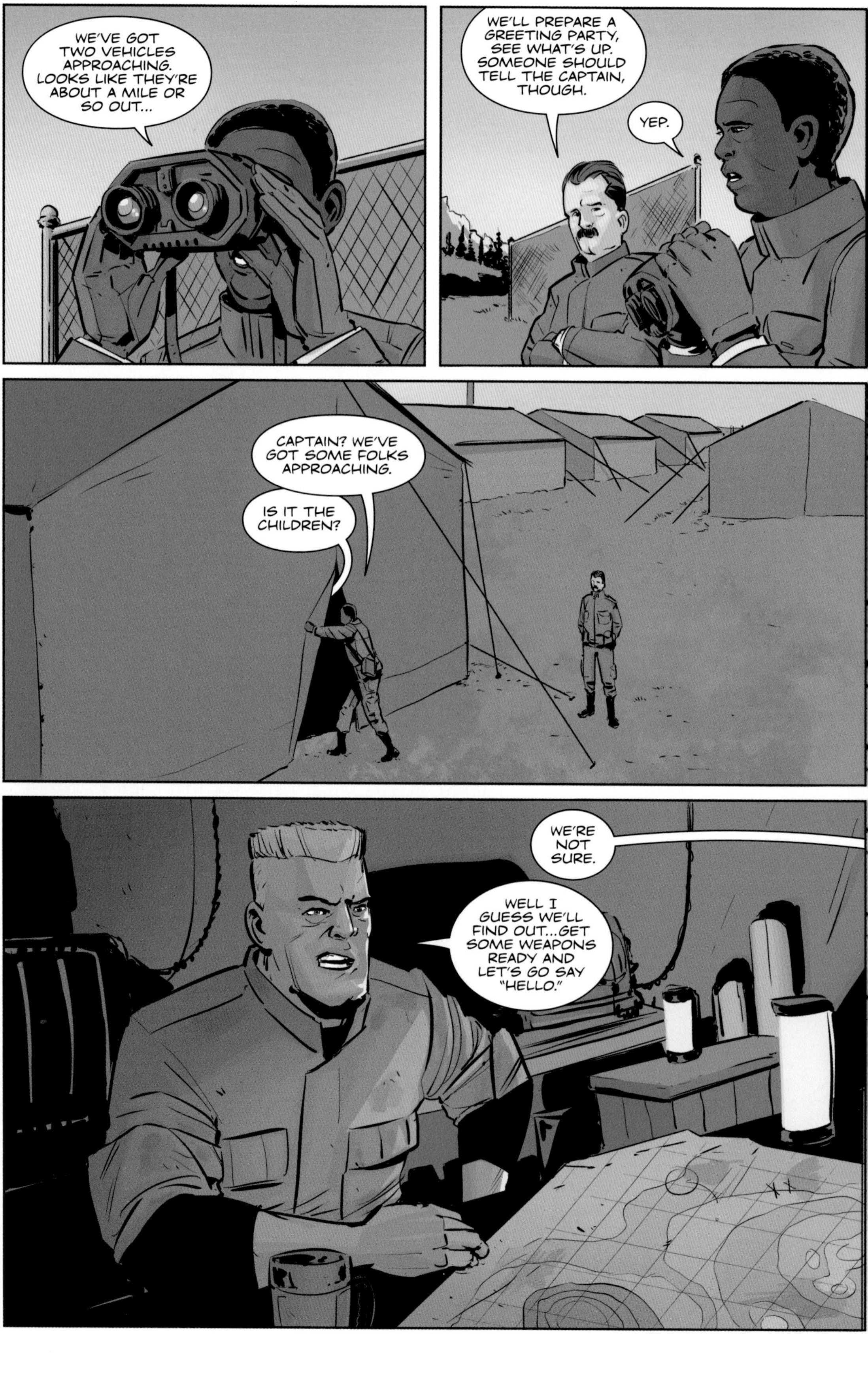
WE'VE GOT TWO VEHICLES APPROACHING. LOOKS LIKE THEY'RE ABOUT A MILE OR SO OUT...
WE'LL PREPARE A GREETING PARTY, SEE WHAT'S UP. SOMEONE SHOULD TELL THE CAPTAIN, THOUGH.
YEP.
CAPTAIN? WE'VE GOT SOME FOLKS APPROACHING.
IS IT THE CHILDREN?
WE'RE NOT SURE.
WELL I GUESS WE'LL FIND OUT...GET SOME WEAPONS READY AND LET'S GO SAY "HELLO."

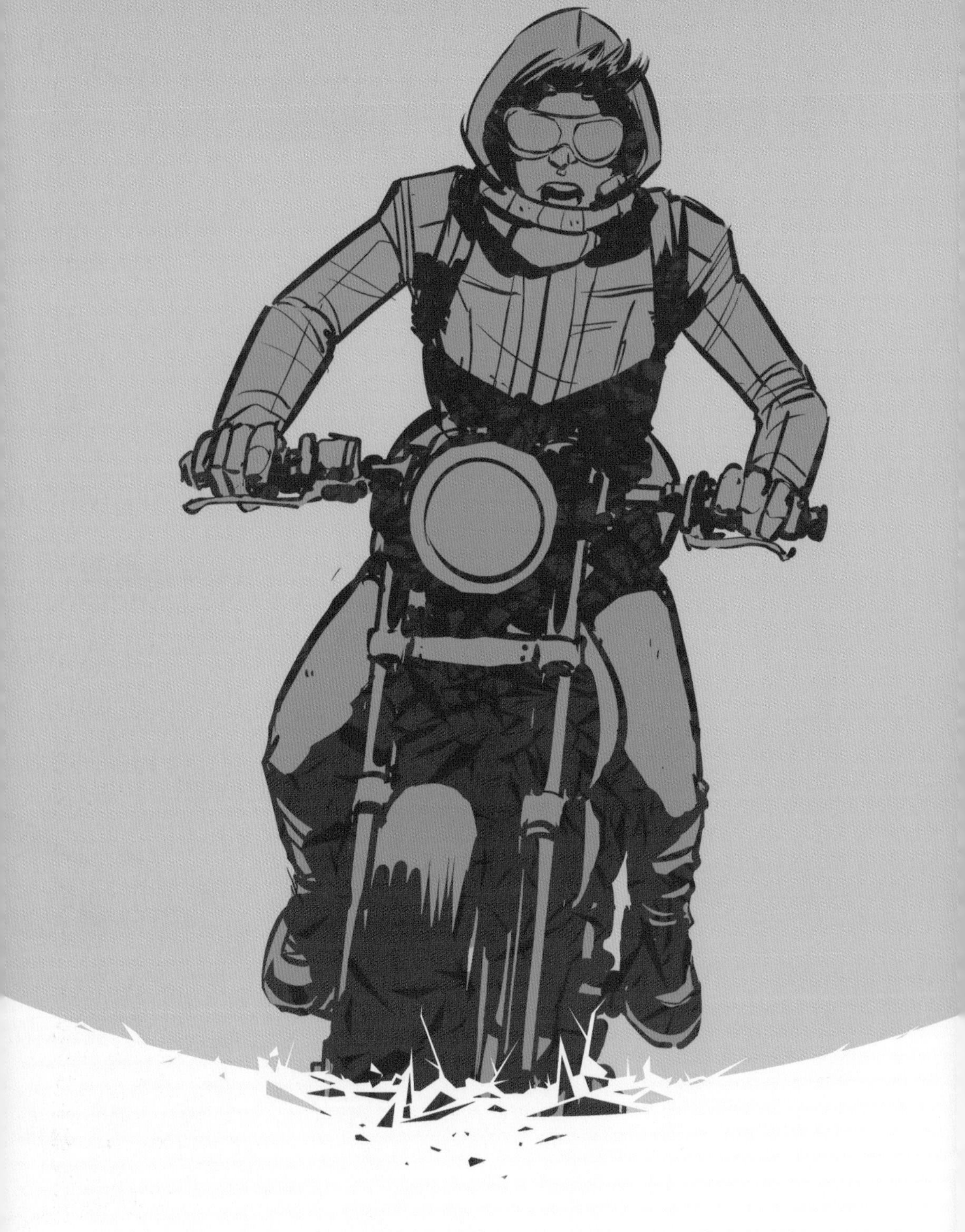

CHAPTER THREE

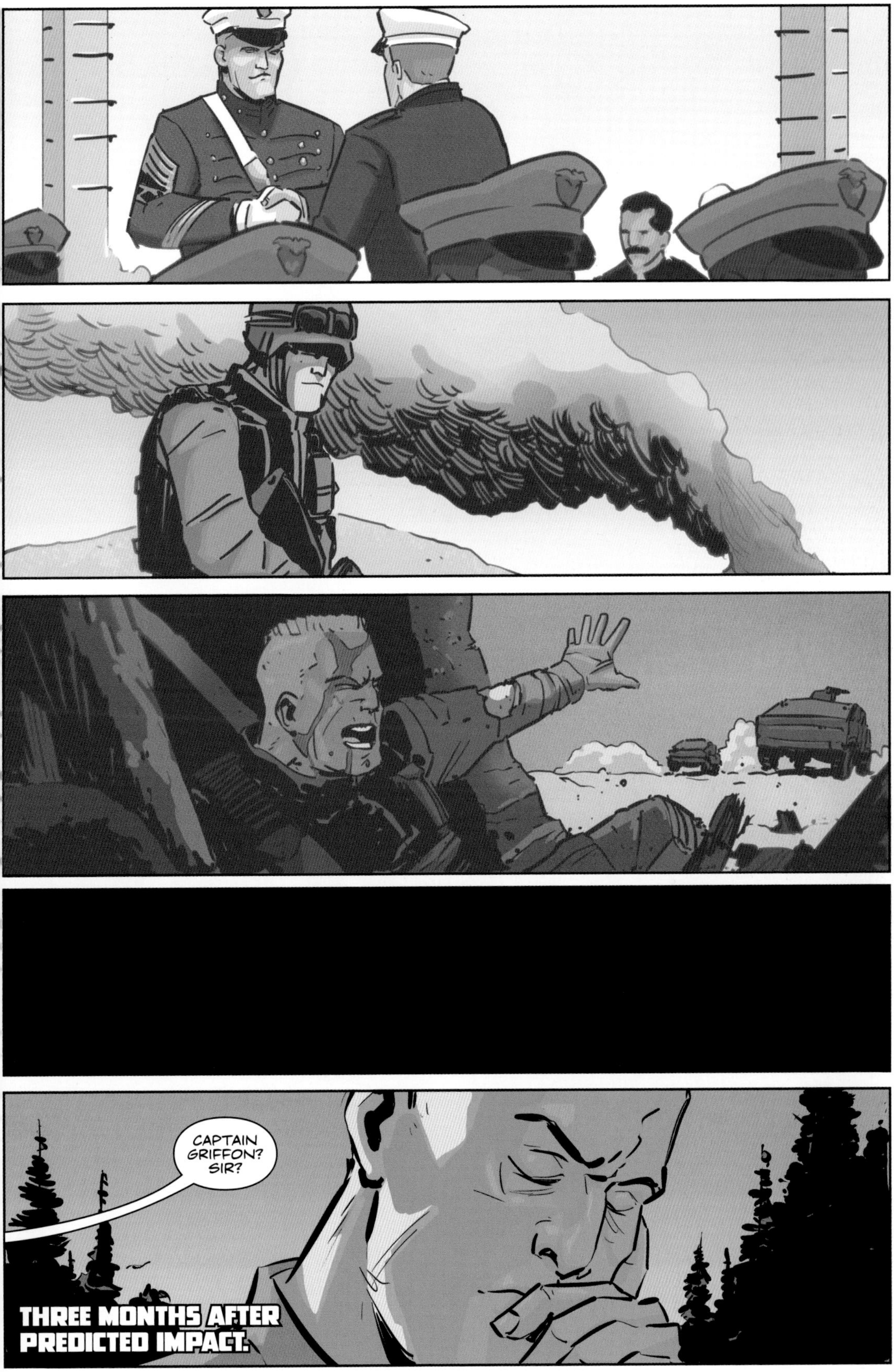
CAPTAIN GRIFFON? SIR?
THREE MONTHS AFTER PREDICTED IMPACT.

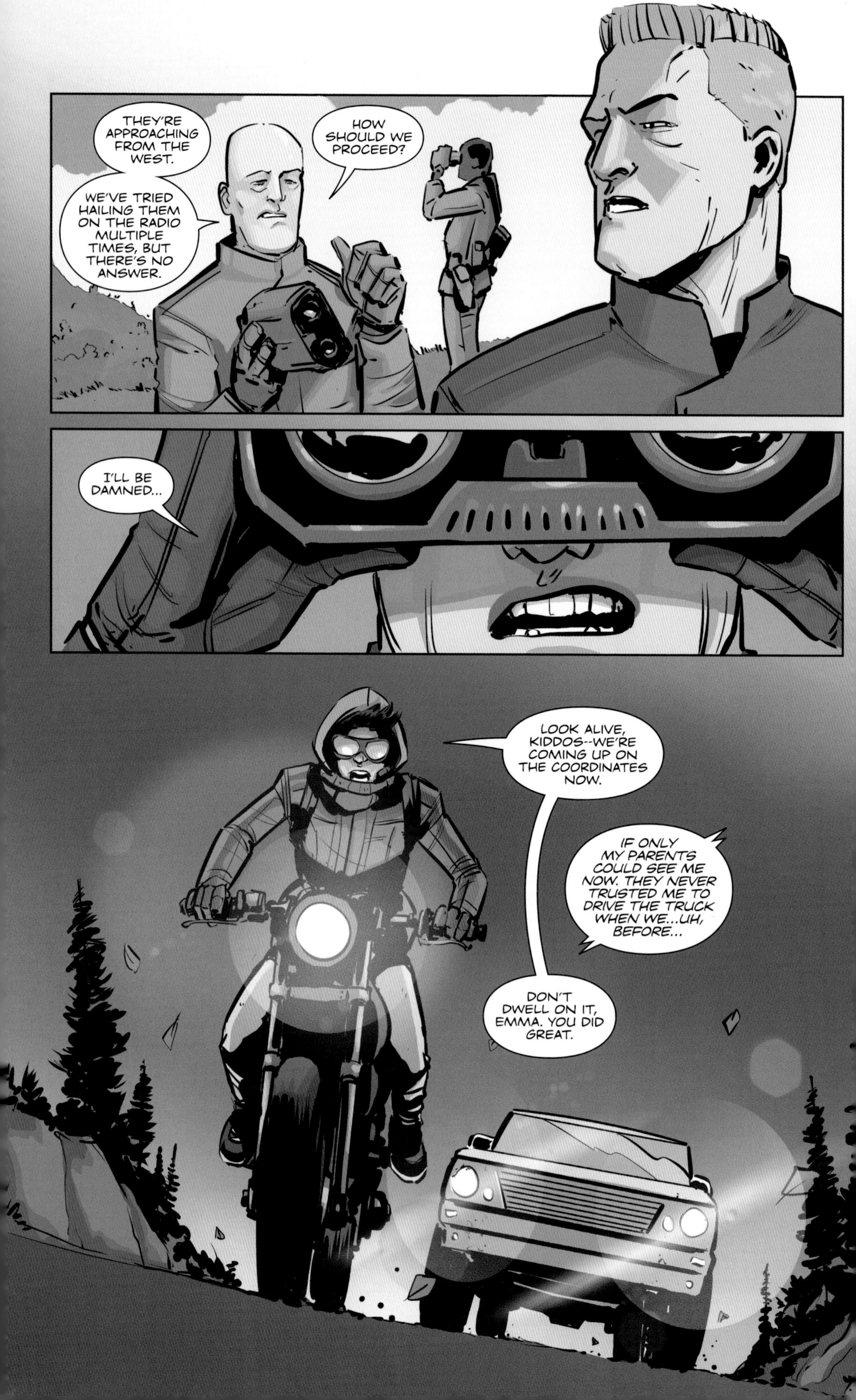

THEY'RE APPROACHING FROM THE WEST.
WE'VE TRIED HAILING THEM ON THE RADIO MULTIPLE TIMES, BUT THERE'S NO ANSWER.
HOW SHOULD WE PROCEED?
I'LL BE DAMNED...
LOOK ALIVE, KIDDOS--WE'RE COMING UP ON THE COORDINATES NOW.
IF ONLY MY PARENTS COULD SEE ME NOW. THEY NEVER TRUSTED ME TO DRIVE THE TRUCK WHEN WE...UH, BEFORE...
DON'T DWELL ON IT, EMMA. YOU DID GREAT.

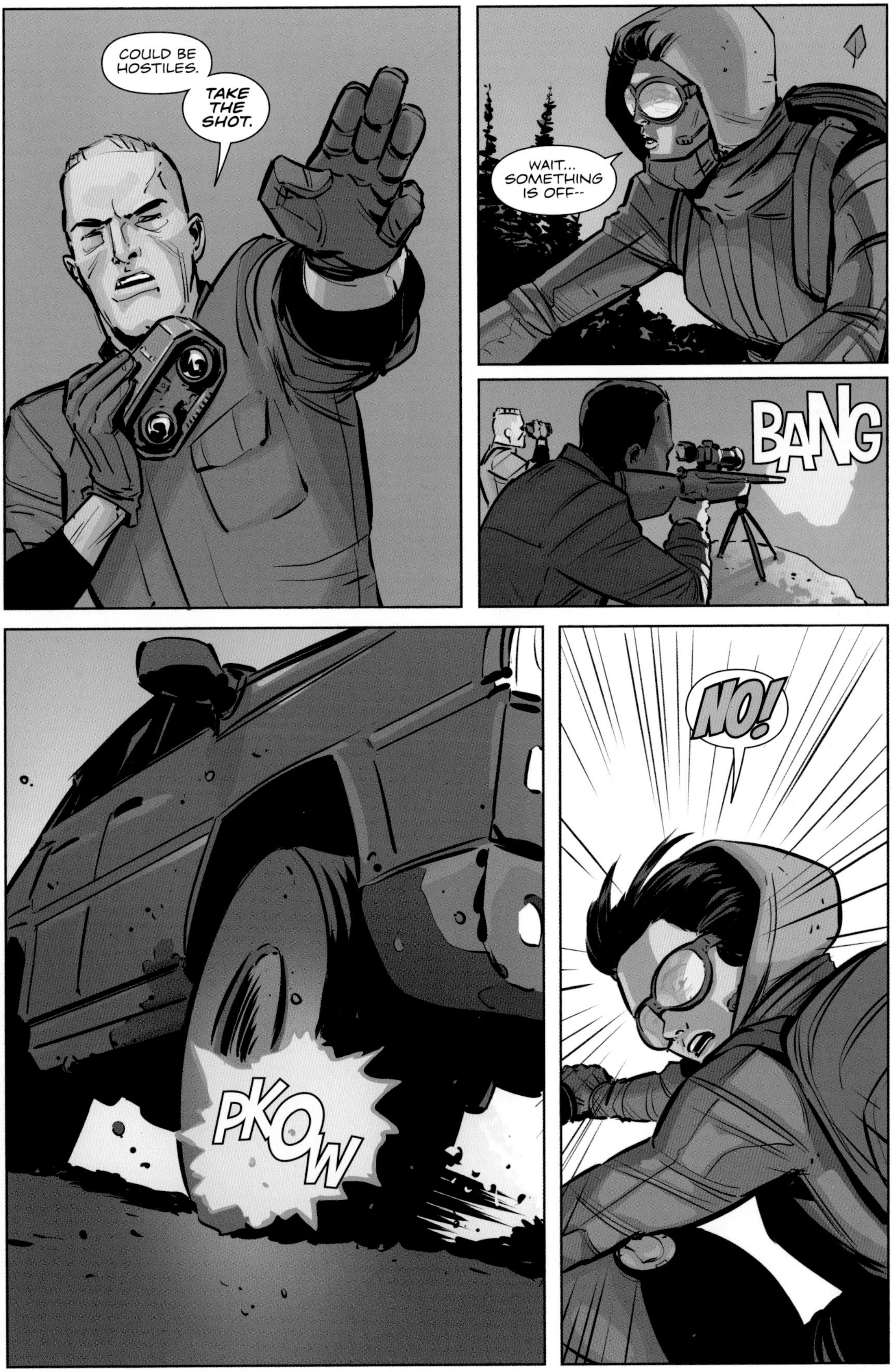

COULD BE HOSTILES.
TAKE THE SHOT.
WAIT... SOMETHING IS OFF--
BANG
PKOW
NO!

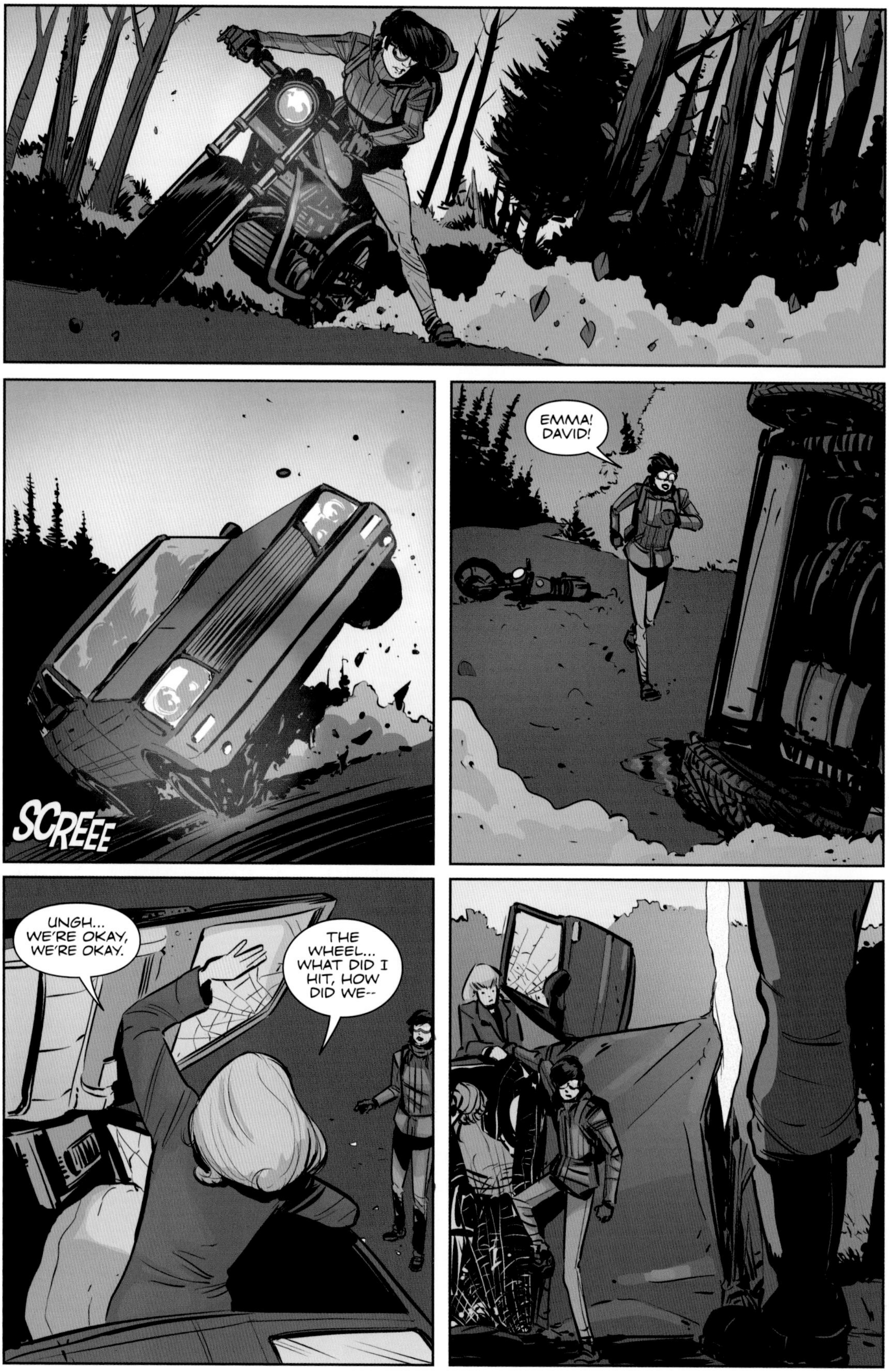
SCREEE
EMMA! DAVID!
UNGH... WE'RE OKAY, WE'RE OKAY.
THE WHEEL... WHAT DID I HIT, HOW DID WE--

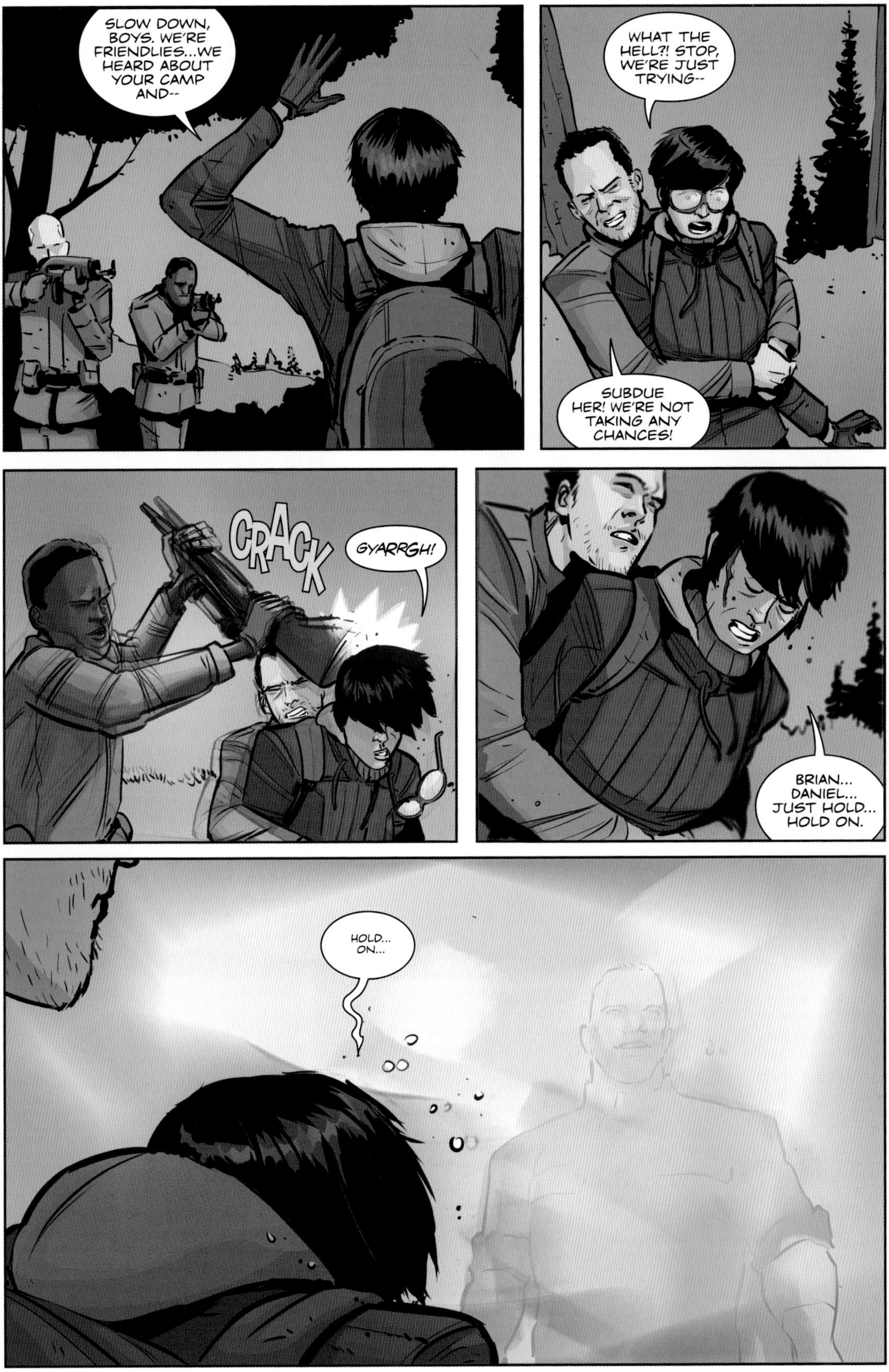
SLOW DOWN, BOYS. WE'RE FRIENDLIES...WE HEARD ABOUT YOUR CAMP AND--
WHAT THE HELL?! STOP, WE'RE JUST TRYING--
SUBDUE HER! WE'RE NOT TAKING ANY CHANCES!
CRACK
GYARRGH!
BRIAN... DANIEL... JUST HOLD... HOLD ON.
HOLD... ON...

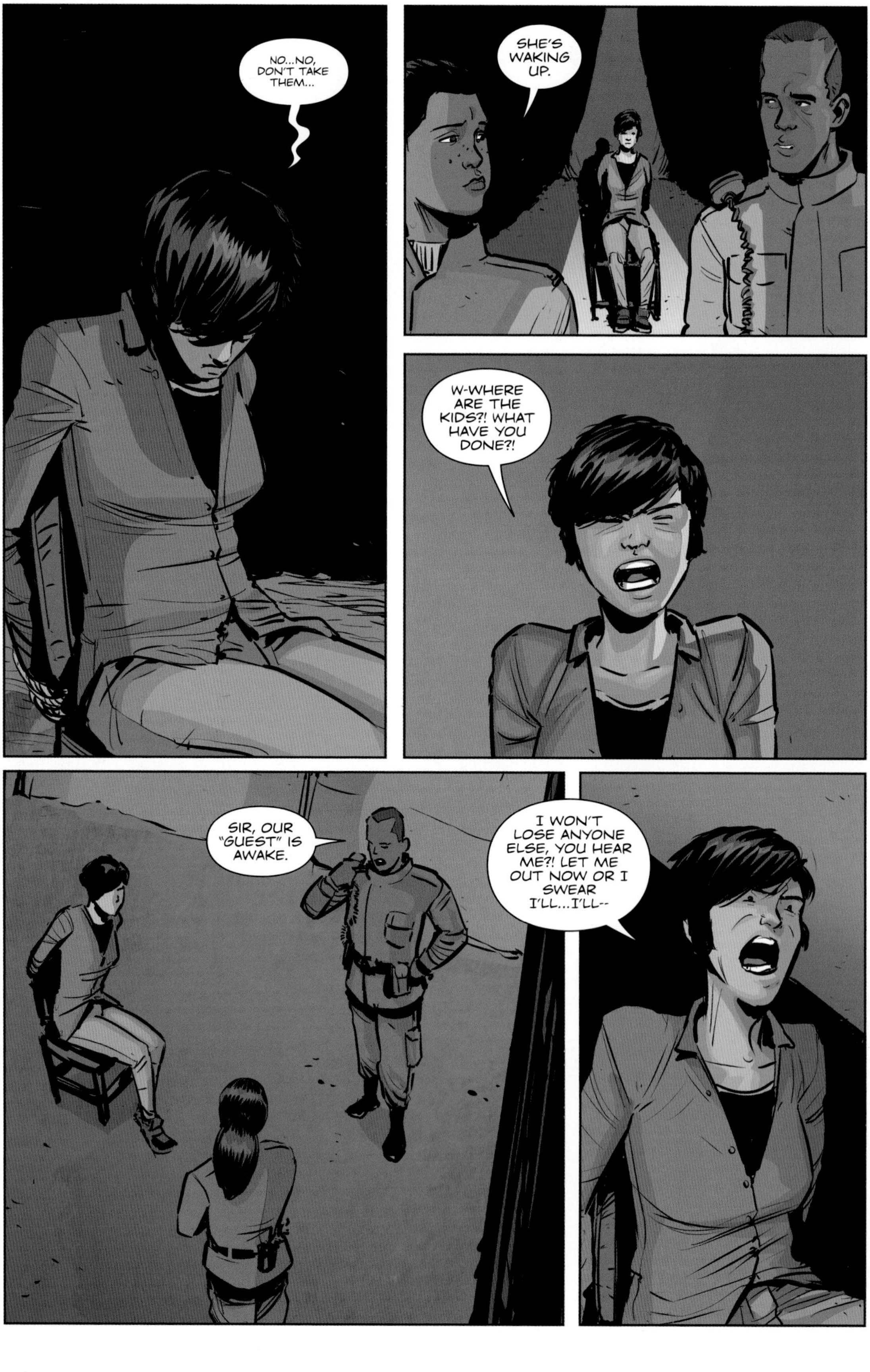
NO...NO, DON'T TAKE THEM...
SHE'S WAKING UP.
W-WHERE ARE THE KIDS?! WHAT HAVE YOU DONE?!
SIR, OUR "GUEST" IS AWAKE.
I WON'T LOSE ANYONE ELSE, YOU HEAR ME?! LET ME OUT NOW OR I SWEAR I'LL...I'LL--

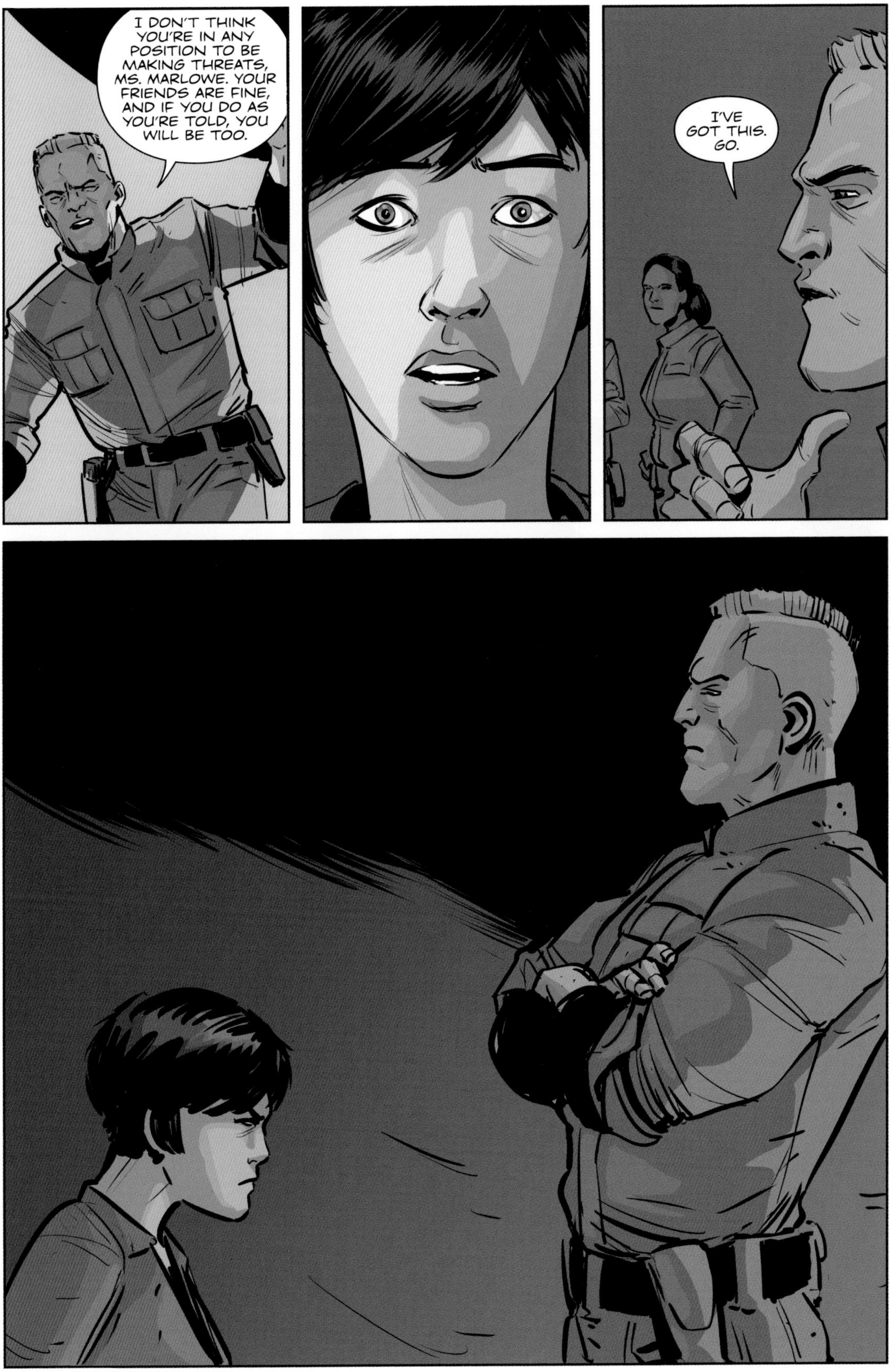
I DON'T THINK YOU'RE IN ANY POSITION TO BE MAKING THREATS, MS. MARLOWE. YOUR FRIENDS ARE FINE, AND IF YOU DO AS YOU'RE TOLD, YOU WILL BE TOO.
I'VE GOT THIS. GO.

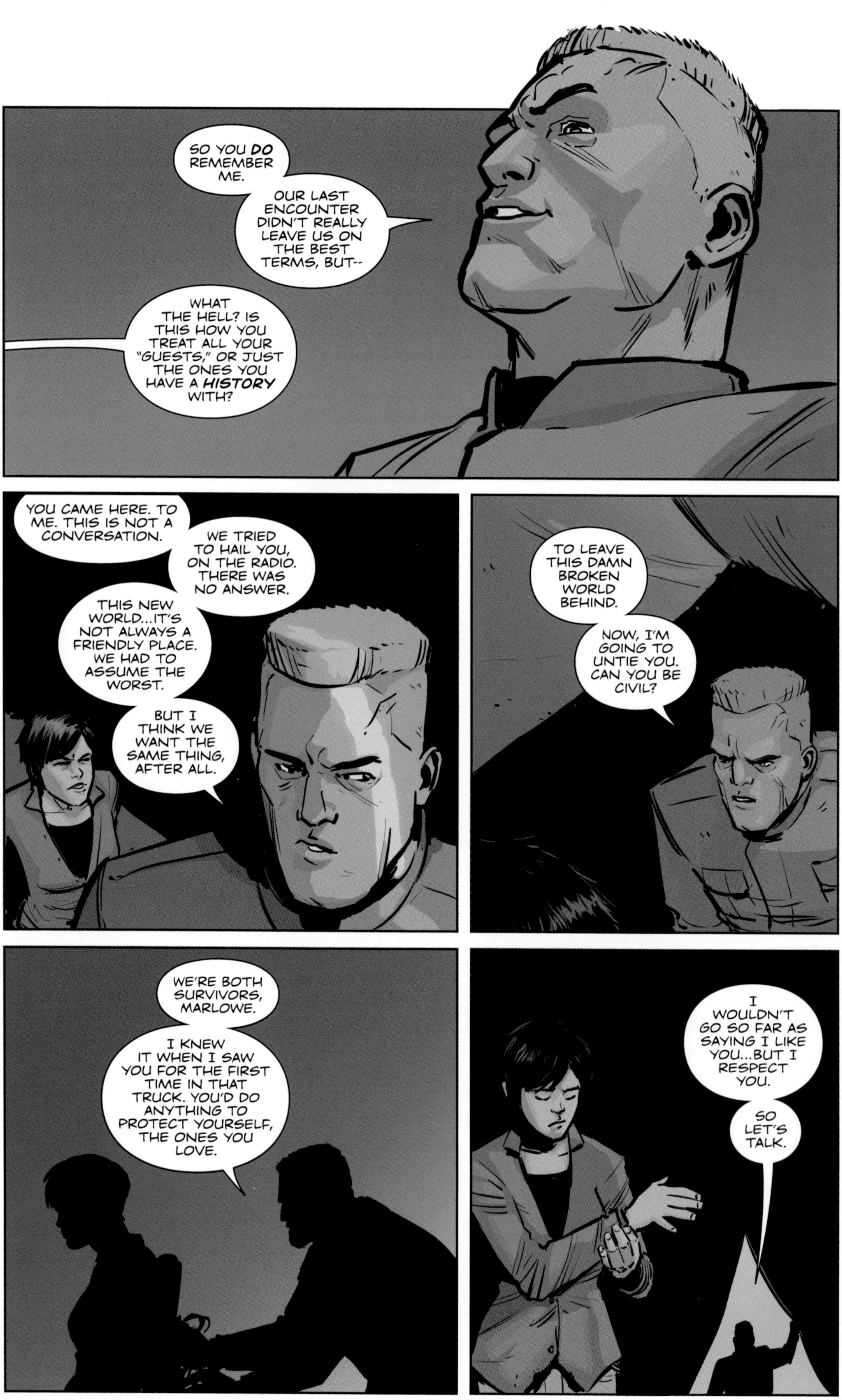
SO YOU DO REMEMBER ME.
OUR LAST ENCOUNTER DIDN'T REALLY LEAVE US ON THE BEST TERMS, BUT--
WHAT THE HELL? IS THIS HOW YOU TREAT ALL YOUR "GUESTS," OR JUST THE ONES YOU HAVE A HISTORY WITH?
YOU CAME HERE. TO ME. THIS IS NOT A CONVERSATION.
WE TRIED TO HAIL YOU, ON THE RADIO. THERE WAS NO ANSWER.
THIS NEW WORLD...IT'S NOT ALWAYS A FRIENDLY PLACE. WE HAD TO ASSUME THE WORST.
BUT I THINK WE WANT THE SAME THING, AFTER ALL.
TO LEAVE THIS DAMN BROKEN WORLD BEHIND.
NOW, I'M GOING TO UNTIE YOU. CAN YOU BE CIVIL?
WE'RE BOTH SURVIVORS, MARLOWE.
I KNEW IT WHEN I SAW YOU FOR THE FIRST TIME IN THAT TRUCK. YOU'D DO ANYTHING TO PROTECT YOURSELF, THE ONES YOU LOVE.
I WOULDN'T GO SO FAR AS SAYING I LIKE YOU...BUT I RESPECT YOU.
SO LET'S TALK.

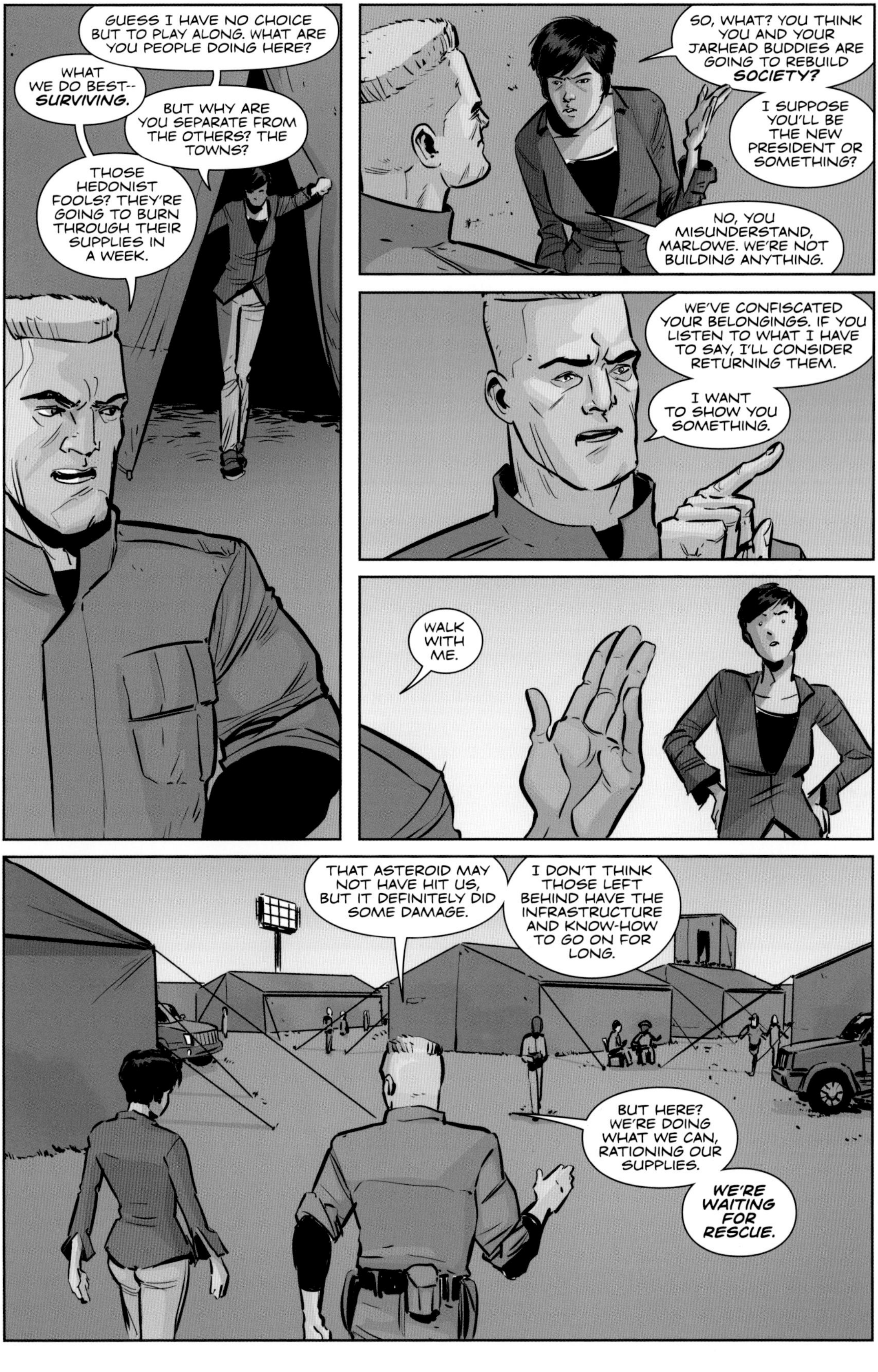
GUESS I HAVE NO CHOICE BUT TO PLAY ALONG. WHAT ARE YOU PEOPLE DOING HERE?
WHAT WE DO BEST-- SURVIVING.
BUT WHY ARE YOU SEPARATE FROM THE OTHERS? THE TOWNS?
THOSE HEDONIST FOOLS? THEY'RE GOING TO BURN THROUGH THEIR SUPPLIES IN A WEEK.
SO, WHAT? YOU THINK YOU AND YOUR JARHEAD BUDDIES ARE GOING TO REBUILD SOCIETY?
I SUPPOSE YOU'LL BE THE NEW PRESIDENT OR SOMETHING?
NO, YOU MISUNDERSTAND, MARLOWE. WE'RE NOT BUILDING ANYTHING.
WE'VE CONFISCATED YOUR BELONGINGS. IF YOU LISTEN TO WHAT I HAVE TO SAY, I'LL CONSIDER RETURNING THEM.
I WANT TO SHOW YOU SOMETHING.
WALK WITH ME.
THAT ASTEROID MAY NOT HAVE HIT US, BUT IT DEFINITELY DID SOME DAMAGE.
I DON'T THINK THOSE LEFT BEHIND HAVE THE INFRASTRUCTURE AND KNOW-HOW TO GO ON FOR LONG.
BUT HERE? WE'RE DOING WHAT WE CAN, RATIONING OUR SUPPLIES.
WE'RE WAITING FOR RESCUE.

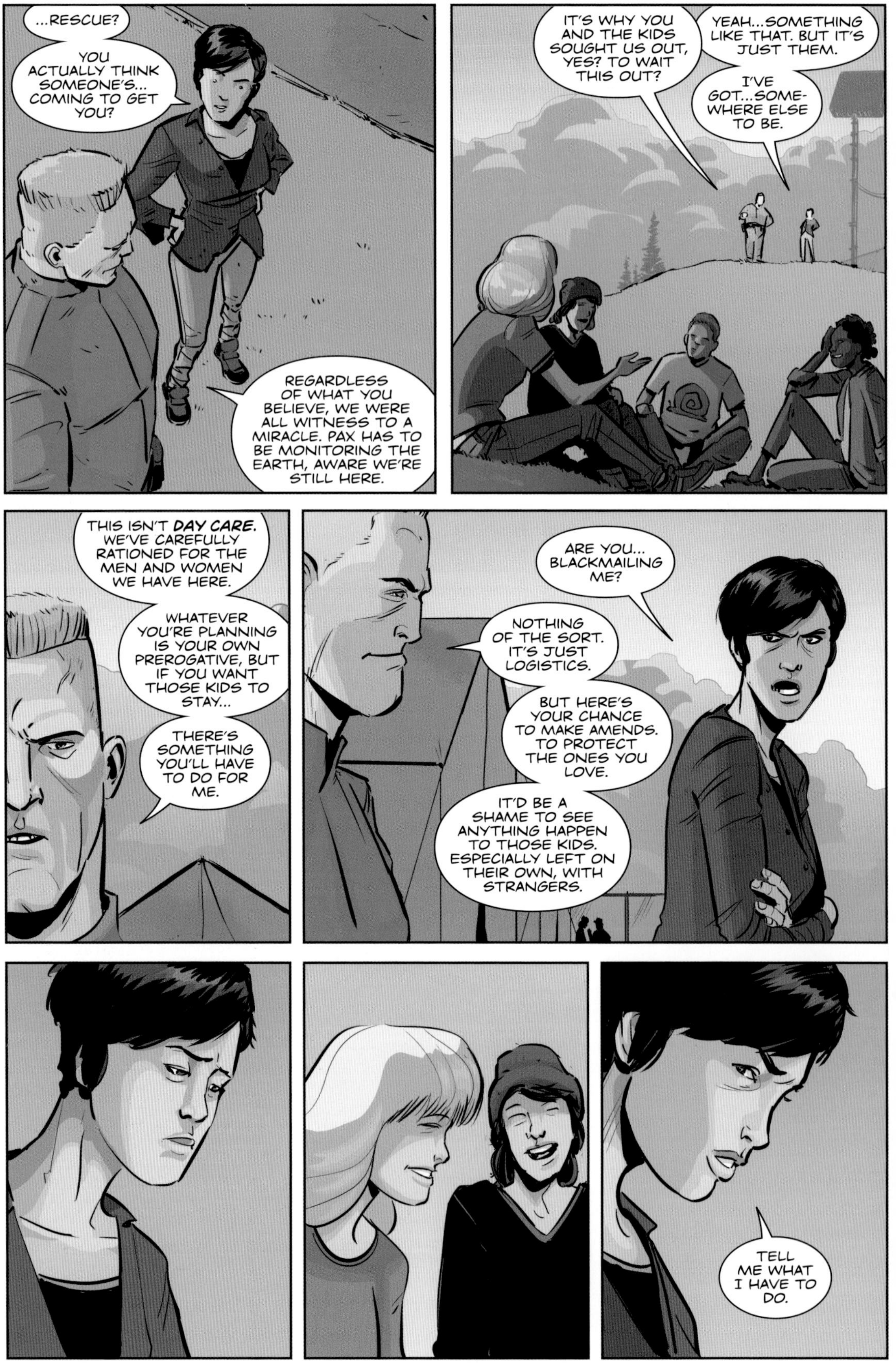
...RESCUE?
YOU ACTUALLY THINK SOMEONE'S... COMING TO GET YOU?
REGARDLESS OF WHAT YOU BELIEVE, WE WERE ALL WITNESS TO A MIRACLE. PAX HAS TO BE MONITORING THE EARTH, AWARE WE'RE STILL HERE.
IT'S WHY YOU AND THE KIDS SOUGHT US OUT, YES? TO WAIT THIS OUT?
YEAH...SOMETHING LIKE THAT. BUT IT'S JUST THEM.
I'VE GOT...SOMEWHERE ELSE TO BE.
THIS ISN'T **DAY CARE.** WE'VE CAREFULLY RATIONED FOR THE MEN AND WOMEN WE HAVE HERE.
WHATEVER YOU'RE PLANNING IS YOUR OWN PREROGATIVE, BUT IF YOU WANT THOSE KIDS TO STAY...
THERE'S SOMETHING YOU'LL HAVE TO DO FOR ME.
ARE YOU... BLACKMAILING ME?
NOTHING OF THE SORT. IT'S JUST LOGISTICS.
BUT HERE'S YOUR CHANCE TO MAKE AMENDS. TO PROTECT THE ONES YOU LOVE.
IT'D BE A SHAME TO SEE ANYTHING HAPPEN TO THOSE KIDS. ESPECIALLY LEFT ON THEIR OWN, WITH STRANGERS.
TELL ME WHAT I HAVE TO DO.

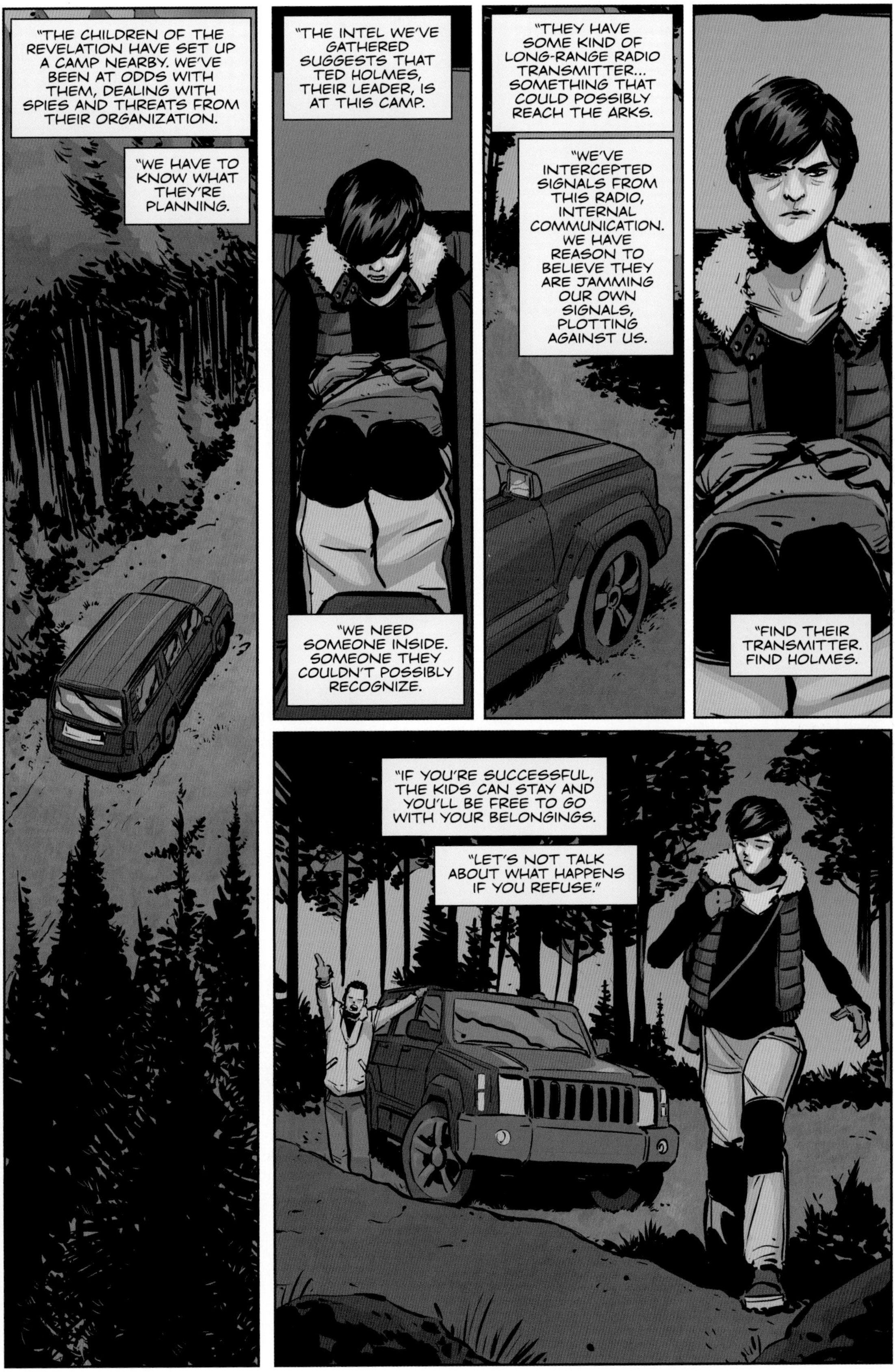
"THE CHILDREN OF THE REVELATION HAVE SET UP A CAMP NEARBY. WE'VE BEEN AT ODDS WITH THEM, DEALING WITH SPIES AND THREATS FROM THEIR ORGANIZATION.
"WE HAVE TO KNOW WHAT THEY'RE PLANNING.
"THE INTEL WE'VE GATHERED SUGGESTS THAT TED HOLMES, THEIR LEADER, IS AT THIS CAMP.
"WE NEED SOMEONE INSIDE. SOMEONE THEY COULDN'T POSSIBLY RECOGNIZE.
"THEY HAVE SOME KIND OF LONG-RANGE RADIO TRANSMITTER... SOMETHING THAT COULD POSSIBLY REACH THE ARKS.
"WE'VE INTERCEPTED SIGNALS FROM THIS RADIO, INTERNAL COMMUNICATION. WE HAVE REASON TO BELIEVE THEY ARE JAMMING OUR OWN SIGNALS, PLOTTING AGAINST US.
"FIND THEIR TRANSMITTER. FIND HOLMES.
"IF YOU'RE SUCCESSFUL, THE KIDS CAN STAY AND YOU'LL BE FREE TO GO WITH YOUR BELONGINGS.
"LET'S NOT TALK ABOUT WHAT HAPPENS IF YOU REFUSE."

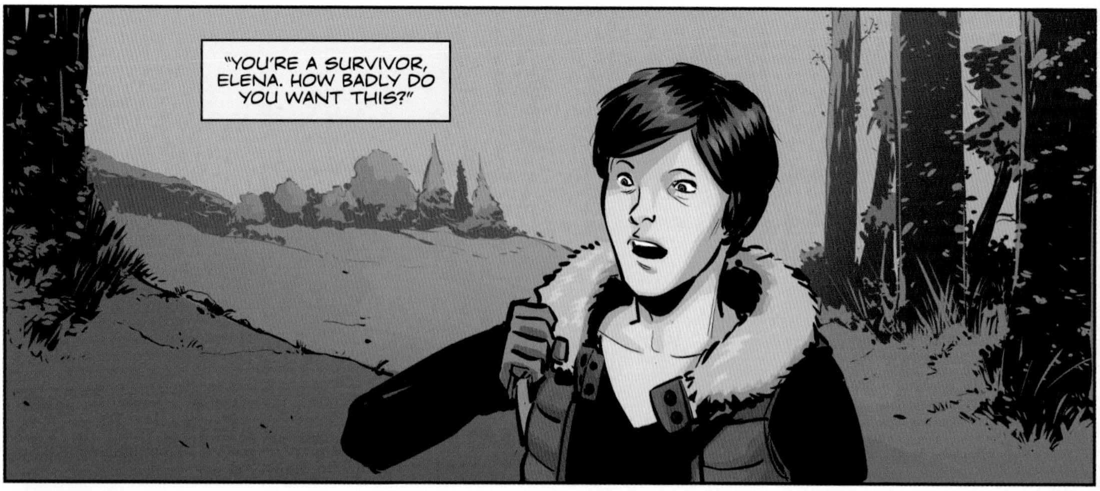
"YOU'RE A SURVIVOR, ELENA. HOW BADLY DO YOU WANT THIS?"

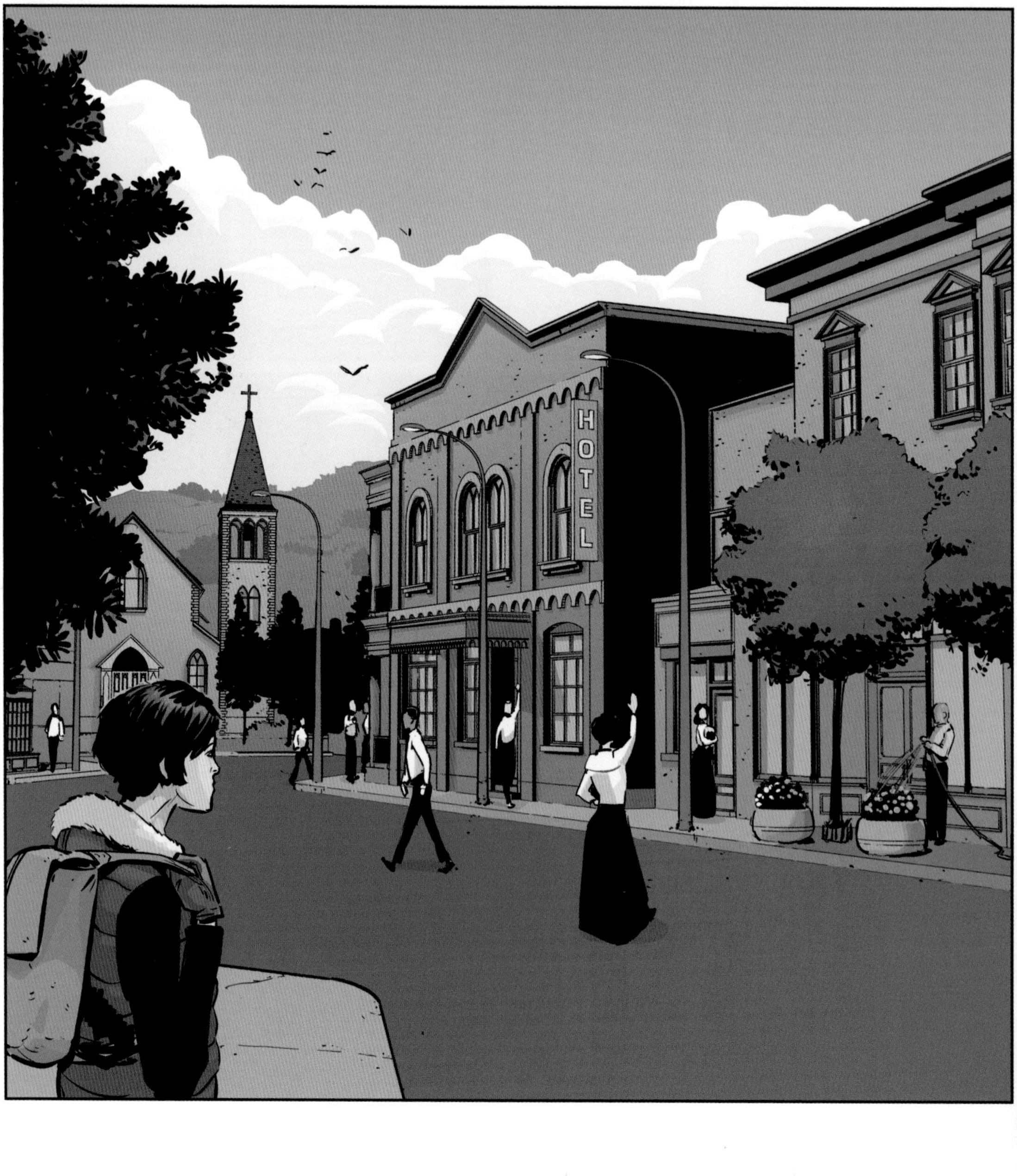
HOTEL

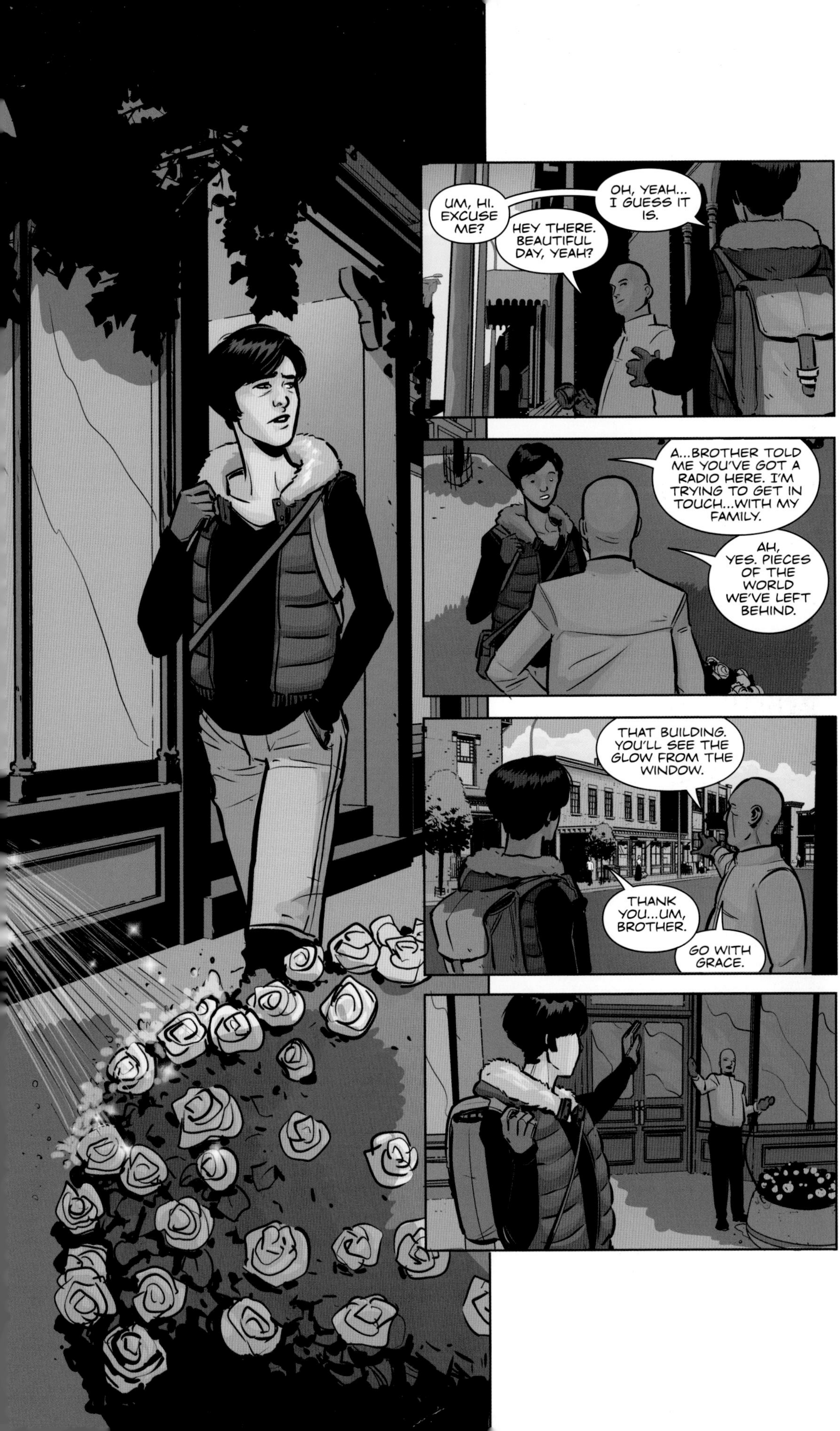
UM, HI. EXCUSE ME?
HEY THERE. BEAUTIFUL DAY, YEAH?
OH, YEAH... I GUESS IT IS.
A...BROTHER TOLD ME YOU'VE GOT A RADIO HERE. I'M TRYING TO GET IN TOUCH...WITH MY FAMILY.
AH, YES. PIECES OF THE WORLD WE'VE LEFT BEHIND.
THAT BUILDING. YOU'LL SEE THE GLOW FROM THE WINDOW.
THANK YOU...UM, BROTHER.
GO WITH GRACE.

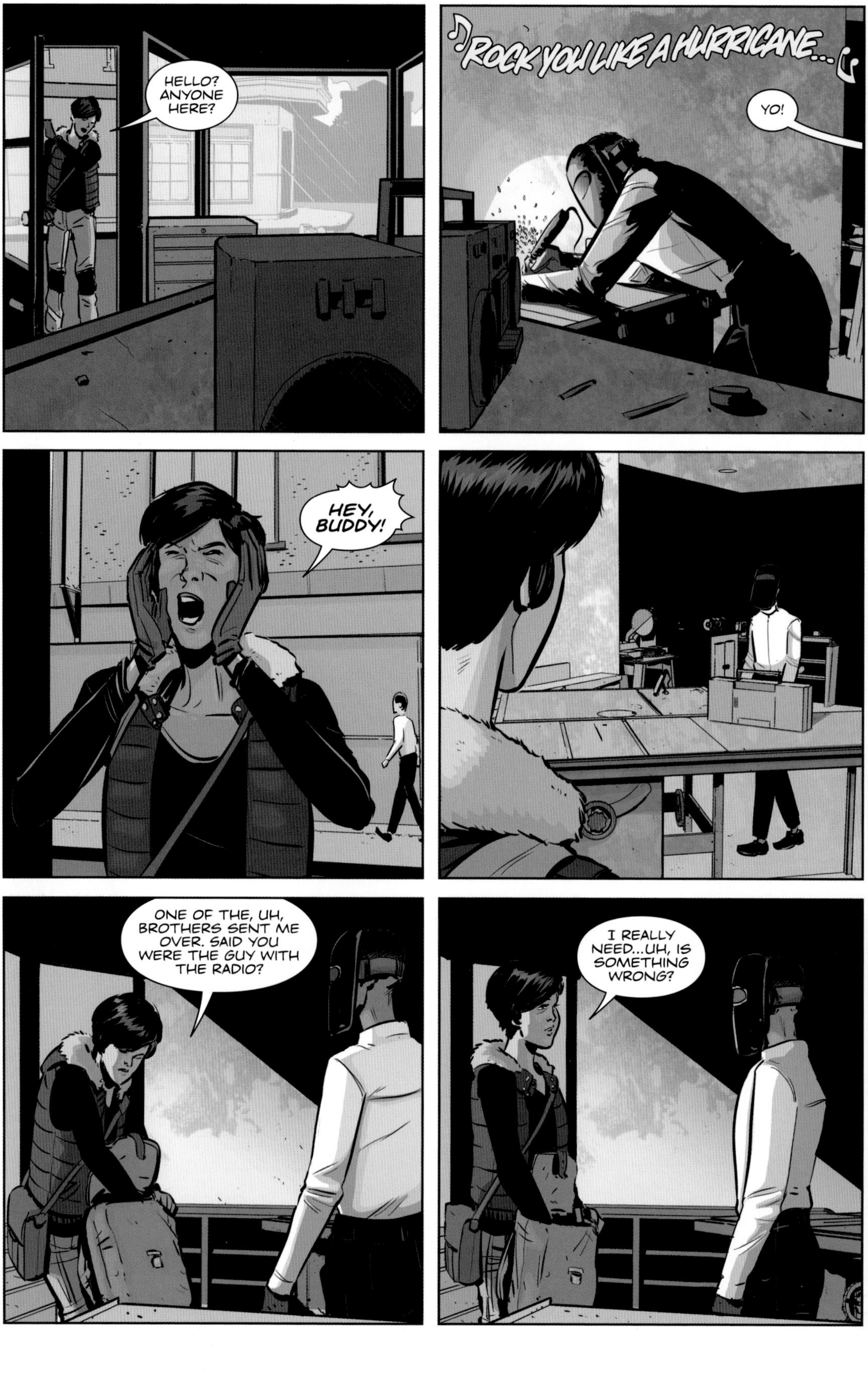
HELLO? ANYONE HERE?
ROCK YOU LIKE A HURRICANE...
YO!
HEY, BUDDY!
ONE OF THE, UH, BROTHERS SENT ME OVER. SAID YOU WERE THE GUY WITH THE RADIO?
I REALLY NEED...UH, IS SOMETHING WRONG?

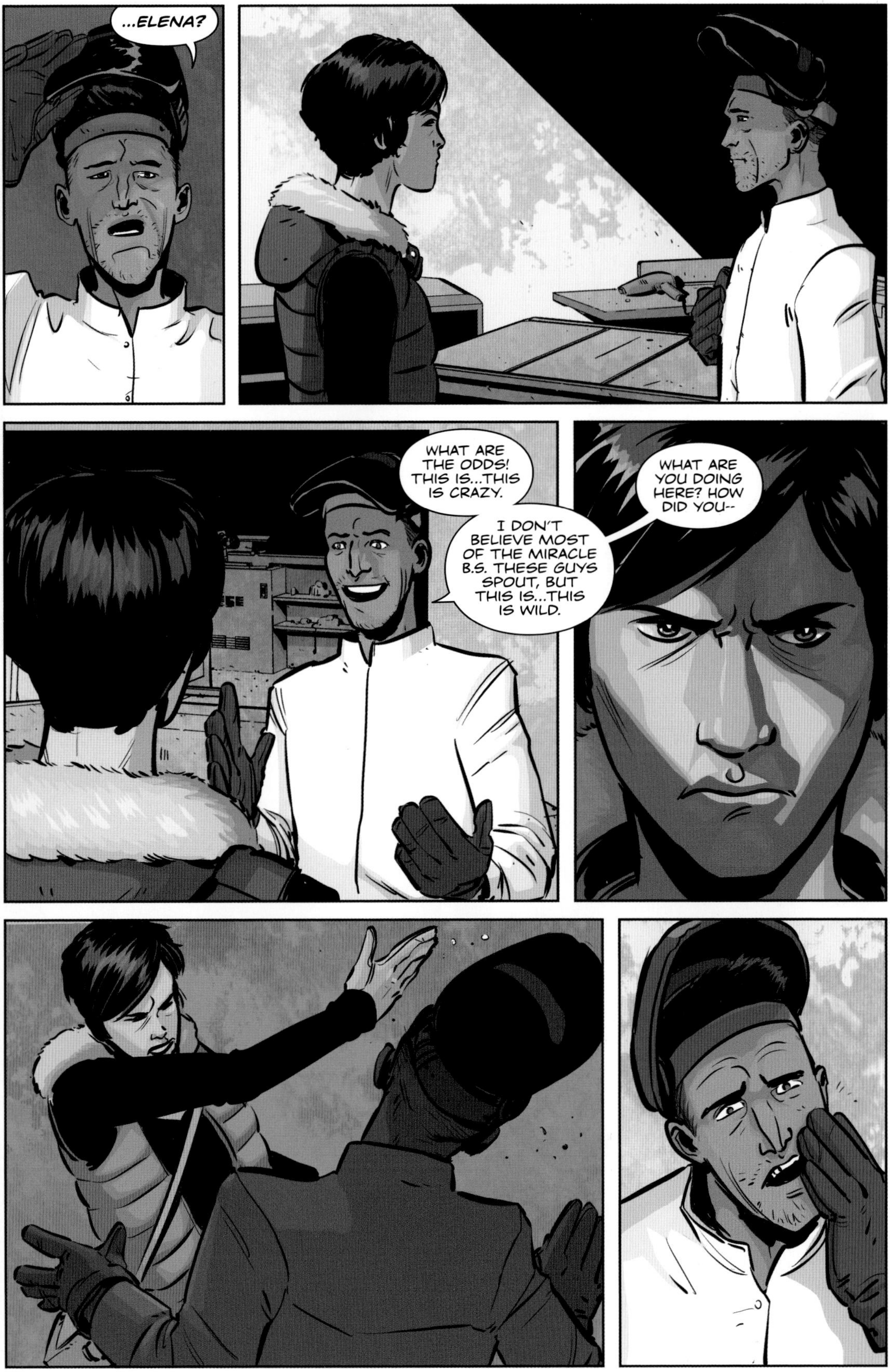
...ELENA?
WHAT ARE THE ODDS! THIS IS...THIS IS CRAZY.
I DON'T BELIEVE MOST OF THE MIRACLE B.S. THESE GUYS SPOUT, BUT THIS IS...THIS IS WILD.
WHAT ARE YOU DOING HERE? HOW DID YOU--

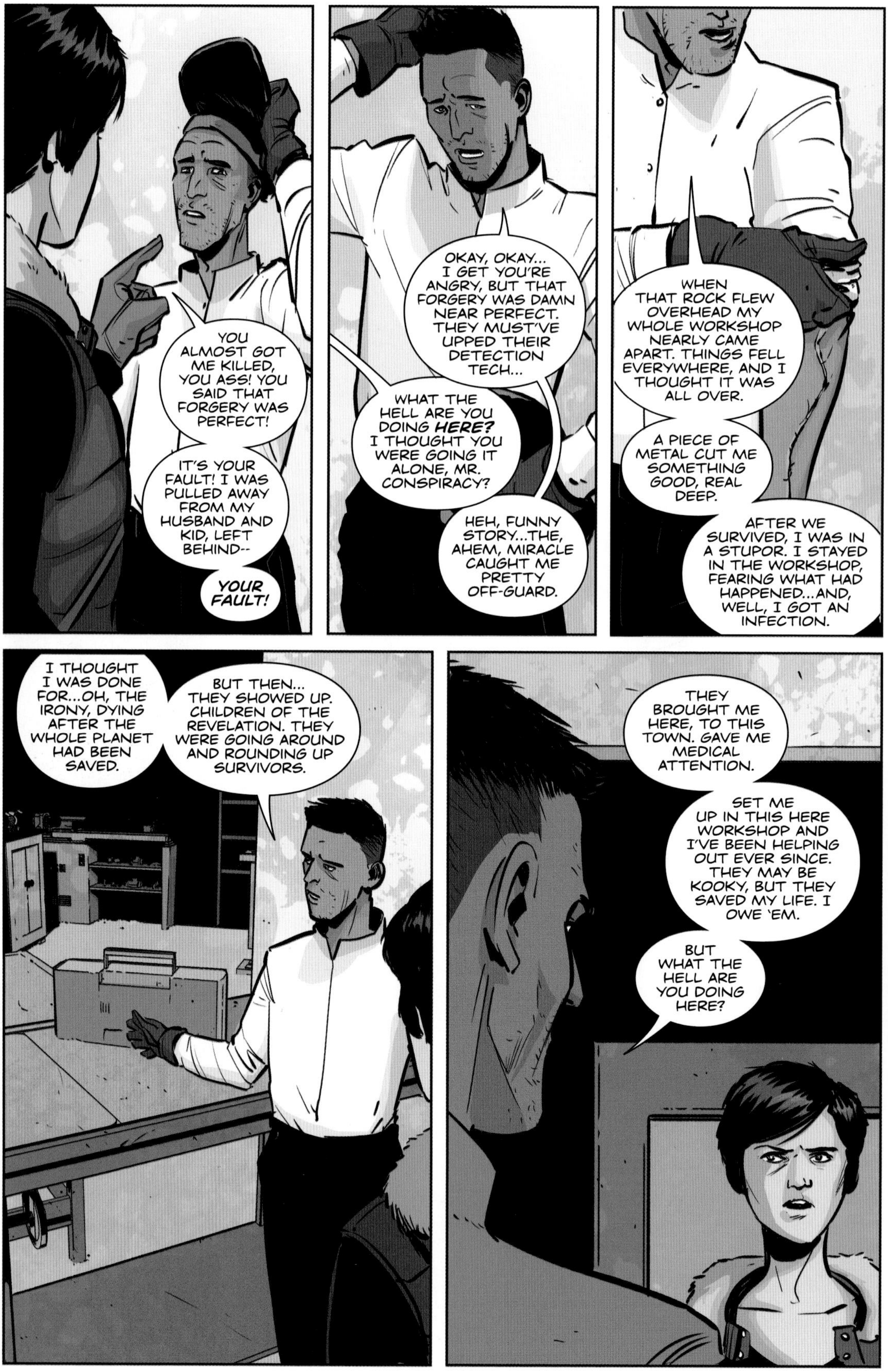
YOU ALMOST GOT ME KILLED, YOU ASS! YOU SAID THAT FORGERY WAS PERFECT!
IT'S YOUR FAULT! I WAS PULLED AWAY FROM MY HUSBAND AND KID, LEFT BEHIND--
YOUR FAULT!
OKAY, OKAY... I GET YOU'RE ANGRY, BUT THAT FORGERY WAS DAMN NEAR PERFECT. THEY MUST'VE UPPED THEIR DETECTION TECH...
WHAT THE HELL ARE YOU DOING HERE? I THOUGHT YOU WERE GOING IT ALONE, MR. CONSPIRACY?
HEH, FUNNY STORY...THE, AHEM, MIRACLE CAUGHT ME PRETTY OFF-GUARD.
WHEN THAT ROCK FLEW OVERHEAD MY WHOLE WORKSHOP NEARLY CAME APART. THINGS FELL EVERYWHERE, AND I THOUGHT IT WAS ALL OVER.
A PIECE OF METAL CUT ME SOMETHING GOOD, REAL DEEP.
AFTER WE SURVIVED, I WAS IN A STUPOR. I STAYED IN THE WORKSHOP, FEARING WHAT HAD HAPPENED...AND, WELL, I GOT AN INFECTION.
I THOUGHT I WAS DONE FOR...OH, THE IRONY, DYING AFTER THE WHOLE PLANET HAD BEEN SAVED.
BUT THEN... THEY SHOWED UP. CHILDREN OF THE REVELATION. THEY WERE GOING AROUND AND ROUNDING UP SURVIVORS.
THEY BROUGHT ME HERE, TO THIS TOWN. GAVE ME MEDICAL ATTENTION.
SET ME UP IN THIS HERE WORKSHOP AND I'VE BEEN HELPING OUT EVER SINCE. THEY MAY BE KOOKY, BUT THEY SAVED MY LIFE. I OWE 'EM.
BUT WHAT THE HELL ARE YOU DOING HERE?

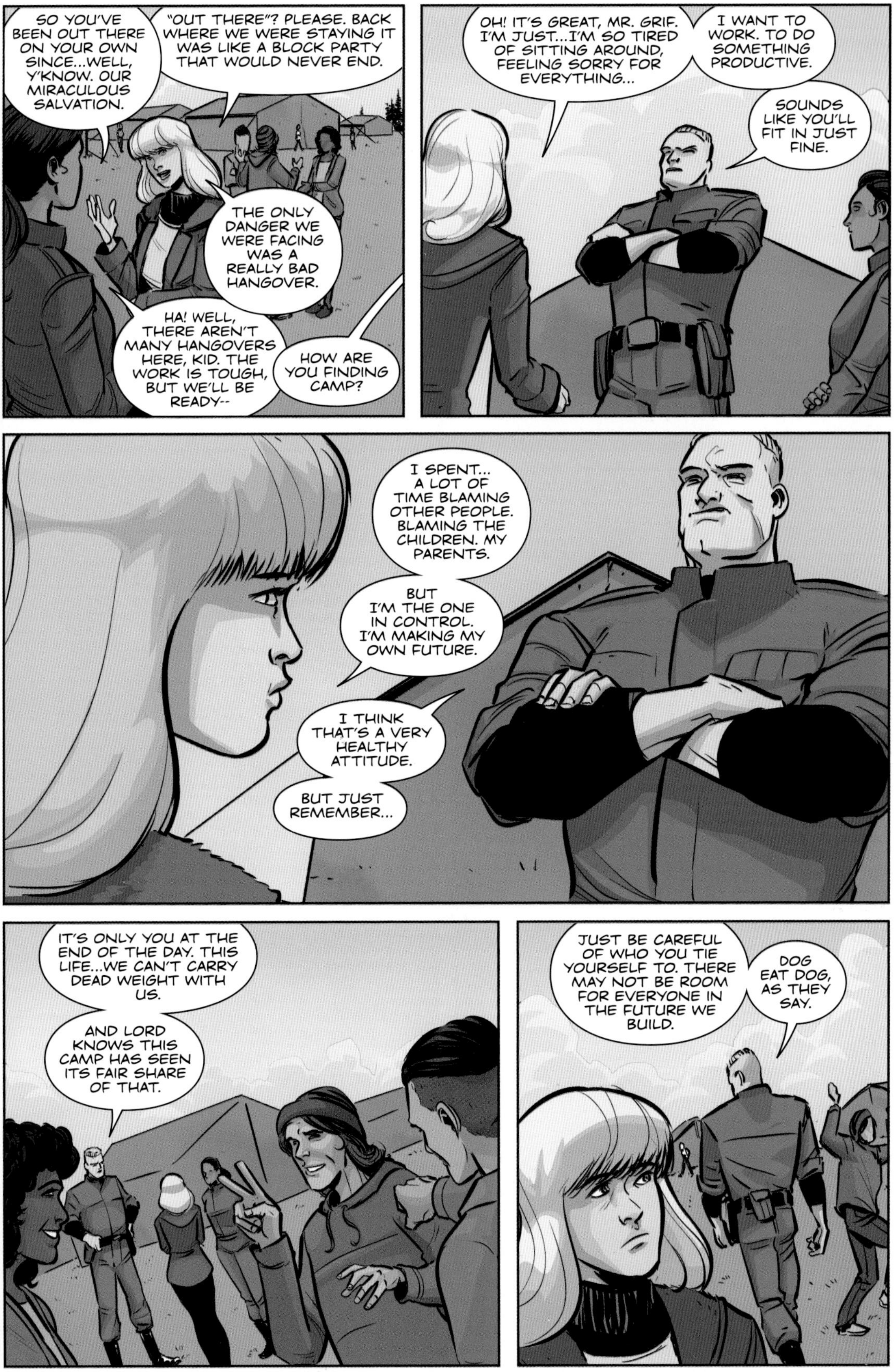

SO YOU'VE BEEN OUT THERE ON YOUR OWN SINCE...WELL, Y'KNOW. OUR MIRACULOUS SALVATION.
"OUT THERE"? PLEASE. BACK WHERE WE WERE STAYING IT WAS LIKE A BLOCK PARTY THAT WOULD NEVER END.
THE ONLY DANGER WE WERE FACING WAS A REALLY BAD HANGOVER.
HA! WELL, THERE AREN'T MANY HANGOVERS HERE, KID. THE WORK IS TOUGH, BUT WE'LL BE READY--
HOW ARE YOU FINDING CAMP?
OH! IT'S GREAT, MR. GRIF. I'M JUST...I'M SO TIRED OF SITTING AROUND, FEELING SORRY FOR EVERYTHING...
I WANT TO WORK. TO DO SOMETHING PRODUCTIVE.
SOUNDS LIKE YOU'LL FIT IN JUST FINE.
I SPENT... A LOT OF TIME BLAMING OTHER PEOPLE. BLAMING THE CHILDREN. MY PARENTS.
BUT I'M THE ONE IN CONTROL. I'M MAKING MY OWN FUTURE.
I THINK THAT'S A VERY HEALTHY ATTITUDE.
BUT JUST REMEMBER...
IT'S ONLY YOU AT THE END OF THE DAY. THIS LIFE...WE CAN'T CARRY DEAD WEIGHT WITH US.
AND LORD KNOWS THIS CAMP HAS SEEN ITS FAIR SHARE OF THAT.
JUST BE CAREFUL OF WHO YOU TIE YOURSELF TO. THERE MAY NOT BE ROOM FOR EVERYONE IN THE FUTURE WE BUILD.
DOG EAT DOG, AS THEY SAY.

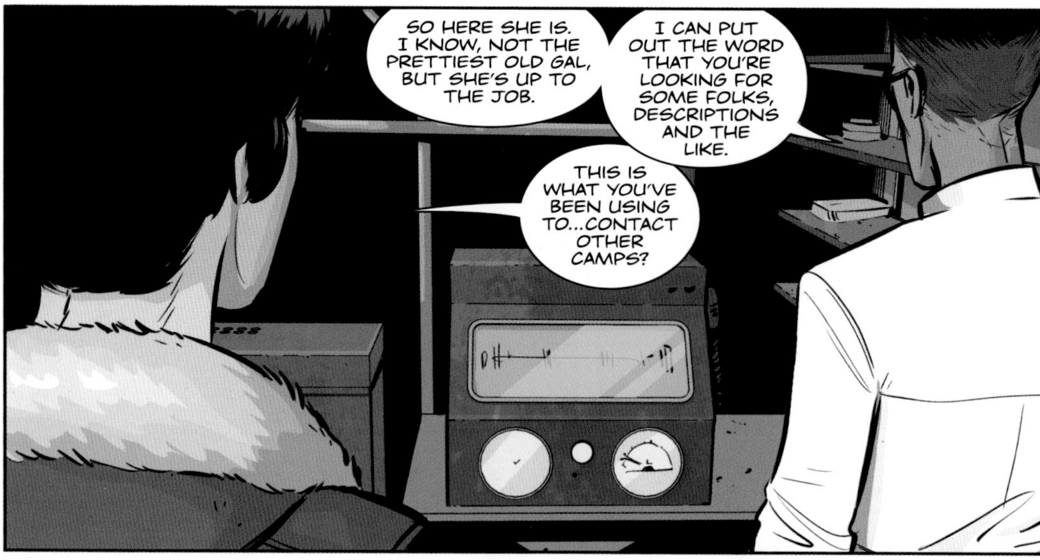
SO HERE SHE IS. I KNOW, NOT THE PRETTIEST OLD GAL, BUT SHE'S UP TO THE JOB.
I CAN PUT OUT THE WORD THAT YOU'RE LOOKING FOR SOME FOLKS, DESCRIPTIONS AND THE LIKE.
THIS IS WHAT YOU'VE BEEN USING TO...CONTACT OTHER CAMPS?

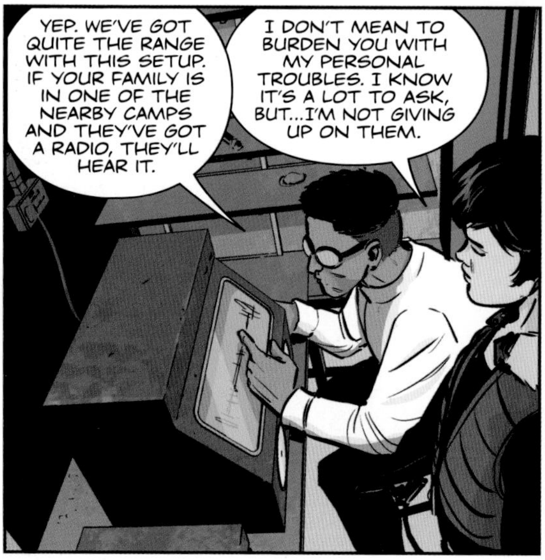
YEP. WE'VE GOT QUITE THE RANGE WITH THIS SETUP. IF YOUR FAMILY IS IN ONE OF THE NEARBY CAMPS AND THEY'VE GOT A RADIO, THEY'LL HEAR IT.
I DON'T MEAN TO BURDEN YOU WITH MY PERSONAL TROUBLES. I KNOW IT'S A LOT TO ASK, BUT...I'M NOT GIVING UP ON THEM.

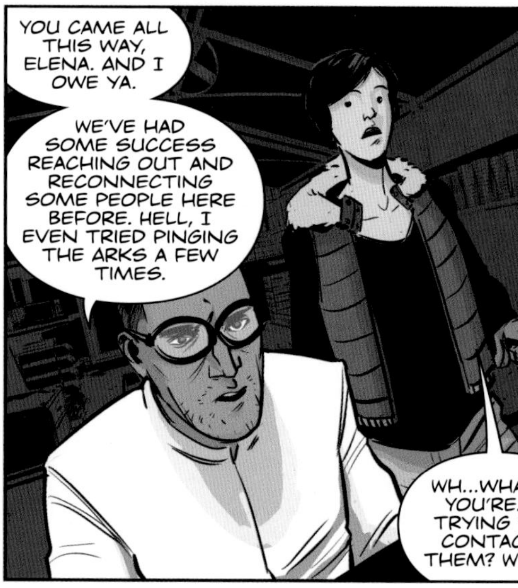
YOU CAME ALL THIS WAY, ELENA. AND I OWE YA.
WE'VE HAD SOME SUCCESS REACHING OUT AND RECONNECTING SOME PEOPLE HERE BEFORE. HELL, I EVEN TRIED PINGING THE ARKS A FEW TIMES.
WH...WHAT? YOU'RE... TRYING TO CONTACT THEM? WHY?

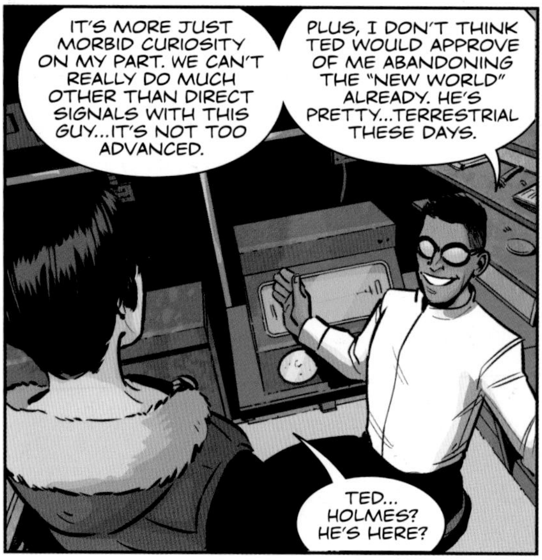
IT'S MORE JUST MORBID CURIOSITY ON MY PART. WE CAN'T REALLY DO MUCH OTHER THAN DIRECT SIGNALS WITH THIS GUY...IT'S NOT TOO ADVANCED.
PLUS, I DON'T THINK TED WOULD APPROVE OF ME ABANDONING THE "NEW WORLD" ALREADY. HE'S PRETTY...TERRESTRIAL THESE DAYS.
TED... HOLMES? HE'S HERE?

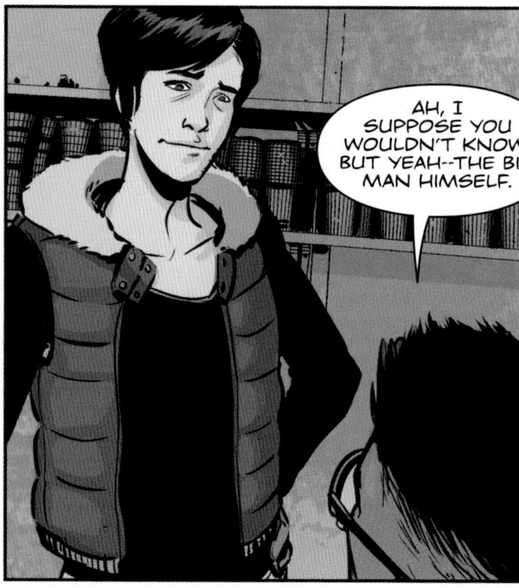
AH, I SUPPOSE YOU WOULDN'T KNOW. BUT YEAH--THE BIG MAN HIMSELF.

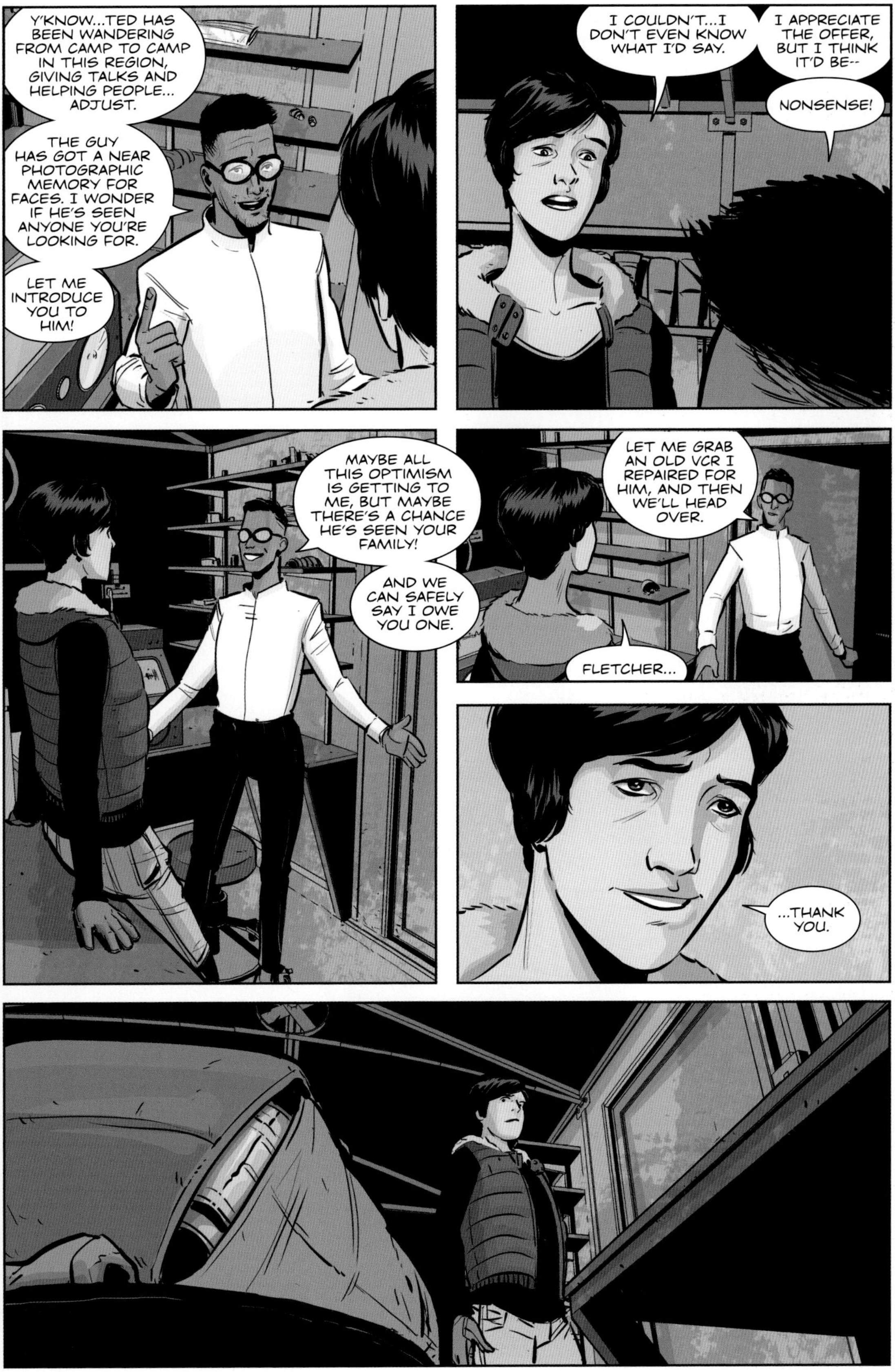
Y'KNOW...TED HAS BEEN WANDERING FROM CAMP TO CAMP IN THIS REGION, GIVING TALKS AND HELPING PEOPLE... ADJUST.
THE GUY HAS GOT A NEAR PHOTOGRAPHIC MEMORY FOR FACES. I WONDER IF HE'S SEEN ANYONE YOU'RE LOOKING FOR.
LET ME INTRODUCE YOU TO HIM!
I COULDN'T...I DON'T EVEN KNOW WHAT I'D SAY.
I APPRECIATE THE OFFER, BUT I THINK IT'D BE--
NONSENSE!
MAYBE ALL THIS OPTIMISM IS GETTING TO ME, BUT MAYBE THERE'S A CHANCE HE'S SEEN YOUR FAMILY!
AND WE CAN SAFELY SAY I OWE YOU ONE.
LET ME GRAB AN OLD VCR I REPAIRED FOR HIM, AND THEN WE'LL HEAD OVER.
FLETCHER...
...THANK YOU.

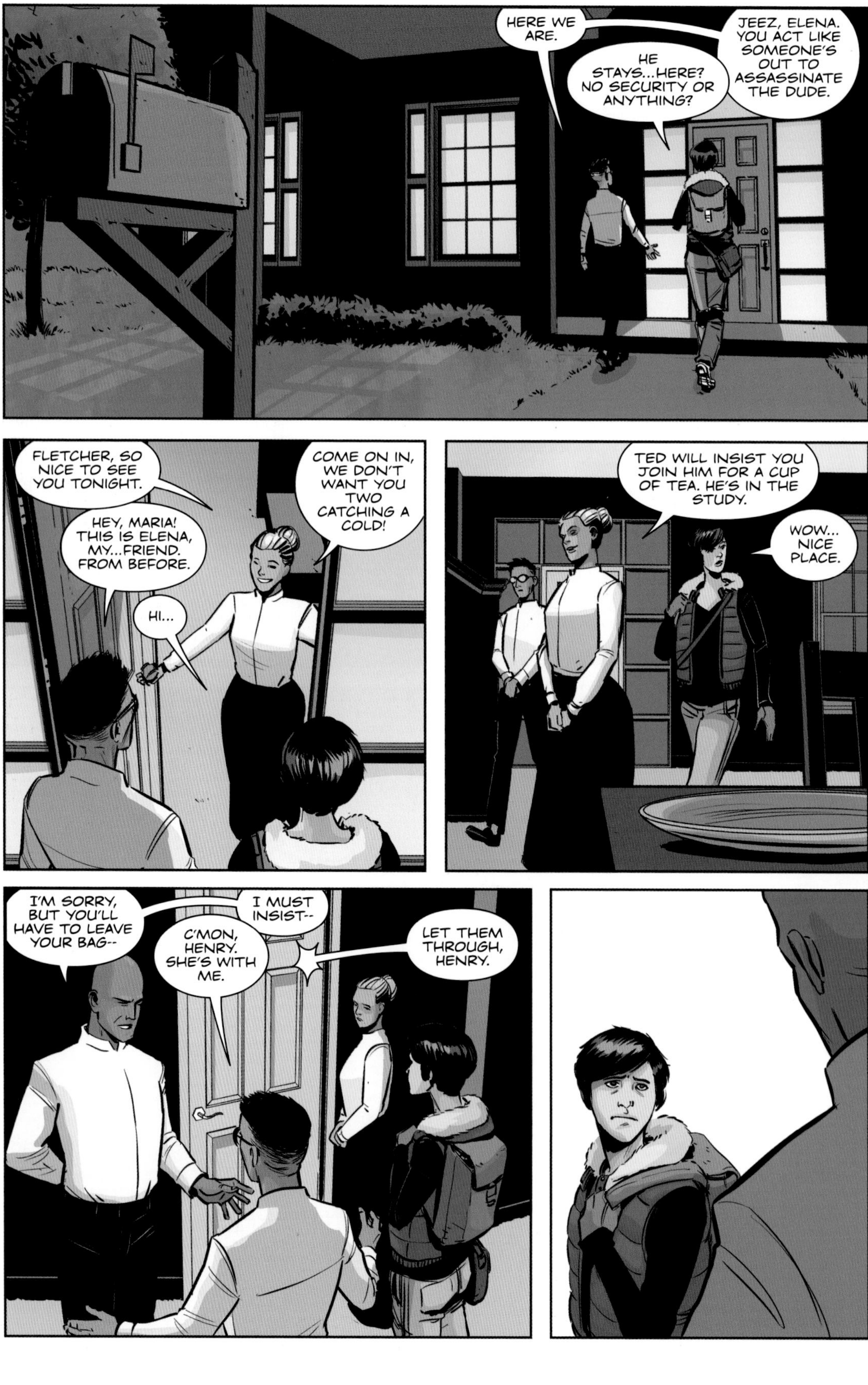
HERE WE ARE.
JEEZ, ELENA. YOU ACT LIKE SOMEONE'S OUT TO ASSASSINATE THE DUDE.
HE STAYS...HERE? NO SECURITY OR ANYTHING?
FLETCHER, SO NICE TO SEE YOU TONIGHT.
HEY, MARIA! THIS IS ELENA, MY...FRIEND. FROM BEFORE.
HI...
COME ON IN, WE DON'T WANT YOU TWO CATCHING A COLD!
TED WILL INSIST YOU JOIN HIM FOR A CUP OF TEA. HE'S IN THE STUDY.
WOW... NICE PLACE.
I'M SORRY, BUT YOU'LL HAVE TO LEAVE YOUR BAG--
I MUST INSIST--
C'MON, HENRY. SHE'S WITH ME.
LET THEM THROUGH, HENRY.

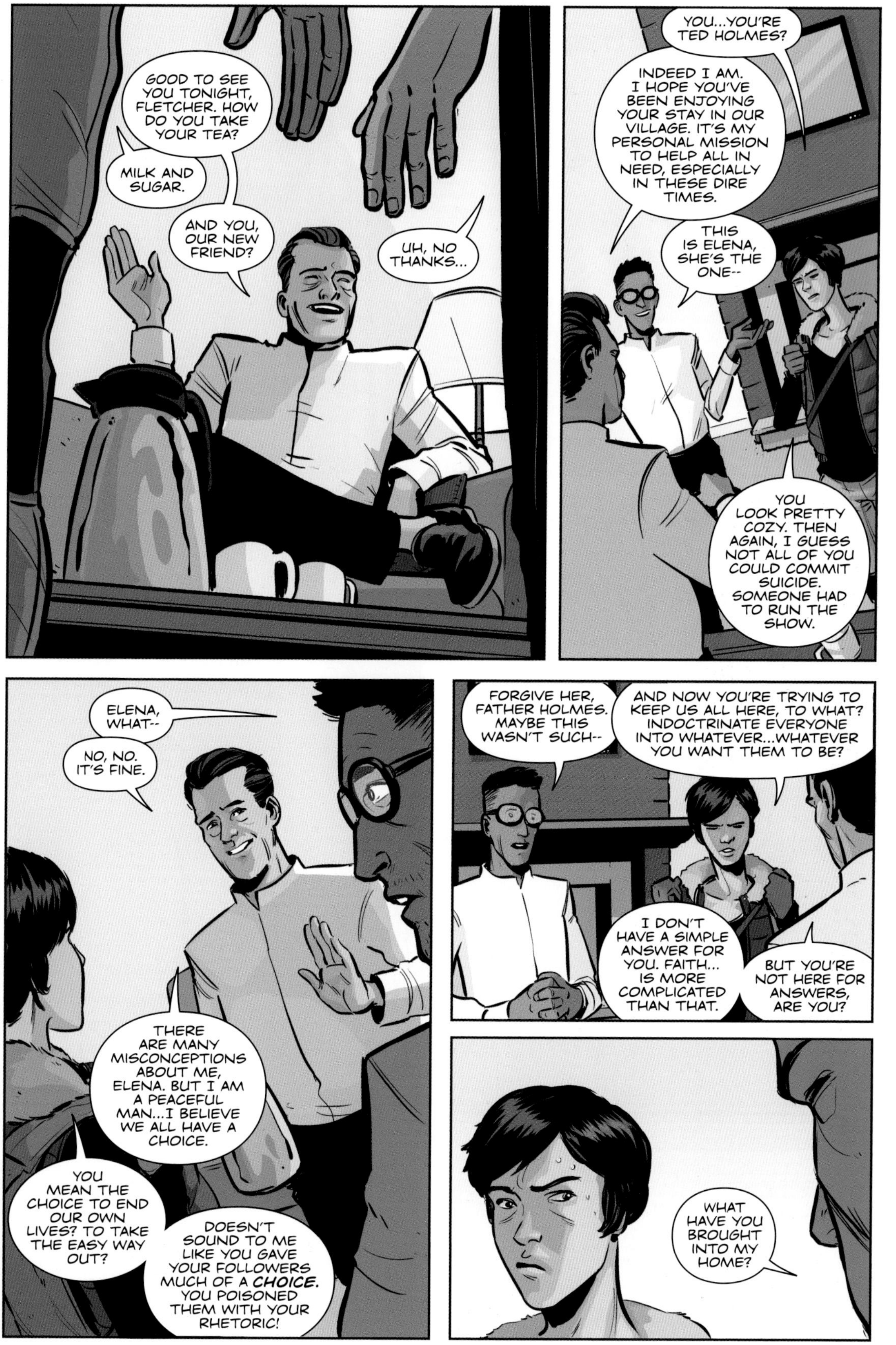
GOOD TO SEE YOU TONIGHT, FLETCHER. HOW DO YOU TAKE YOUR TEA?
MILK AND SUGAR.
AND YOU, OUR NEW FRIEND?
UH, NO THANKS...
YOU...YOU'RE TED HOLMES?
INDEED I AM. I HOPE YOU'VE BEEN ENJOYING YOUR STAY IN OUR VILLAGE. IT'S MY PERSONAL MISSION TO HELP ALL IN NEED, ESPECIALLY IN THESE DIRE TIMES.
THIS IS ELENA, SHE'S THE ONE--
YOU LOOK PRETTY COZY. THEN AGAIN, I GUESS NOT ALL OF YOU COULD COMMIT SUICIDE. SOMEONE HAD TO RUN THE SHOW.
ELENA, WHAT--
NO, NO. IT'S FINE.
THERE ARE MANY MISCONCEPTIONS ABOUT ME, ELENA. BUT I AM A PEACEFUL MAN...I BELIEVE WE ALL HAVE A CHOICE.
YOU MEAN THE CHOICE TO END OUR OWN LIVES? TO TAKE THE EASY WAY OUT?
DOESN'T SOUND TO ME LIKE YOU GAVE YOUR FOLLOWERS MUCH OF A **CHOICE.** YOU POISONED THEM WITH YOUR RHETORIC!
FORGIVE HER, FATHER HOLMES. MAYBE THIS WASN'T SUCH--
AND NOW YOU'RE TRYING TO KEEP US ALL HERE, TO WHAT? INDOCTRINATE EVERYONE INTO WHATEVER...WHATEVER YOU WANT THEM TO BE?
I DON'T HAVE A SIMPLE ANSWER FOR YOU. FAITH... IS MORE COMPLICATED THAN THAT.
BUT YOU'RE NOT HERE FOR ANSWERS, ARE YOU?
WHAT HAVE YOU BROUGHT INTO MY HOME?

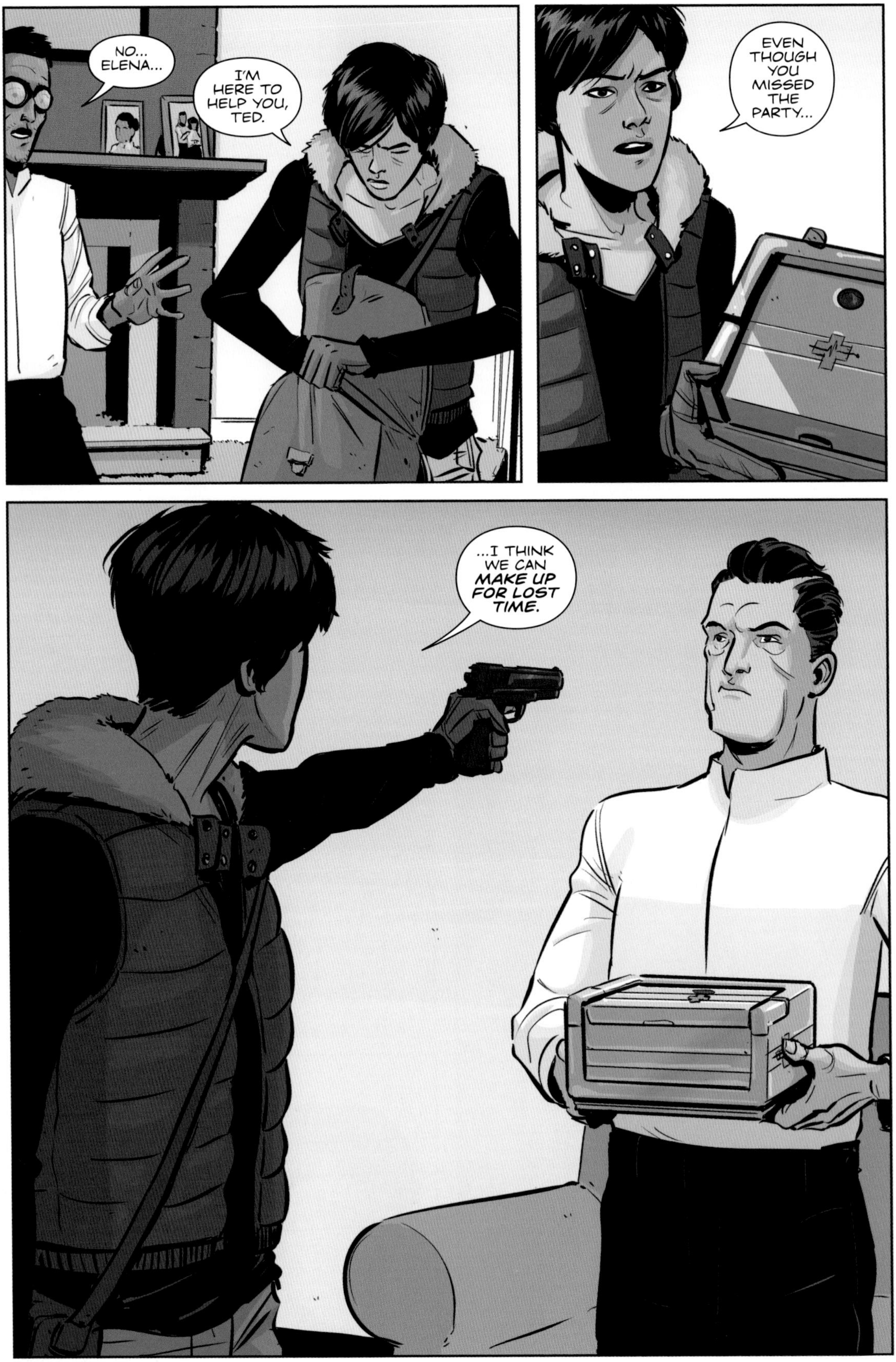
NO... ELENA...
I'M HERE TO HELP YOU, TED.
EVEN THOUGH YOU MISSED THE PARTY...
...I THINK WE CAN ***MAKE UP FOR LOST TIME.***

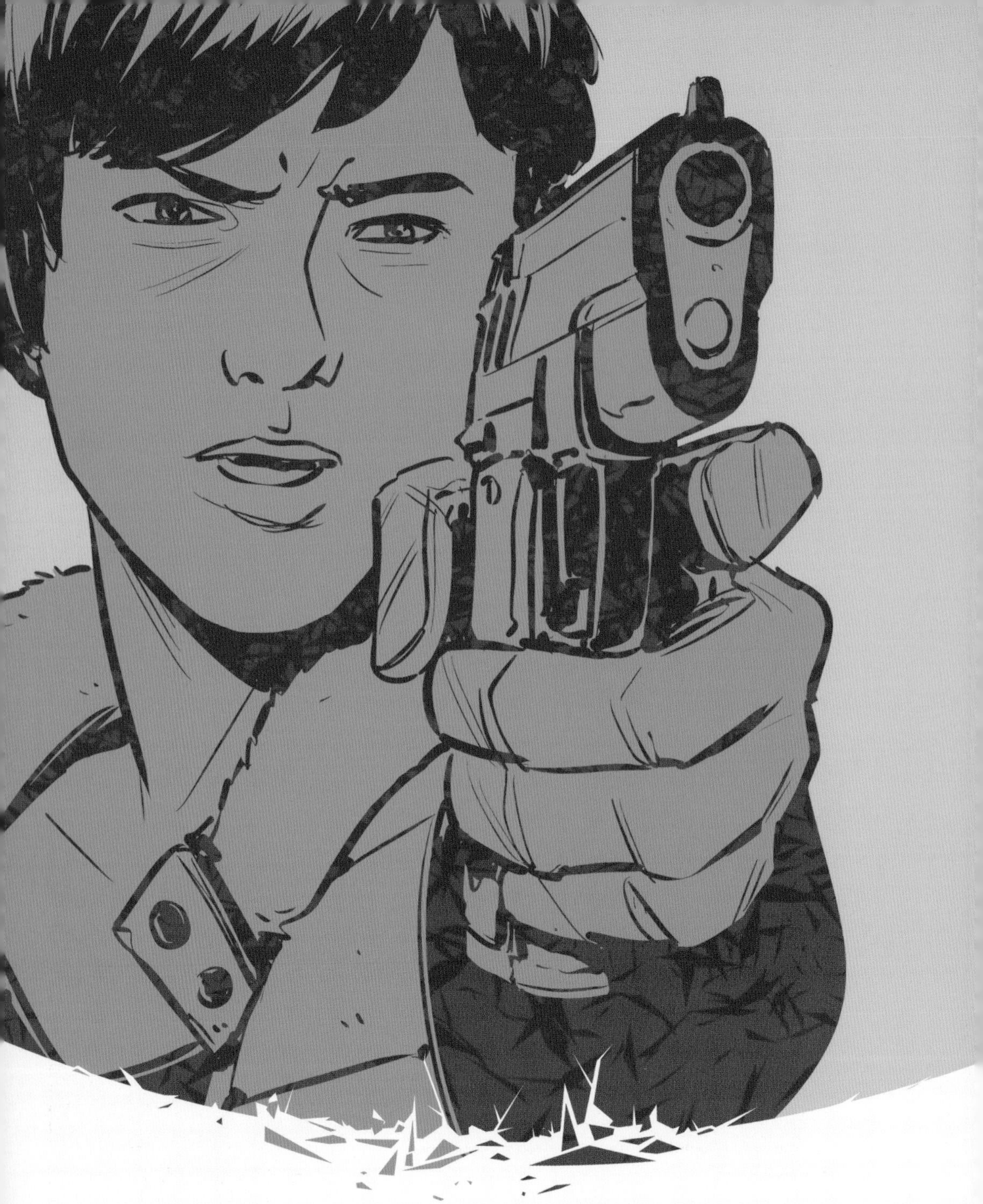

CHAPTER FOUR

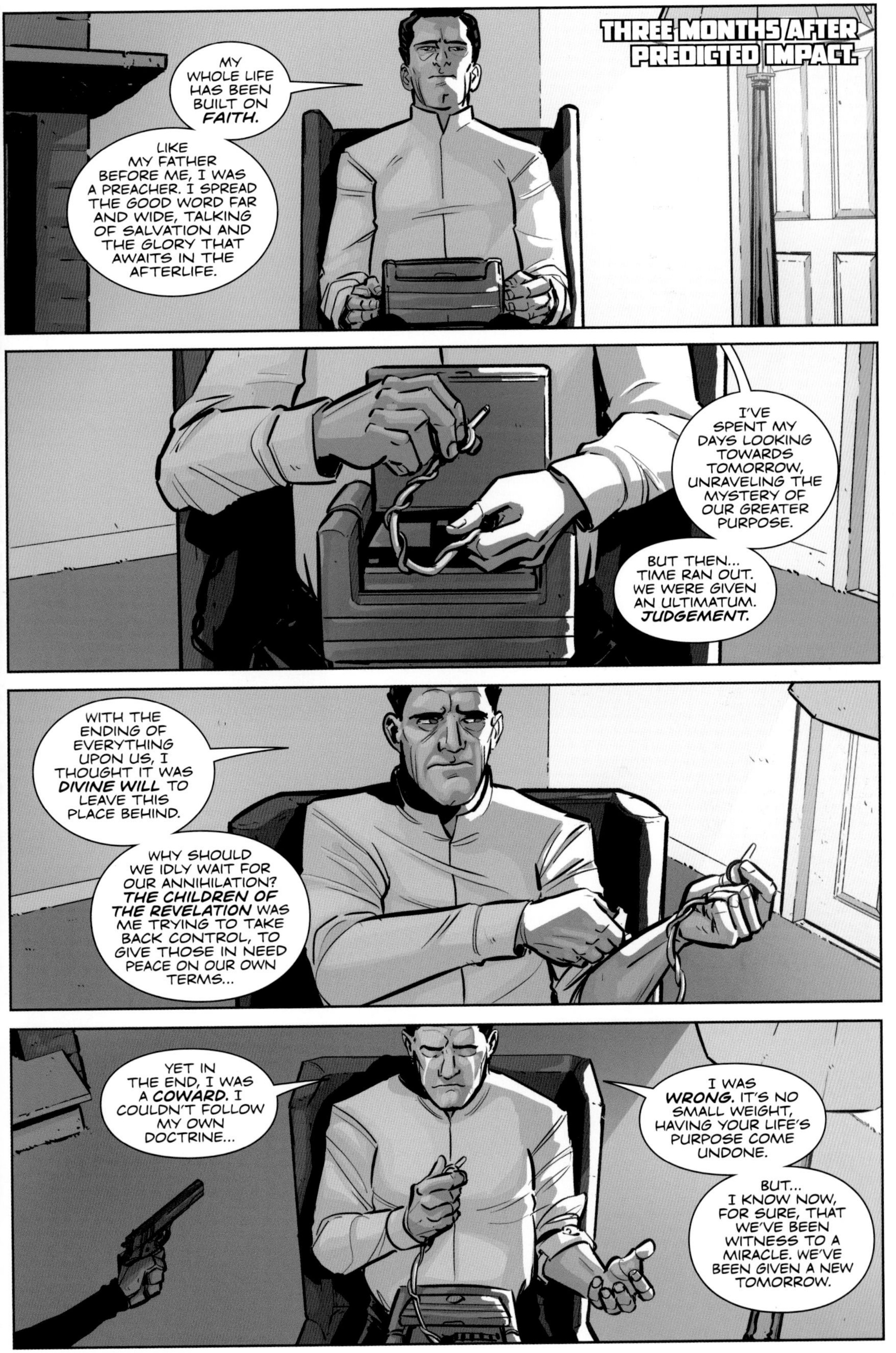

THREE MONTHS AFTER PREDICTED IMPACT.
MY WHOLE LIFE HAS BEEN BUILT ON FAITH.
LIKE MY FATHER BEFORE ME, I WAS A PREACHER. I SPREAD THE GOOD WORD FAR AND WIDE, TALKING OF SALVATION AND THE GLORY THAT AWAITS IN THE AFTERLIFE.
I'VE SPENT MY DAYS LOOKING TOWARDS TOMORROW, UNRAVELING THE MYSTERY OF OUR GREATER PURPOSE.
BUT THEN... TIME RAN OUT. WE WERE GIVEN AN ULTIMATUM. JUDGEMENT.
WITH THE ENDING OF EVERYTHING UPON US, I THOUGHT IT WAS DIVINE WILL TO LEAVE THIS PLACE BEHIND.
WHY SHOULD WE IDLY WAIT FOR OUR ANNIHILATION? THE CHILDREN OF THE REVELATION WAS ME TRYING TO TAKE BACK CONTROL, TO GIVE THOSE IN NEED PEACE ON OUR OWN TERMS...
YET IN THE END, I WAS A COWARD. I COULDN'T FOLLOW MY OWN DOCTRINE...
I WAS WRONG. IT'S NO SMALL WEIGHT, HAVING YOUR LIFE'S PURPOSE COME UNDONE.
BUT... I KNOW NOW, FOR SURE, THAT WE'VE BEEN WITNESS TO A MIRACLE. WE'VE BEEN GIVEN A NEW TOMORROW.

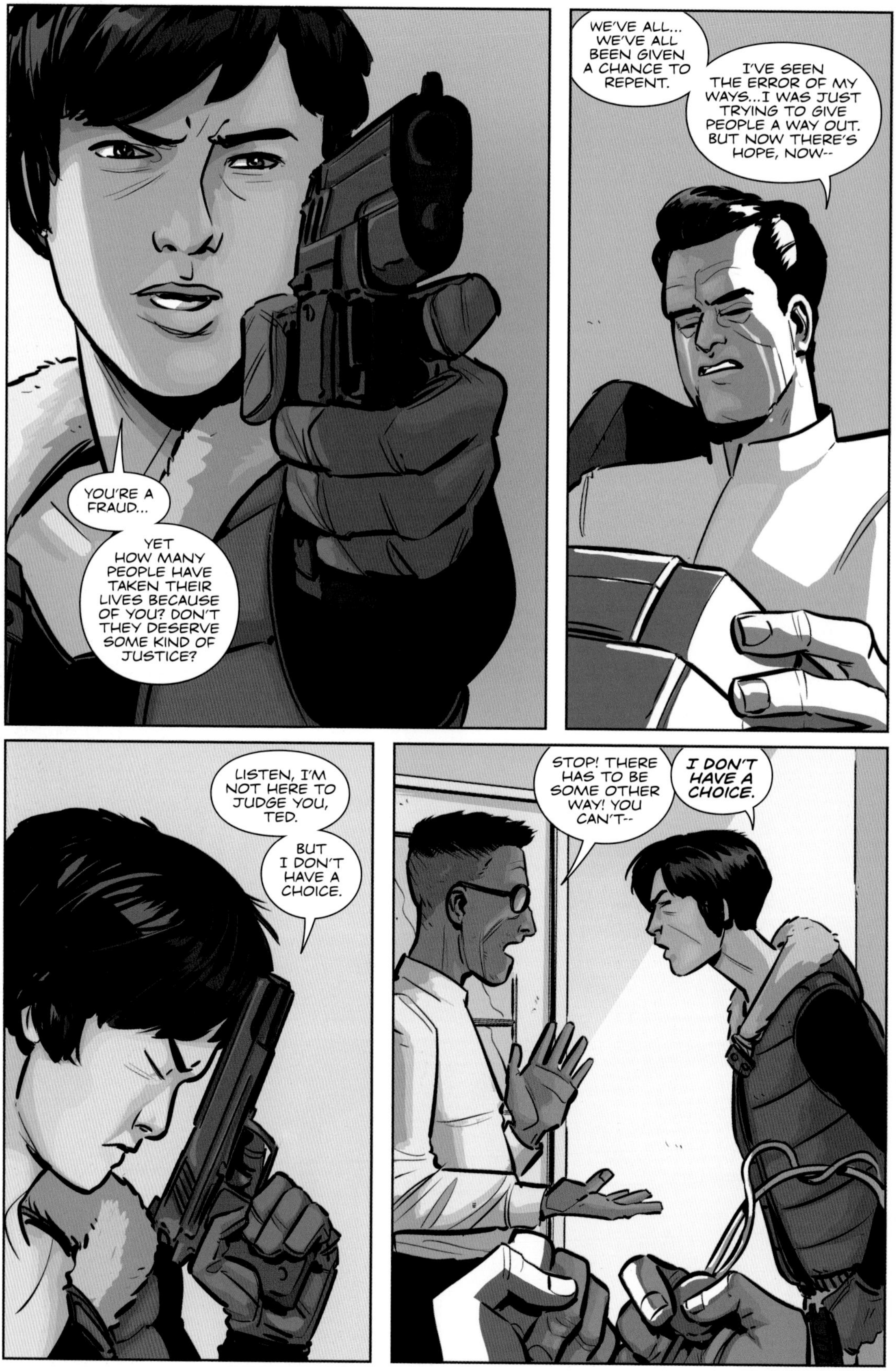
YOU'RE A FRAUD...
YET HOW MANY PEOPLE HAVE TAKEN THEIR LIVES BECAUSE OF YOU? DON'T THEY DESERVE SOME KIND OF JUSTICE?
WE'VE ALL... WE'VE ALL BEEN GIVEN A CHANCE TO REPENT.
I'VE SEEN THE ERROR OF MY WAYS...I WAS JUST TRYING TO GIVE PEOPLE A WAY OUT. BUT NOW THERE'S HOPE, NOW--
LISTEN, I'M NOT HERE TO JUDGE YOU, TED.
BUT I DON'T HAVE A CHOICE.
STOP! THERE HAS TO BE SOME OTHER WAY! YOU CAN'T--
I DON'T HAVE A CHOICE.

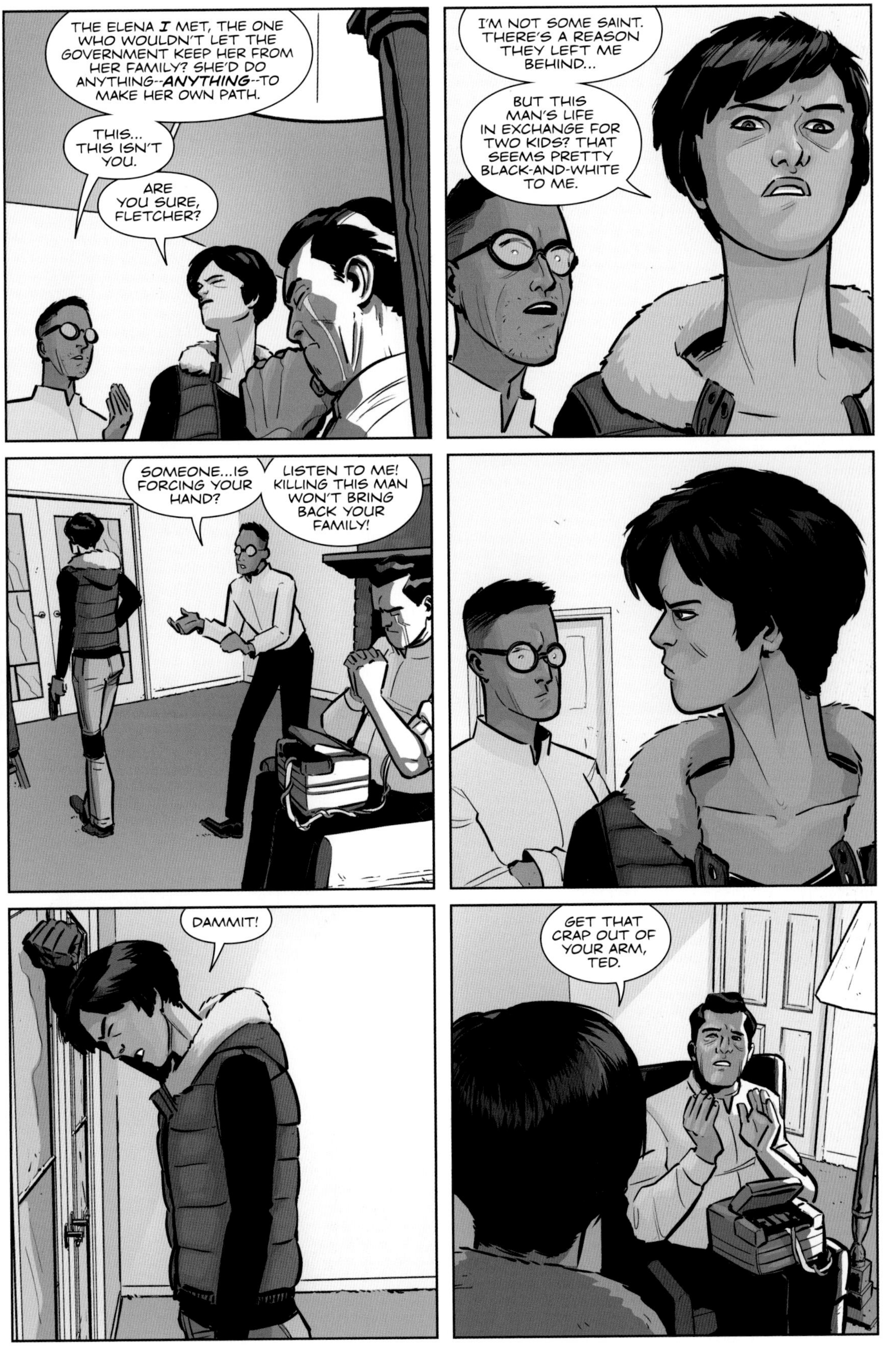
THE ELENA I MET, THE ONE WHO WOULDN'T LET THE GOVERNMENT KEEP HER FROM HER FAMILY? SHE'D DO ANYTHING--ANYTHING--TO MAKE HER OWN PATH.
THIS... THIS ISN'T YOU.
ARE YOU SURE, FLETCHER?
I'M NOT SOME SAINT. THERE'S A REASON THEY LEFT ME BEHIND...
BUT THIS MAN'S LIFE IN EXCHANGE FOR TWO KIDS? THAT SEEMS PRETTY BLACK-AND-WHITE TO ME.
SOMEONE...IS FORCING YOUR HAND?
LISTEN TO ME! KILLING THIS MAN WON'T BRING BACK YOUR FAMILY!
DAMMIT!
GET THAT CRAP OUT OF YOUR ARM, TED.

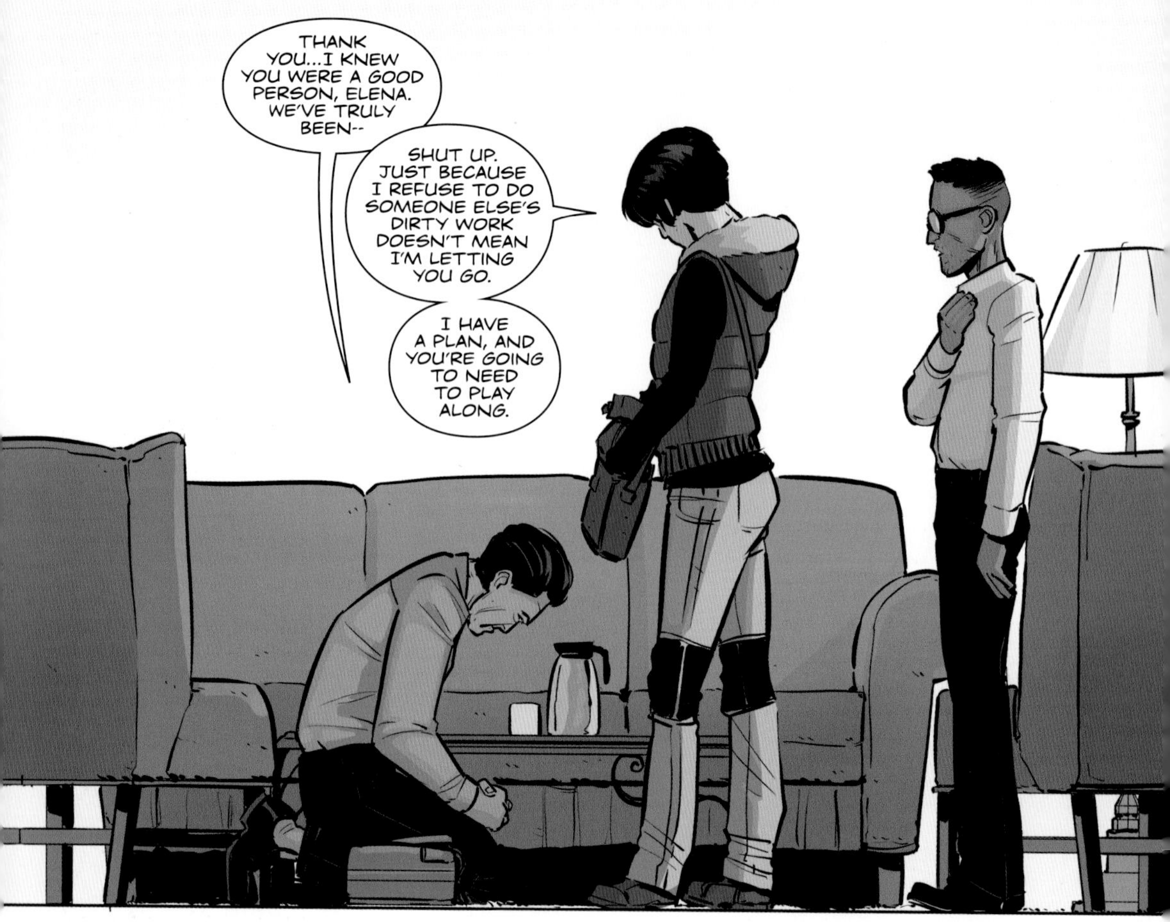
THANK YOU...I KNEW YOU WERE A GOOD PERSON, ELENA. WE'VE TRULY BEEN--
SHUT UP. JUST BECAUSE I REFUSE TO DO SOMEONE ELSE'S DIRTY WORK DOESN'T MEAN I'M LETTING YOU GO.
I HAVE A PLAN, AND YOU'RE GOING TO NEED TO PLAY ALONG.

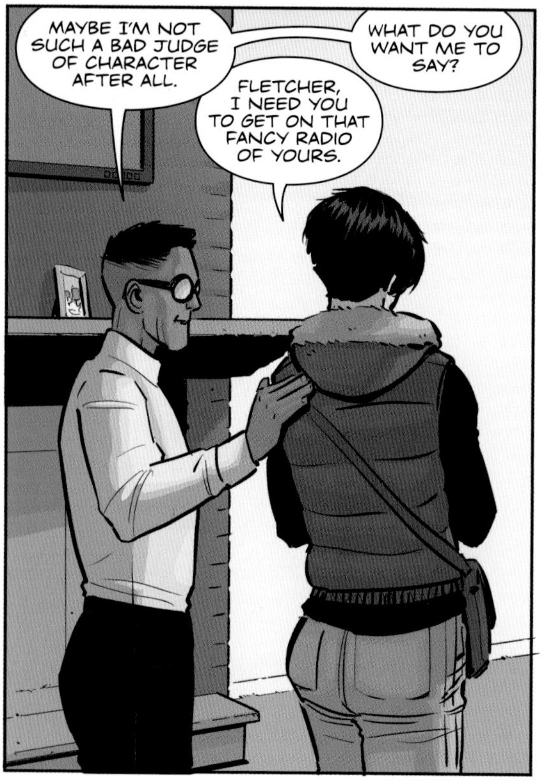
MAYBE I'M NOT SUCH A BAD JUDGE OF CHARACTER AFTER ALL.
WHAT DO YOU WANT ME TO SAY?
FLETCHER, I NEED YOU TO GET ON THAT FANCY RADIO OF YOURS.

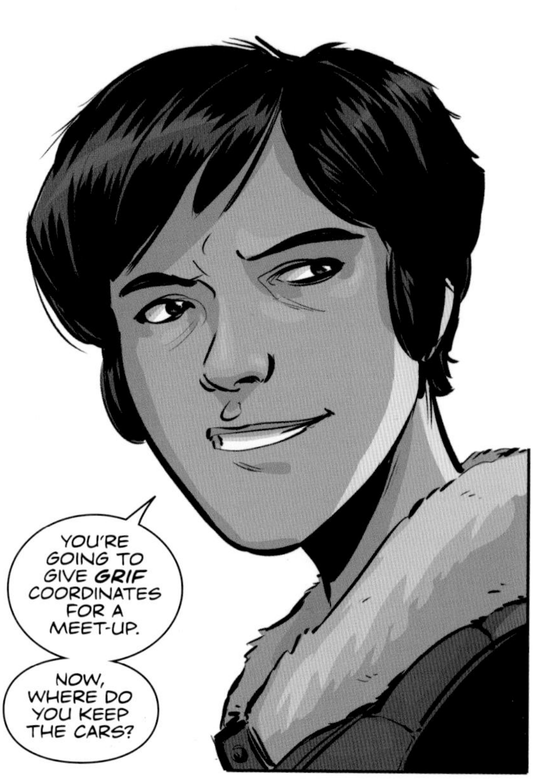
YOU'RE GOING TO GIVE **GRIF** COORDINATES FOR A MEET-UP.
NOW, WHERE DO YOU KEEP THE CARS?

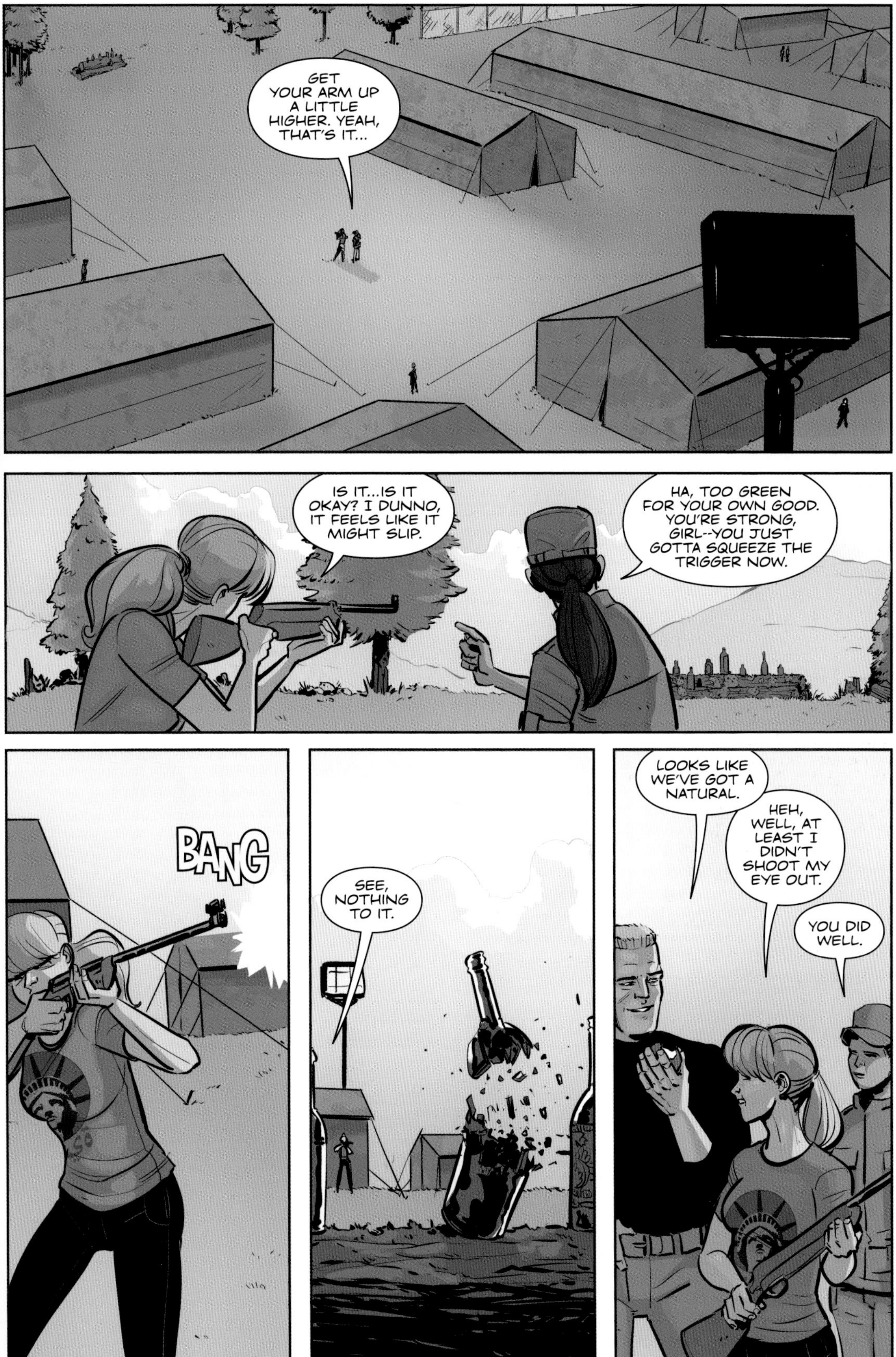
GET YOUR ARM UP A LITTLE HIGHER. YEAH, THAT'S IT...
IS IT...IS IT OKAY? I DUNNO, IT FEELS LIKE IT MIGHT SLIP.
HA, TOO GREEN FOR YOUR OWN GOOD. YOU'RE STRONG, GIRL--YOU JUST GOTTA SQUEEZE THE TRIGGER NOW.
BANG
SEE, NOTHING TO IT.
LOOKS LIKE WE'VE GOT A NATURAL.
HEH, WELL, AT LEAST I DIDN'T SHOOT MY EYE OUT.
YOU DID WELL.

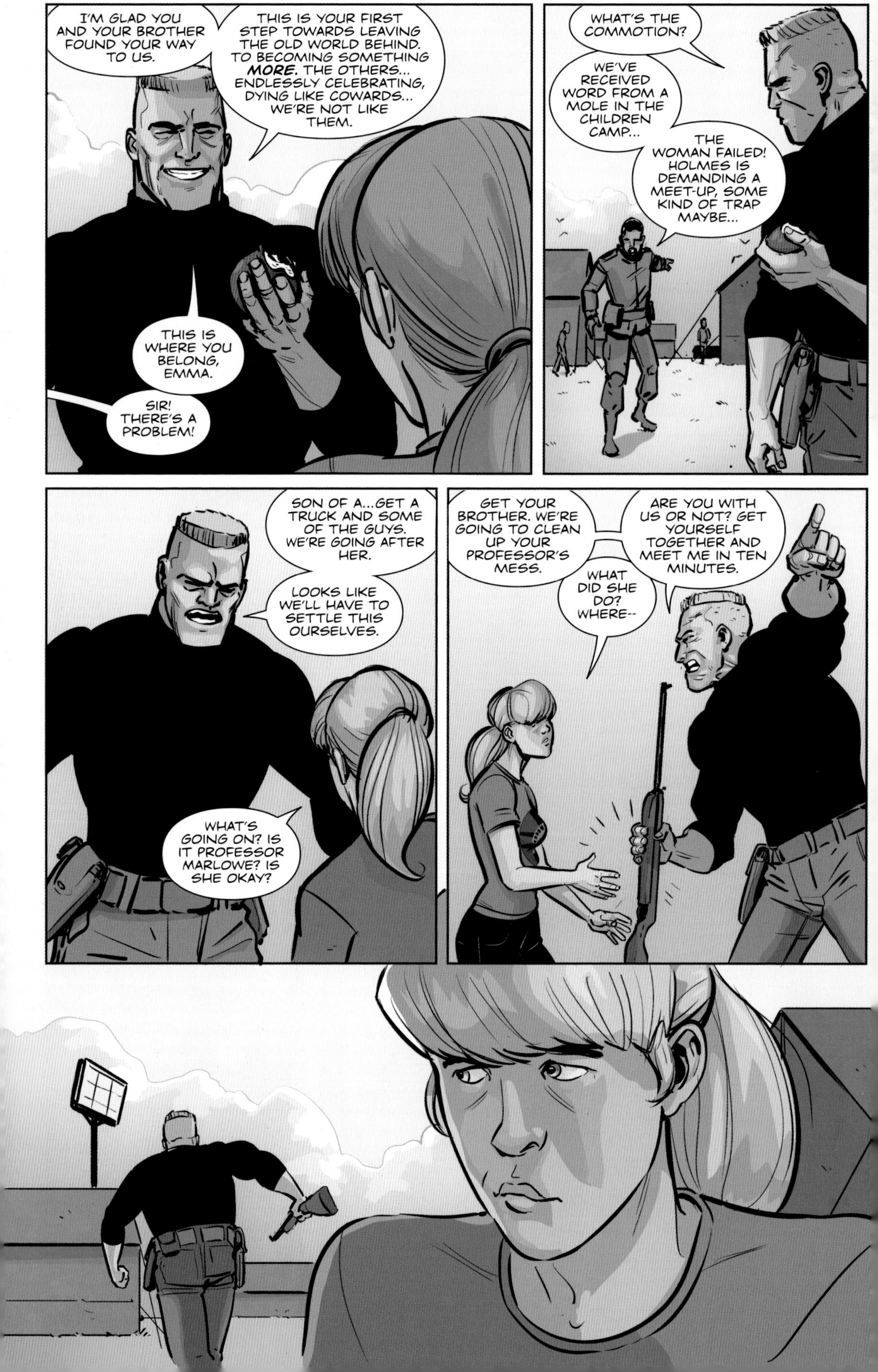
I'M GLAD YOU AND YOUR BROTHER FOUND YOUR WAY TO US.
THIS IS YOUR FIRST STEP TOWARDS LEAVING THE OLD WORLD BEHIND. TO BECOMING SOMETHING *MORE.* THE OTHERS... ENDLESSLY CELEBRATING, DYING LIKE COWARDS... WE'RE NOT LIKE THEM.
THIS IS WHERE YOU BELONG, EMMA.
SIR! THERE'S A PROBLEM!
WHAT'S THE COMMOTION?
WE'VE RECEIVED WORD FROM A MOLE IN THE CHILDREN CAMP...
THE WOMAN FAILED! HOLMES IS DEMANDING A MEET-UP, SOME KIND OF TRAP MAYBE...
SON OF A...GET A TRUCK AND SOME OF THE GUYS. WE'RE GOING AFTER HER.
LOOKS LIKE WE'LL HAVE TO SETTLE THIS OURSELVES.
WHAT'S GOING ON? IS IT PROFESSOR MARLOWE? IS SHE OKAY?
GET YOUR BROTHER. WE'RE GOING TO CLEAN UP YOUR PROFESSOR'S MESS.
WHAT DID SHE DO? WHERE--
ARE YOU WITH US OR NOT? GET YOURSELF TOGETHER AND MEET ME IN TEN MINUTES.

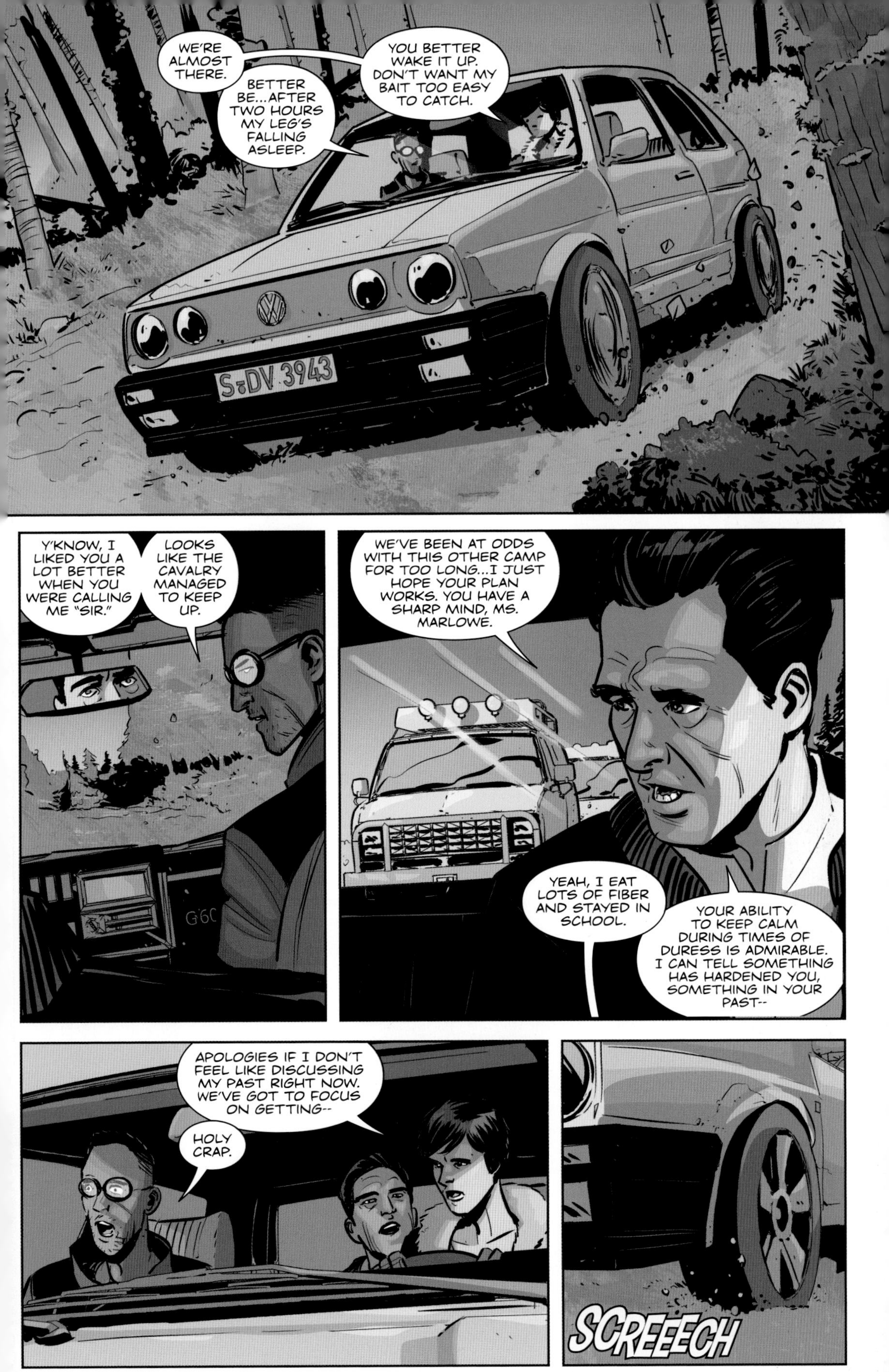
WE'RE ALMOST THERE.
YOU BETTER WAKE IT UP. DON'T WANT MY BAIT TOO EASY TO CATCH.
BETTER BE...AFTER TWO HOURS MY LEG'S FALLING ASLEEP.
S-DV 3943
Y'KNOW, I LIKED YOU A LOT BETTER WHEN YOU WERE CALLING ME "SIR."
LOOKS LIKE THE CAVALRY MANAGED TO KEEP UP.
G60
WE'VE BEEN AT ODDS WITH THIS OTHER CAMP FOR TOO LONG...I JUST HOPE YOUR PLAN WORKS. YOU HAVE A SHARP MIND, MS. MARLOWE.
YEAH, I EAT LOTS OF FIBER AND STAYED IN SCHOOL.
YOUR ABILITY TO KEEP CALM DURING TIMES OF DURESS IS ADMIRABLE. I CAN TELL SOMETHING HAS HARDENED YOU, SOMETHING IN YOUR PAST--
APOLOGIES IF I DON'T FEEL LIKE DISCUSSING MY PAST RIGHT NOW. WE'VE GOT TO FOCUS ON GETTING--
HOLY CRAP.
SCREEECH

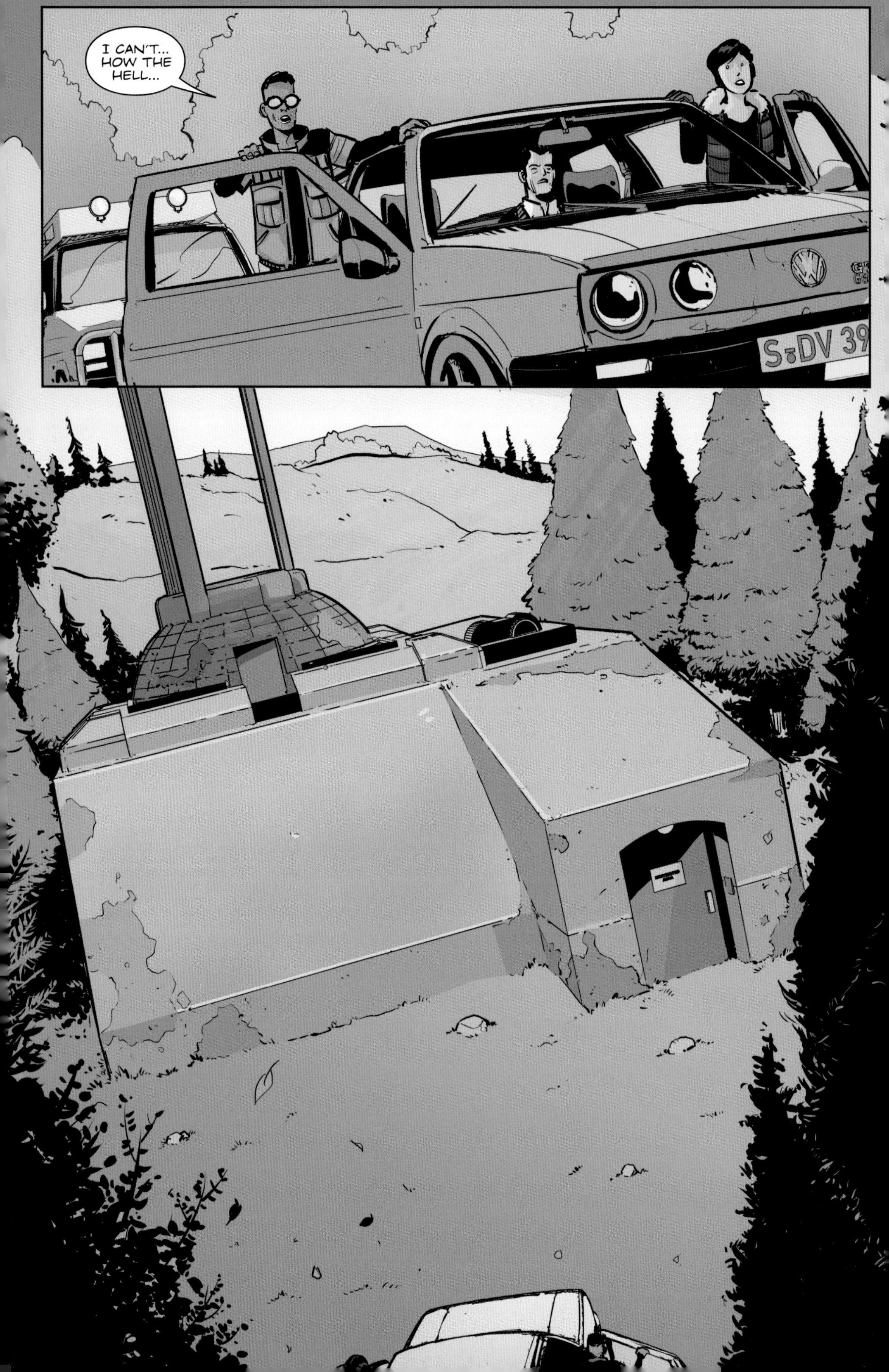
I CAN'T... HOW THE HELL...
S-DV 39

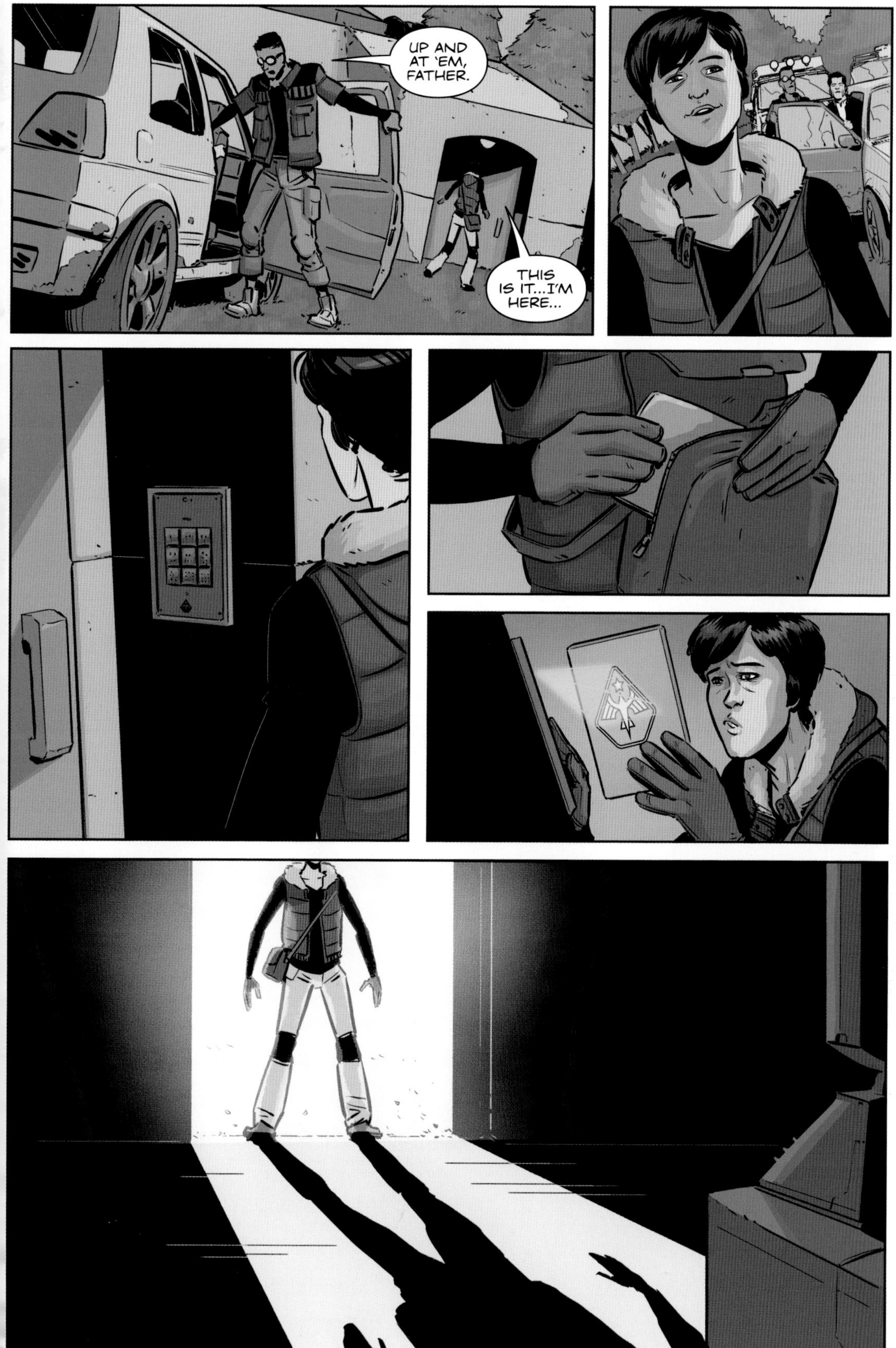
UP AND AT 'EM, FATHER.
THIS IS IT...I'M HERE...

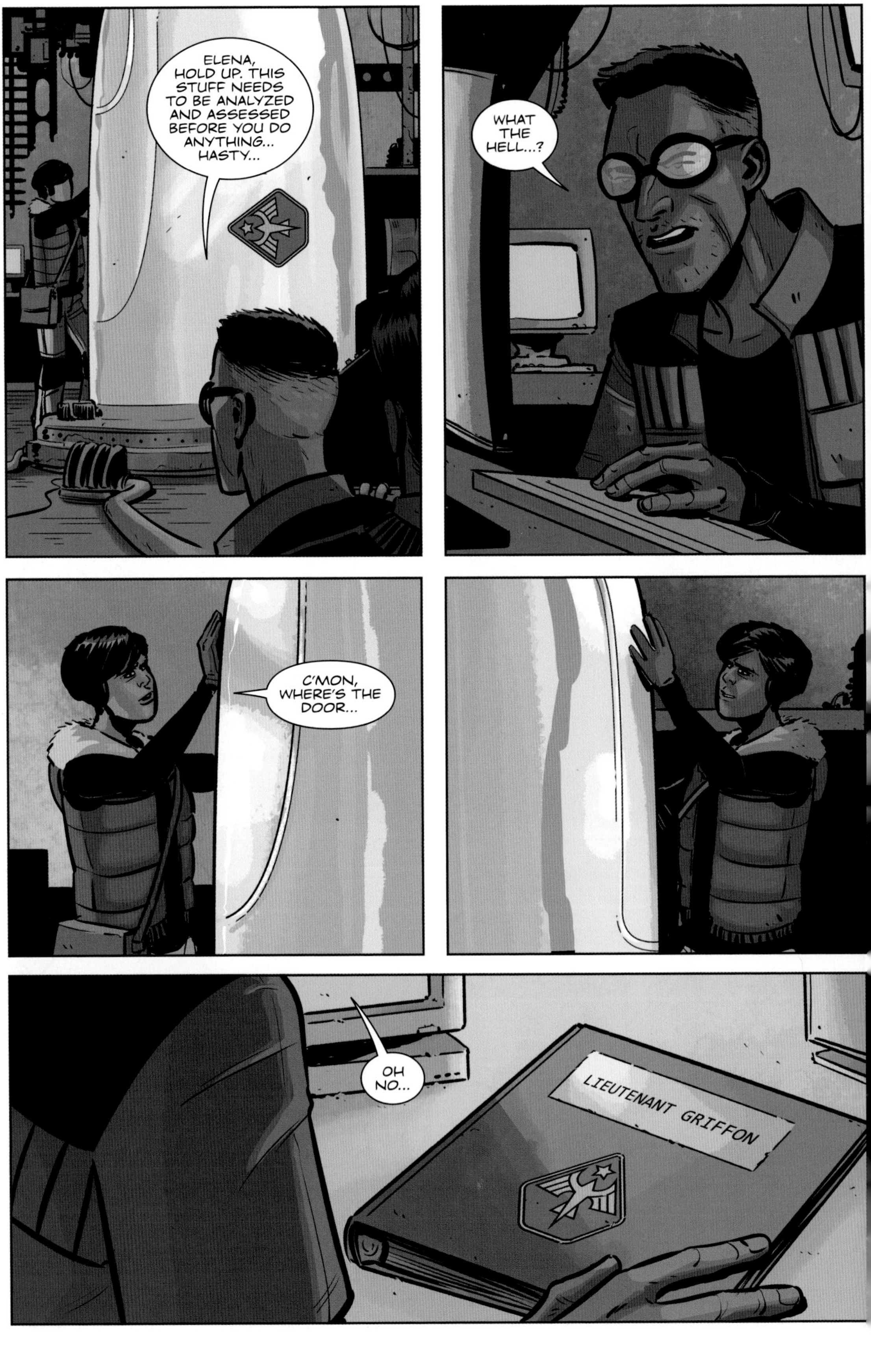
ELENA, HOLD UP. THIS STUFF NEEDS TO BE ANALYZED AND ASSESSED BEFORE YOU DO ANYTHING... HASTY...
WHAT THE HELL...?
C'MON, WHERE'S THE DOOR...
OH NO...
LIEUTENANT GRIFFON

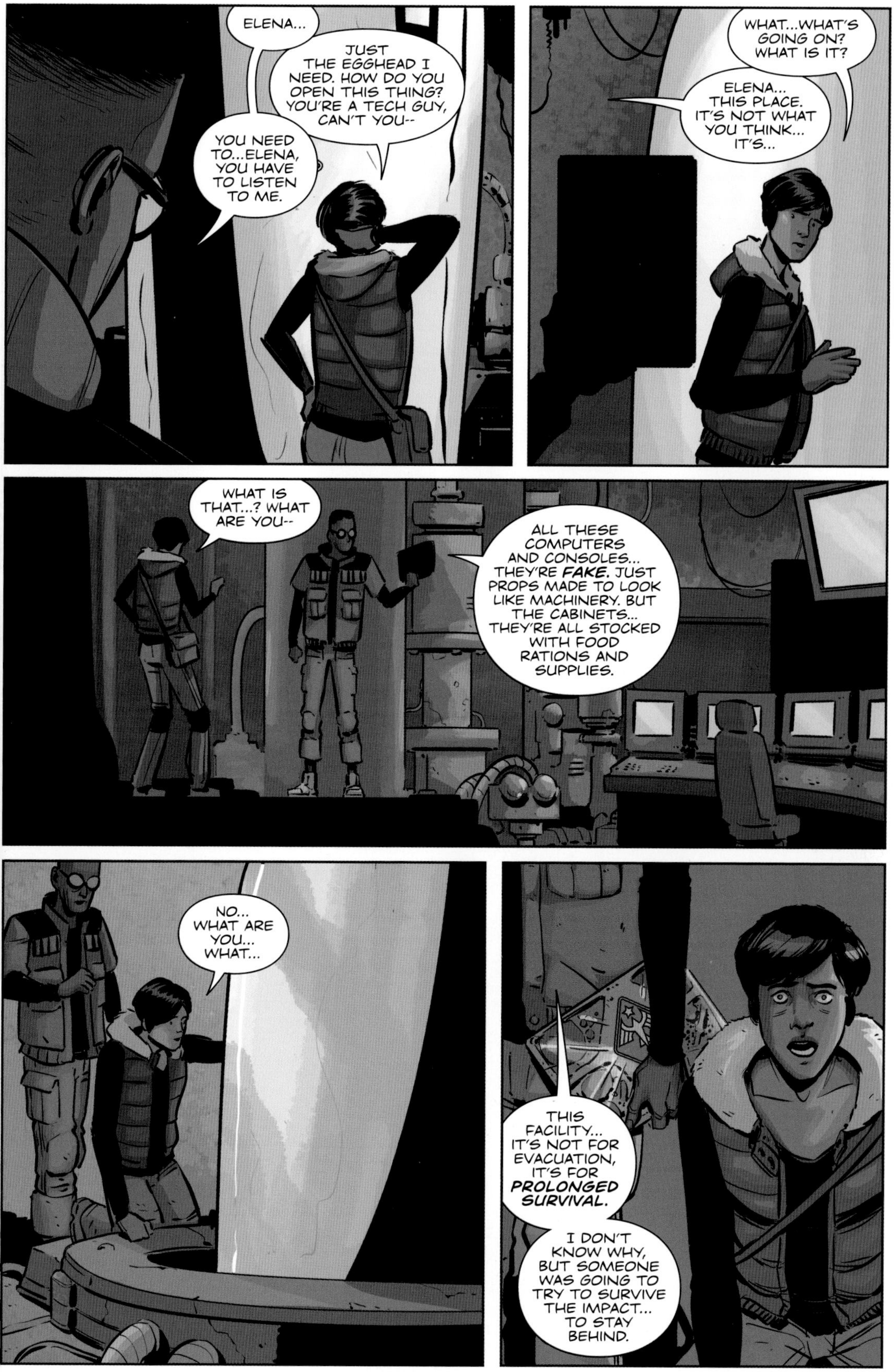
ELENA...
JUST THE EGGHEAD I NEED. HOW DO YOU OPEN THIS THING? YOU'RE A TECH GUY, CAN'T YOU--
YOU NEED TO...ELENA, YOU HAVE TO LISTEN TO ME.
WHAT...WHAT'S GOING ON? WHAT IS IT?
ELENA... THIS PLACE. IT'S NOT WHAT YOU THINK... IT'S...
WHAT IS THAT...? WHAT ARE YOU--
ALL THESE COMPUTERS AND CONSOLES... THEY'RE ***FAKE***. JUST PROPS MADE TO LOOK LIKE MACHINERY. BUT THE CABINETS... THEY'RE ALL STOCKED WITH FOOD RATIONS AND SUPPLIES.
NO... WHAT ARE YOU... WHAT...
THIS FACILITY... IT'S NOT FOR EVACUATION, IT'S FOR ***PROLONGED SURVIVAL.***
I DON'T KNOW WHY, BUT SOMEONE WAS GOING TO TRY TO SURVIVE THE IMPACT... TO STAY BEHIND.

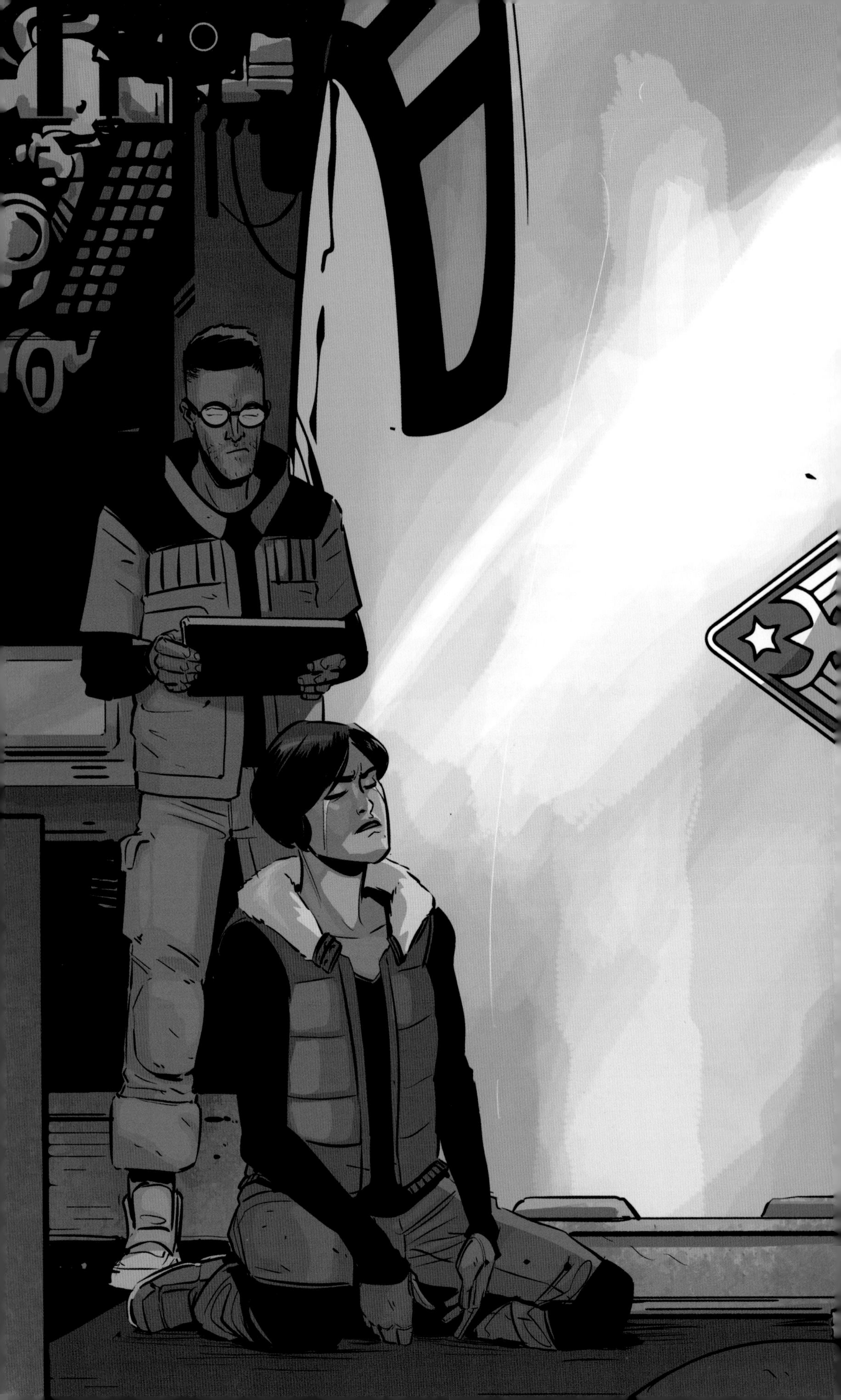

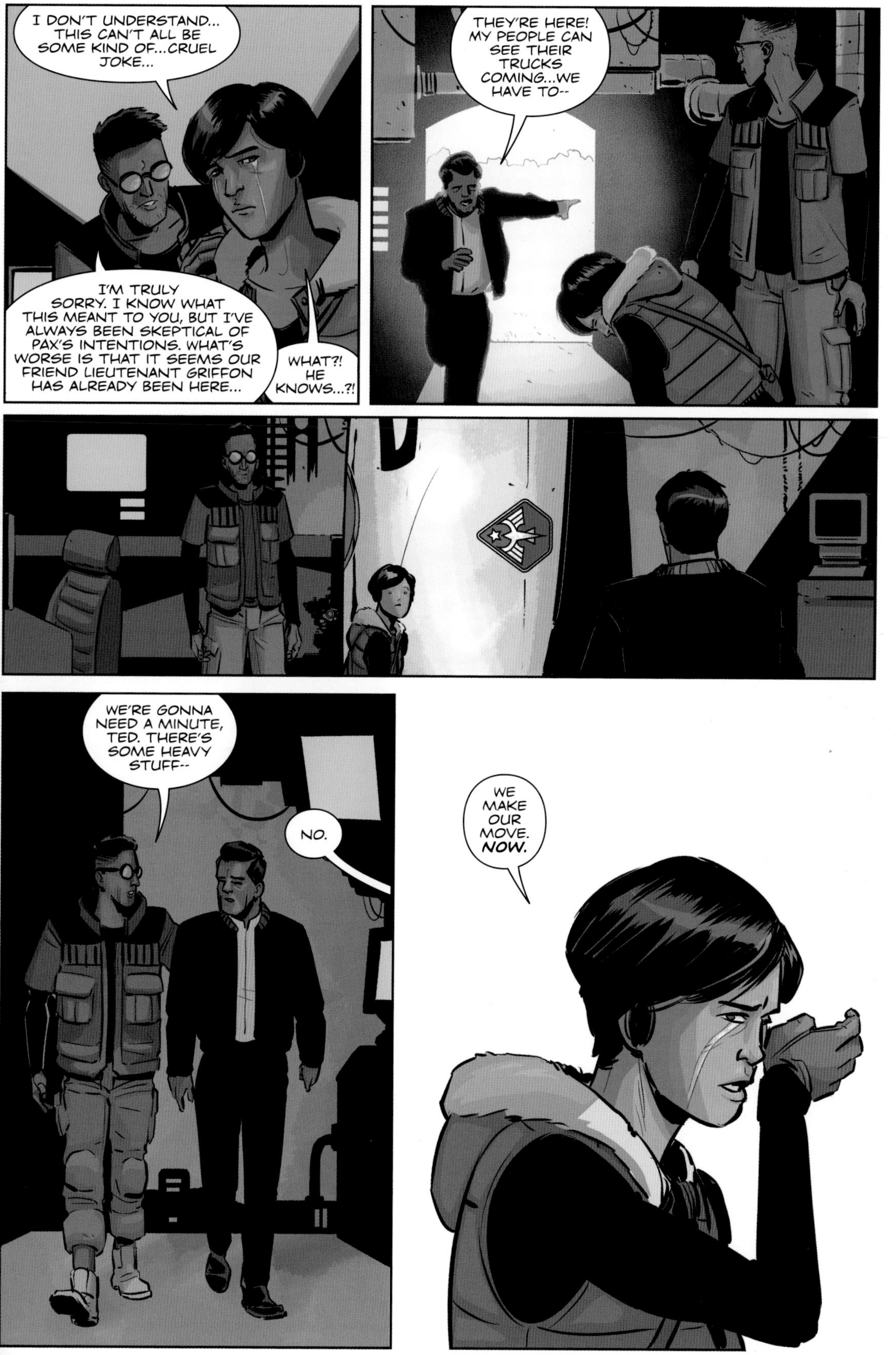
I DON'T UNDERSTAND... THIS CAN'T ALL BE SOME KIND OF...CRUEL JOKE...
I'M TRULY SORRY. I KNOW WHAT THIS MEANT TO YOU, BUT I'VE ALWAYS BEEN SKEPTICAL OF PAX'S INTENTIONS. WHAT'S WORSE IS THAT IT SEEMS OUR FRIEND LIEUTENANT GRIFFON HAS ALREADY BEEN HERE...
WHAT?! HE KNOWS...?!
THEY'RE HERE! MY PEOPLE CAN SEE THEIR TRUCKS COMING...WE HAVE TO--
WE'RE GONNA NEED A MINUTE, TED. THERE'S SOME HEAVY STUFF--
NO.
WE MAKE OUR MOVE. **NOW.**

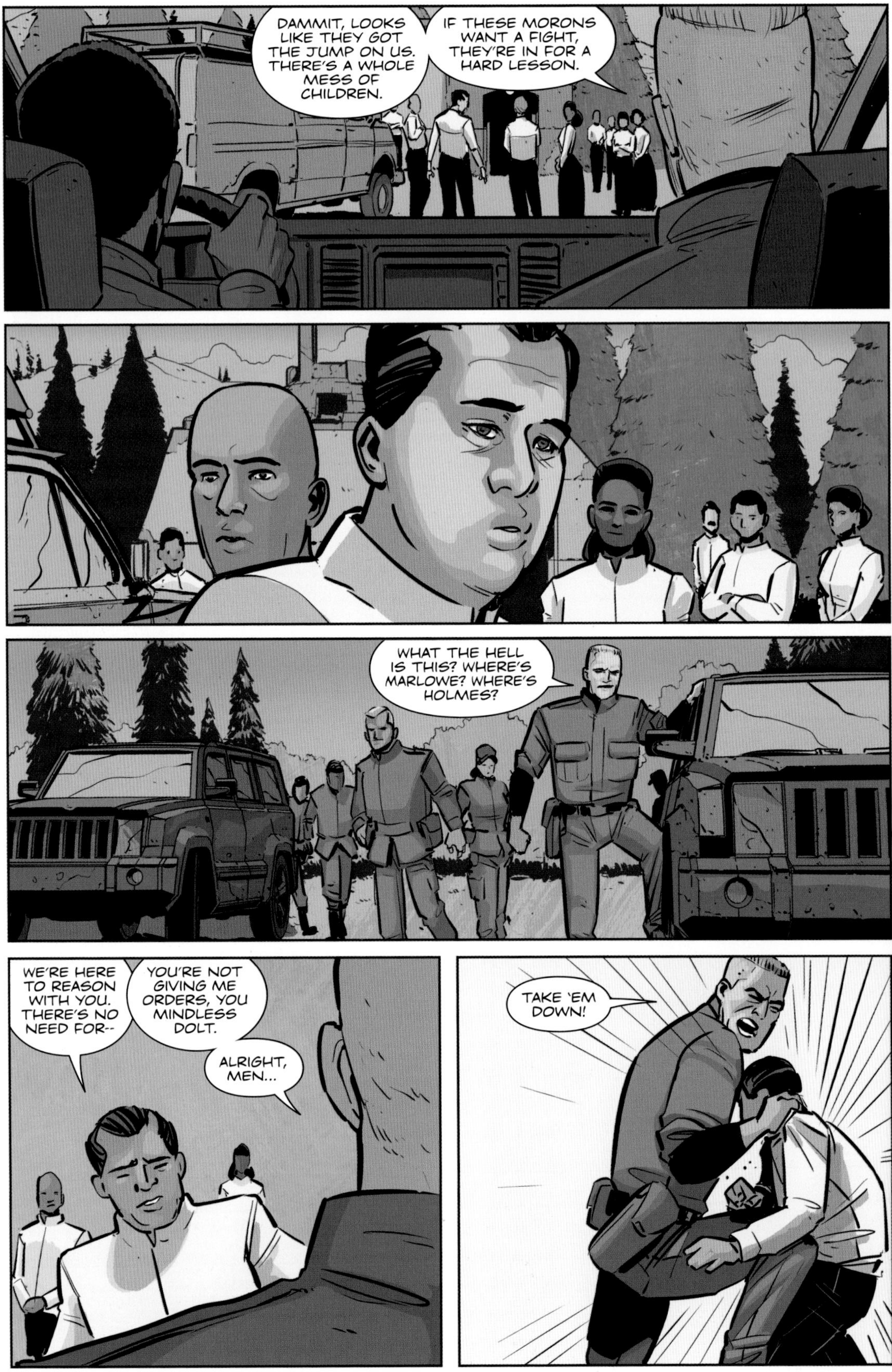
DAMMIT, LOOKS LIKE THEY GOT THE JUMP ON US. THERE'S A WHOLE MESS OF CHILDREN.
IF THESE MORONS WANT A FIGHT, THEY'RE IN FOR A HARD LESSON.
WHAT THE HELL IS THIS? WHERE'S MARLOWE? WHERE'S HOLMES?
WE'RE HERE TO REASON WITH YOU. THERE'S NO NEED FOR--
YOU'RE NOT GIVING ME ORDERS, YOU MINDLESS DOLT.
ALRIGHT, MEN...
TAKE 'EM DOWN!

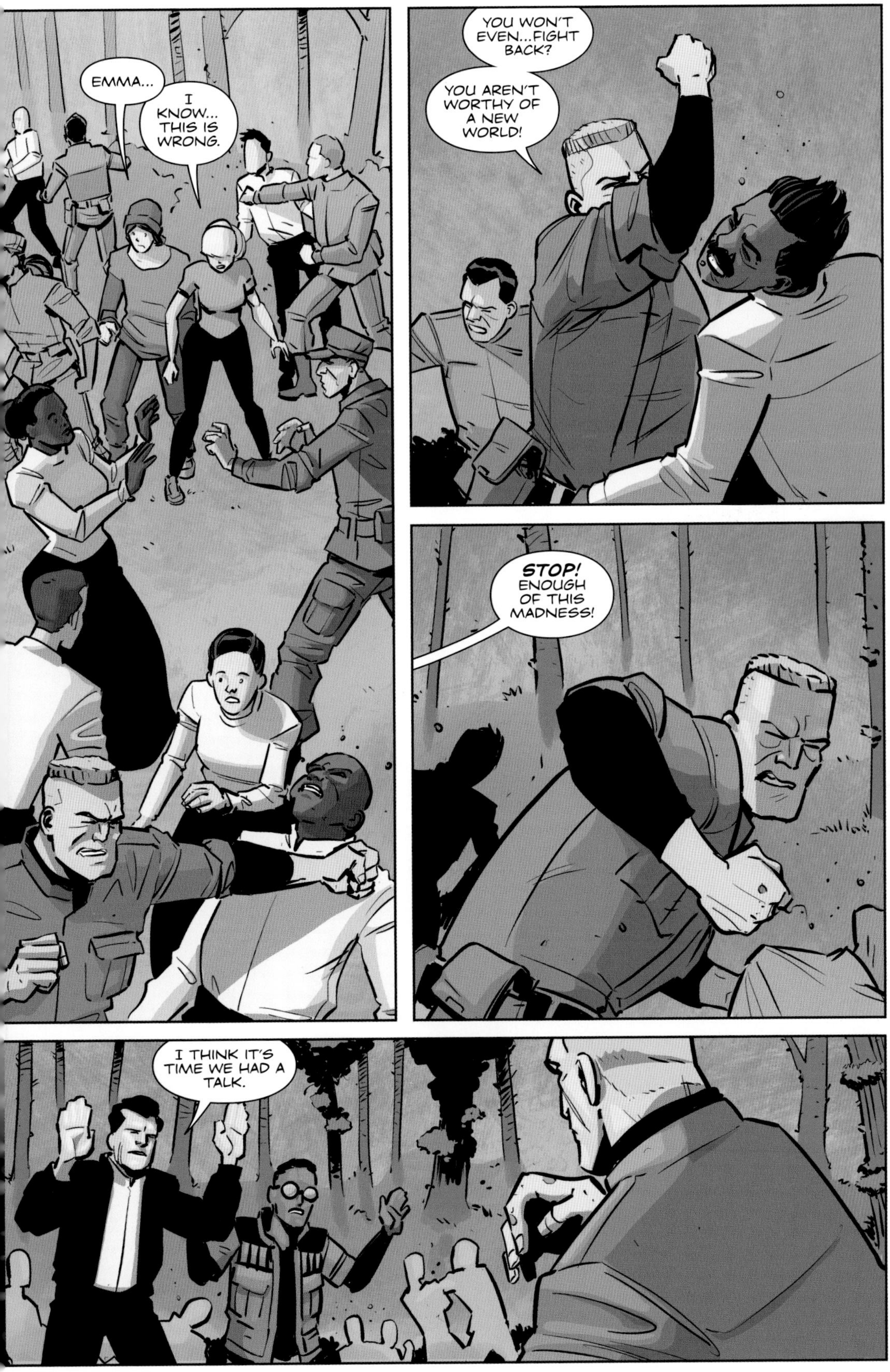

EMMA...
I KNOW... THIS IS WRONG.
YOU WON'T EVEN...FIGHT BACK?
YOU AREN'T WORTHY OF A NEW WORLD!
STOP! ENOUGH OF THIS MADNESS!
I THINK IT'S TIME WE HAD A TALK.

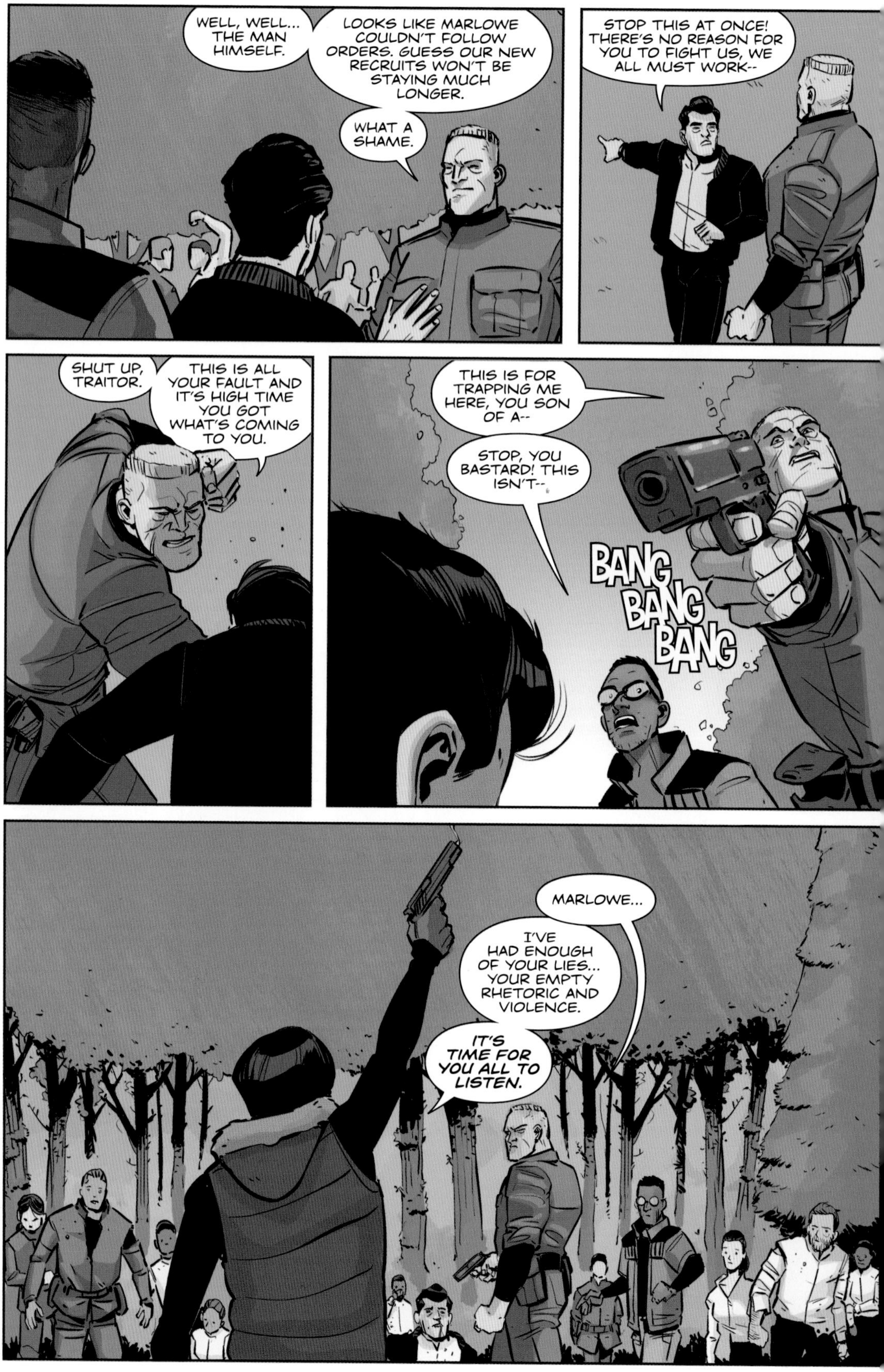
WELL, WELL... THE MAN HIMSELF.
LOOKS LIKE MARLOWE COULDN'T FOLLOW ORDERS. GUESS OUR NEW RECRUITS WON'T BE STAYING MUCH LONGER.
WHAT A SHAME.
STOP THIS AT ONCE! THERE'S NO REASON FOR YOU TO FIGHT US, WE ALL MUST WORK--
SHUT UP, TRAITOR.
THIS IS ALL YOUR FAULT AND IT'S HIGH TIME YOU GOT WHAT'S COMING TO YOU.
THIS IS FOR TRAPPING ME HERE, YOU SON OF A--
STOP, YOU BASTARD! THIS ISN'T--
BANG
BANG
BANG
MARLOWE...
I'VE HAD ENOUGH OF YOUR LIES... YOUR EMPTY RHETORIC AND VIOLENCE.
IT'S TIME FOR YOU ALL TO LISTEN.

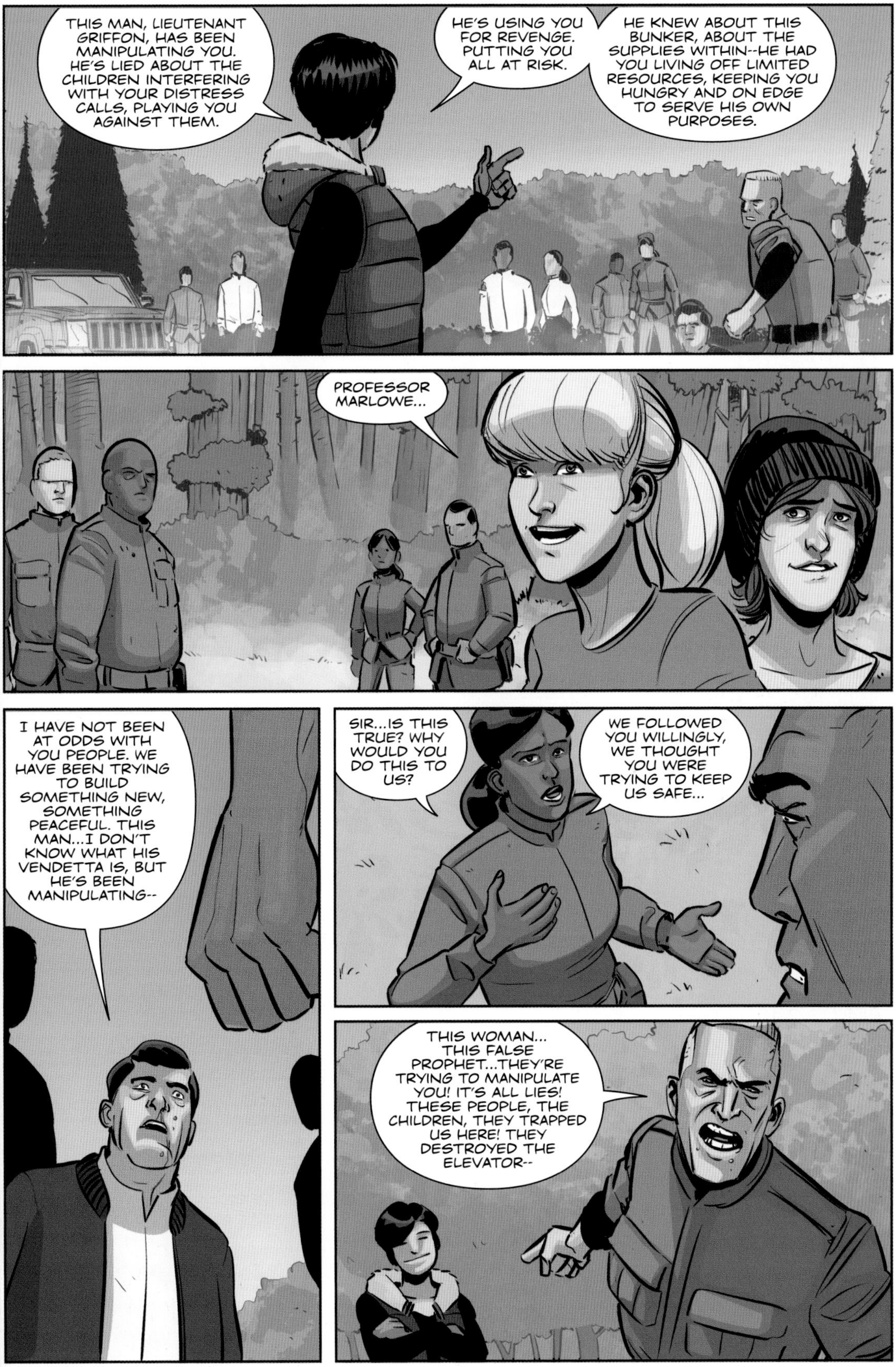

THIS MAN, LIEUTENANT GRIFFON, HAS BEEN MANIPULATING YOU. HE'S LIED ABOUT THE CHILDREN INTERFERING WITH YOUR DISTRESS CALLS, PLAYING YOU AGAINST THEM.
HE'S USING YOU FOR REVENGE. PUTTING YOU ALL AT RISK.
HE KNEW ABOUT THIS BUNKER, ABOUT THE SUPPLIES WITHIN--HE HAD YOU LIVING OFF LIMITED RESOURCES, KEEPING YOU HUNGRY AND ON EDGE TO SERVE HIS OWN PURPOSES.
PROFESSOR MARLOWE...
I HAVE NOT BEEN AT ODDS WITH YOU PEOPLE. WE HAVE BEEN TRYING TO BUILD SOMETHING NEW, SOMETHING PEACEFUL. THIS MAN...I DON'T KNOW WHAT HIS VENDETTA IS, BUT HE'S BEEN MANIPULATING--
SIR...IS THIS TRUE? WHY WOULD YOU DO THIS TO US?
WE FOLLOWED YOU WILLINGLY, WE THOUGHT YOU WERE TRYING TO KEEP US SAFE...
THIS WOMAN... THIS FALSE PROPHET...THEY'RE TRYING TO MANIPULATE YOU! IT'S ALL LIES! THESE PEOPLE, THE CHILDREN, THEY TRAPPED US HERE! THEY DESTROYED THE ELEVATOR--

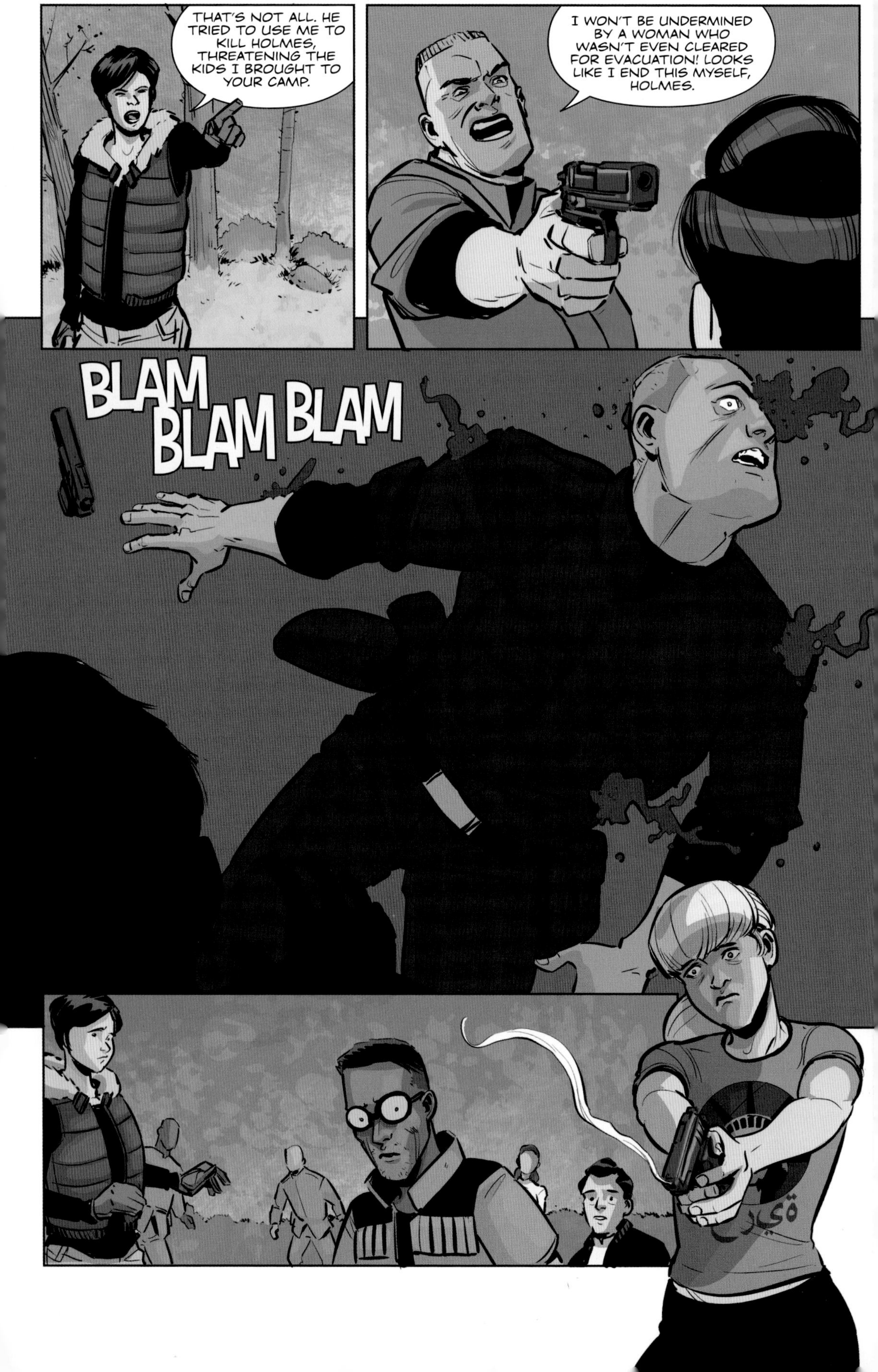
THAT'S NOT ALL. HE TRIED TO USE ME TO KILL HOLMES, THREATENING THE KIDS I BROUGHT TO YOUR CAMP.
I WON'T BE UNDERMINED BY A WOMAN WHO WASN'T EVEN CLEARED FOR EVACUATION! LOOKS LIKE I END THIS MYSELF, HOLMES.
BLAM BLAM BLAM

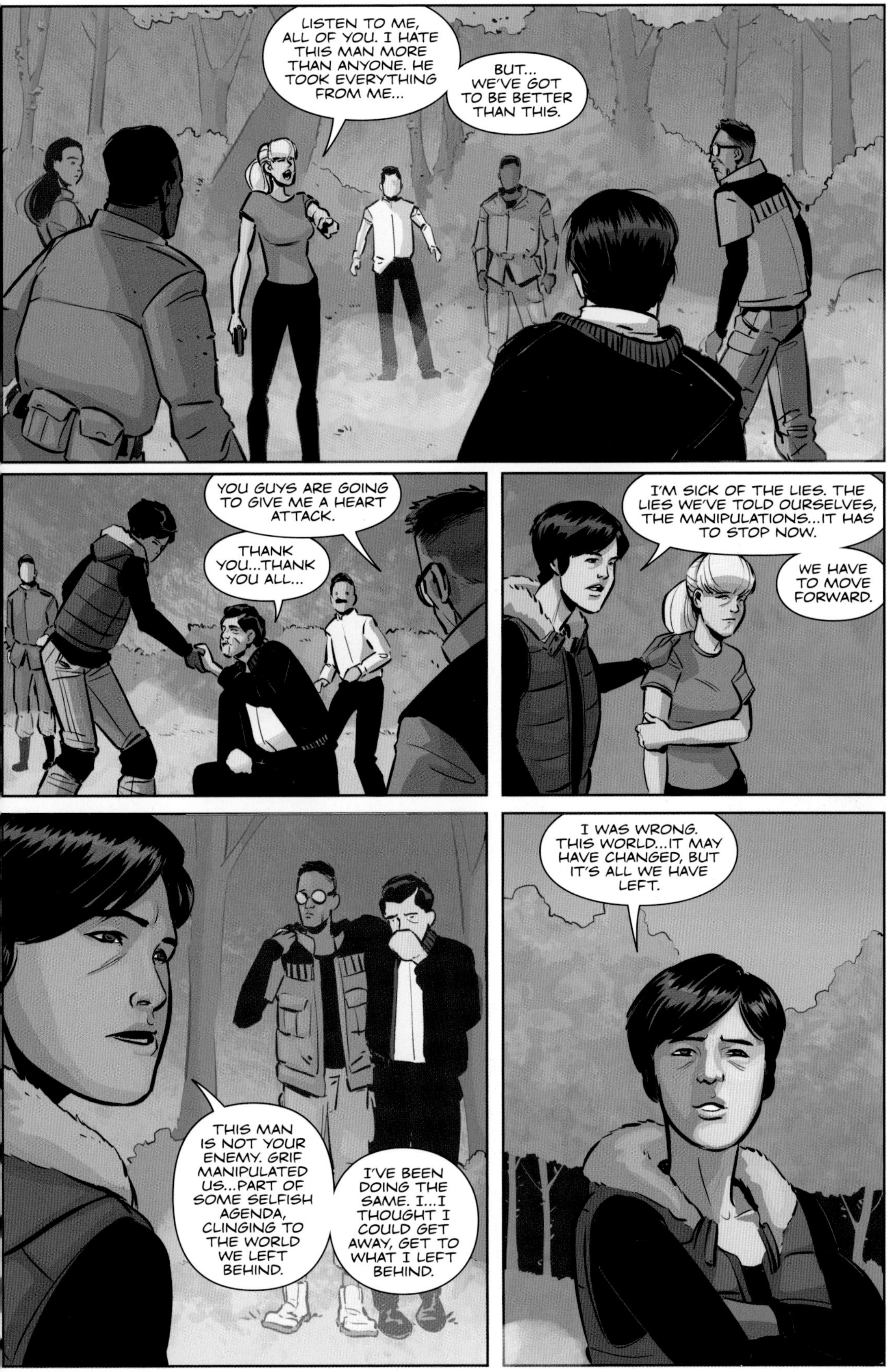
LISTEN TO ME, ALL OF YOU. I HATE THIS MAN MORE THAN ANYONE. HE TOOK EVERYTHING FROM ME...
BUT... WE'VE GOT TO BE BETTER THAN THIS.
YOU GUYS ARE GOING TO GIVE ME A HEART ATTACK.
THANK YOU...THANK YOU ALL...
I'M SICK OF THE LIES. THE LIES WE'VE TOLD OURSELVES, THE MANIPULATIONS...IT HAS TO STOP NOW.
WE HAVE TO MOVE FORWARD.
THIS MAN IS NOT YOUR ENEMY. GRIF MANIPULATED US...PART OF SOME SELFISH AGENDA, CLINGING TO THE WORLD WE LEFT BEHIND.
I'VE BEEN DOING THE SAME. I...I THOUGHT I COULD GET AWAY, GET TO WHAT I LEFT BEHIND.
I WAS WRONG. THIS WORLD...IT MAY HAVE CHANGED, BUT IT'S ALL WE HAVE LEFT.

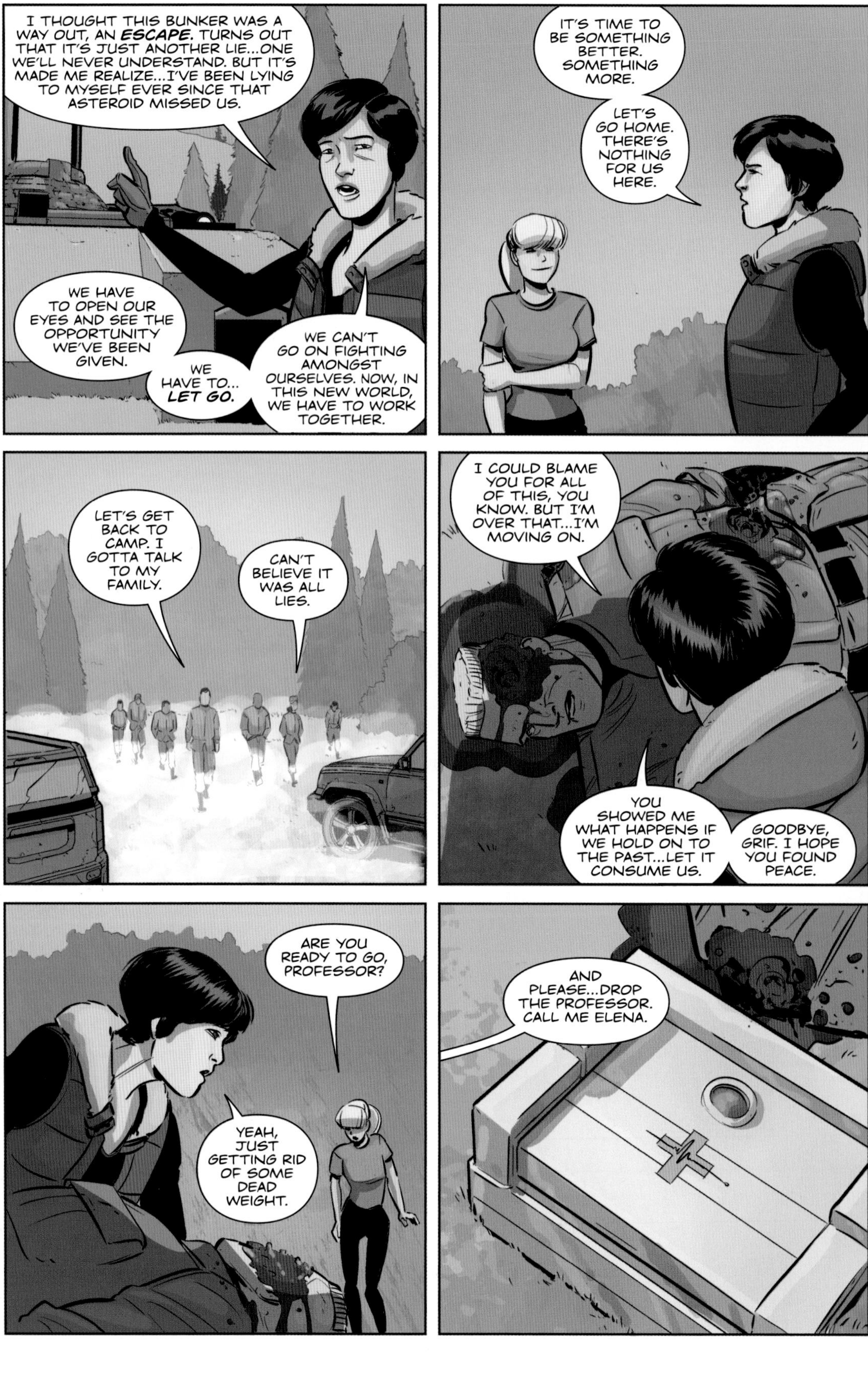
I THOUGHT THIS BUNKER WAS A WAY OUT, AN *ESCAPE.* TURNS OUT THAT IT'S JUST ANOTHER LIE...ONE WE'LL NEVER UNDERSTAND. BUT IT'S MADE ME REALIZE...I'VE BEEN LYING TO MYSELF EVER SINCE THAT ASTEROID MISSED US.
WE HAVE TO OPEN OUR EYES AND SEE THE OPPORTUNITY WE'VE BEEN GIVEN.
WE HAVE TO... *LET GO.*
WE CAN'T GO ON FIGHTING AMONGST OURSELVES. NOW, IN THIS NEW WORLD, WE HAVE TO WORK TOGETHER.
IT'S TIME TO BE SOMETHING BETTER. SOMETHING MORE.
LET'S GO HOME. THERE'S NOTHING FOR US HERE.
LET'S GET BACK TO CAMP. I GOTTA TALK TO MY FAMILY.
CAN'T BELIEVE IT WAS ALL LIES.
I COULD BLAME YOU FOR ALL OF THIS, YOU KNOW. BUT I'M OVER THAT...I'M MOVING ON.
YOU SHOWED ME WHAT HAPPENS IF WE HOLD ON TO THE PAST...LET IT CONSUME US.
GOODBYE, GRIF. I HOPE YOU FOUND PEACE.
ARE YOU READY TO GO, PROFESSOR?
YEAH, JUST GETTING RID OF SOME DEAD WEIGHT.
AND PLEASE...DROP THE PROFESSOR. CALL ME ELENA.

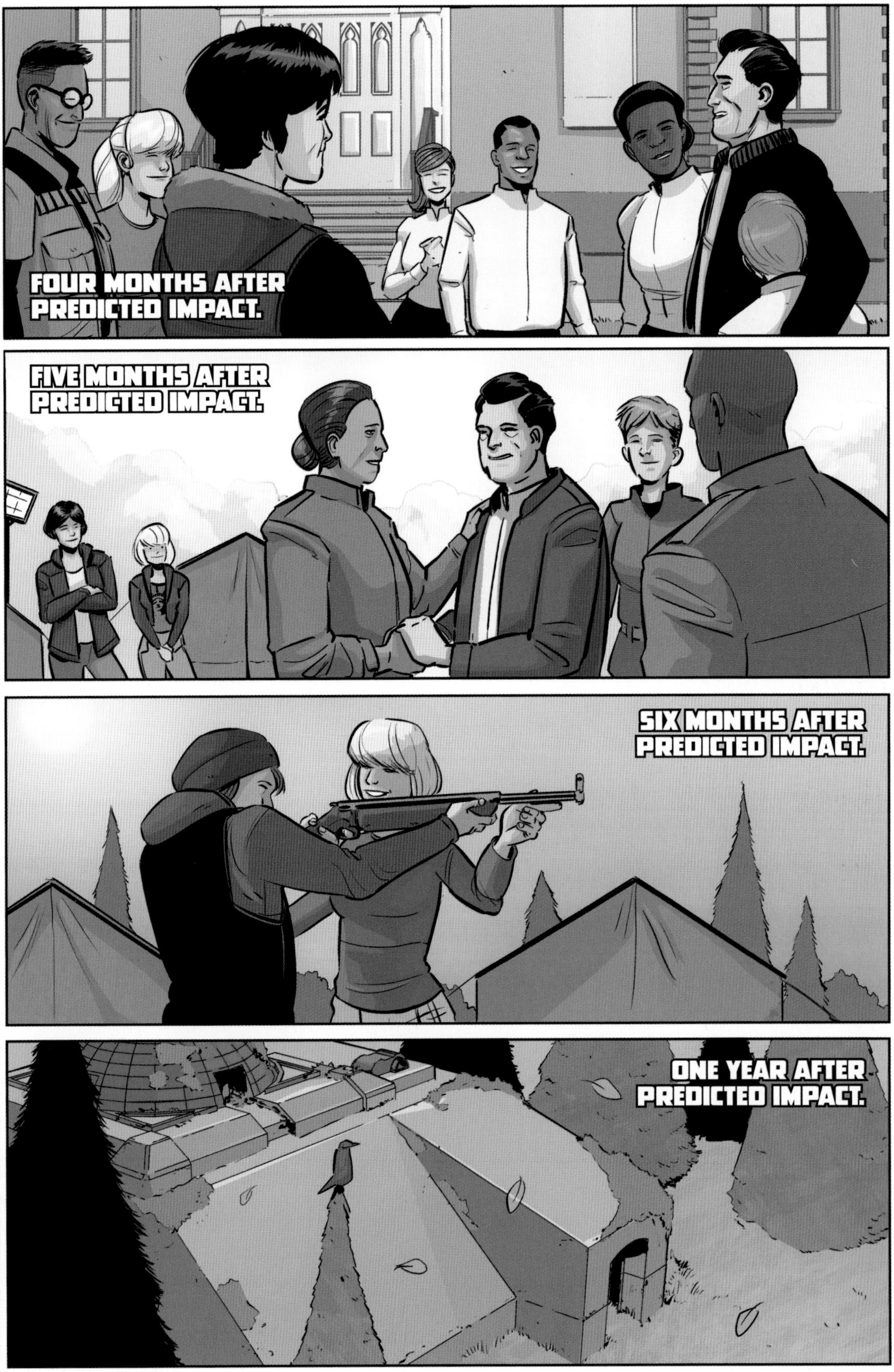
FOUR MONTHS AFTER PREDICTED IMPACT.
FIVE MONTHS AFTER PREDICTED IMPACT.
SIX MONTHS AFTER PREDICTED IMPACT.
ONE YEAR AFTER PREDICTED IMPACT.

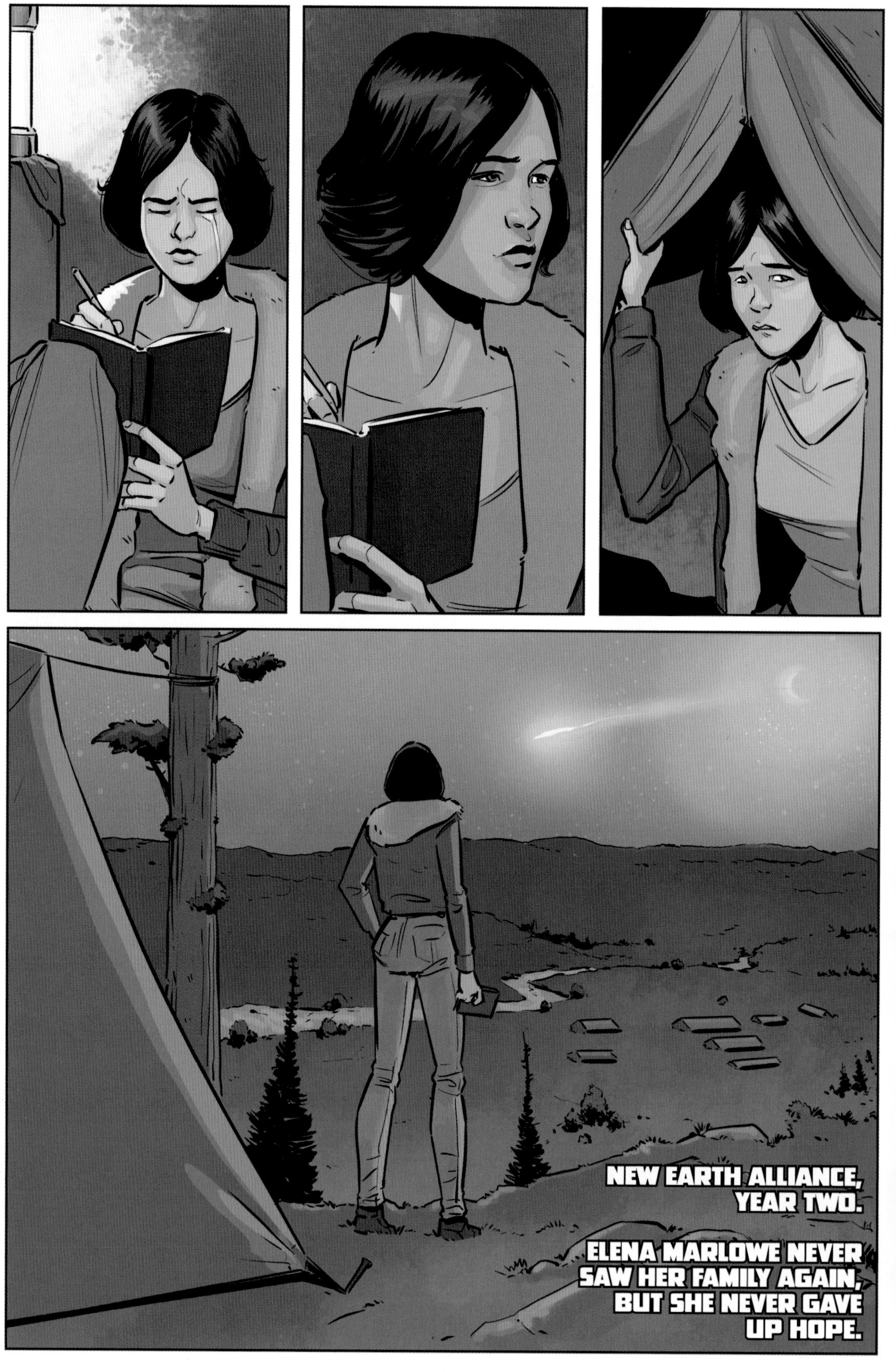
NEW EARTH ALLIANCE, YEAR TWO.
ELENA MARLOWE NEVER SAW HER FAMILY AGAIN, BUT SHE NEVER GAVE UP HOPE.

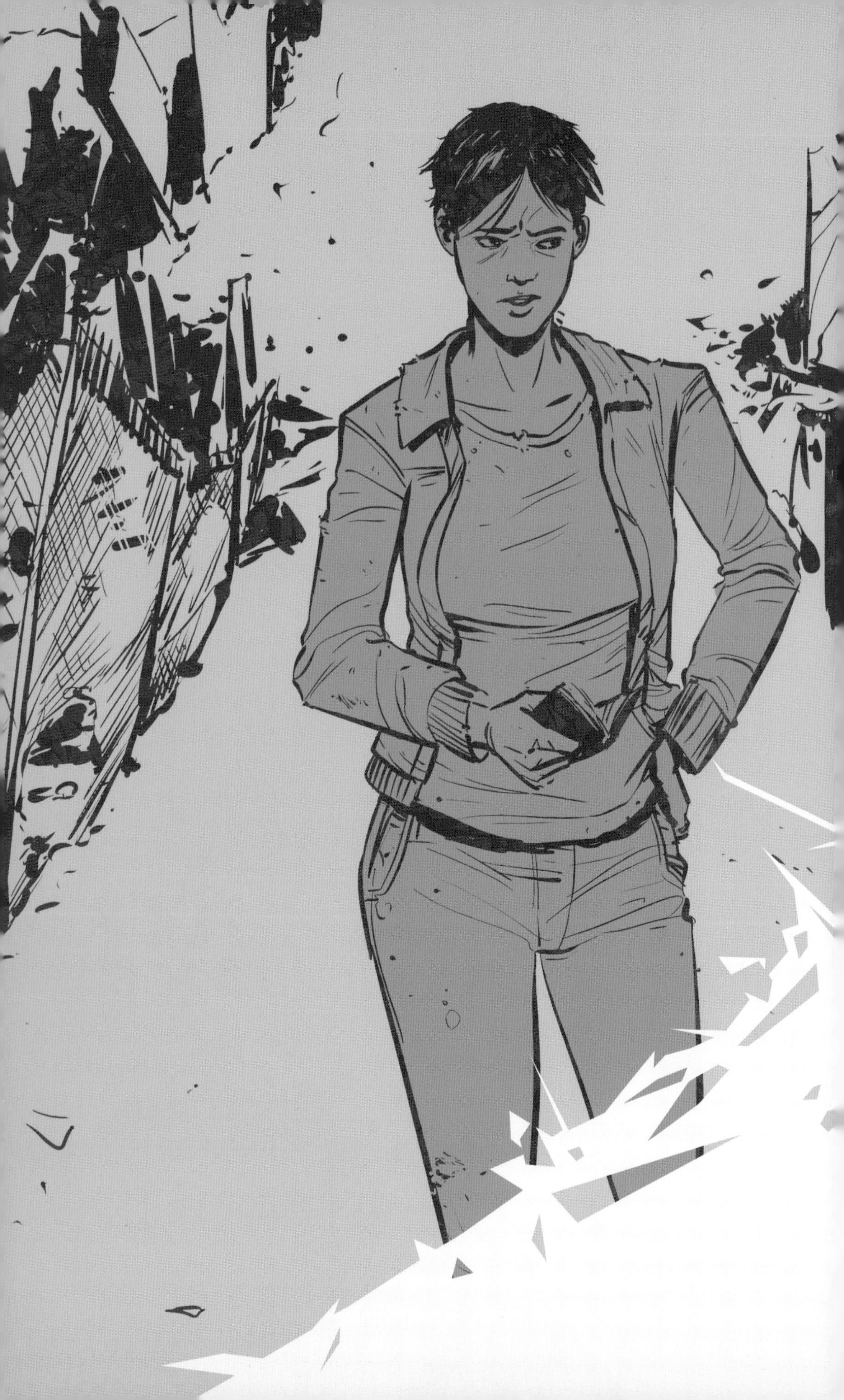

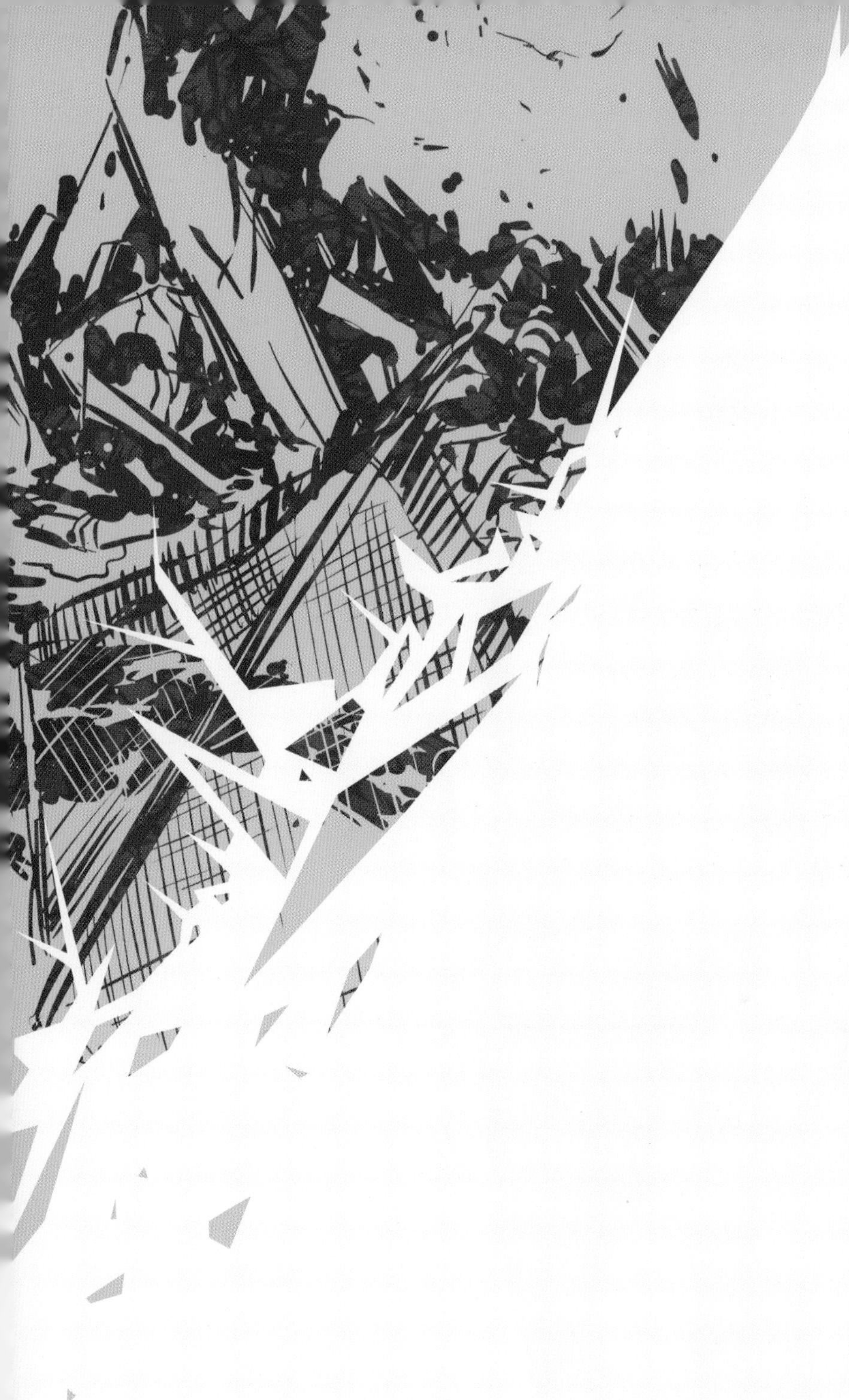

COVER GALLERY

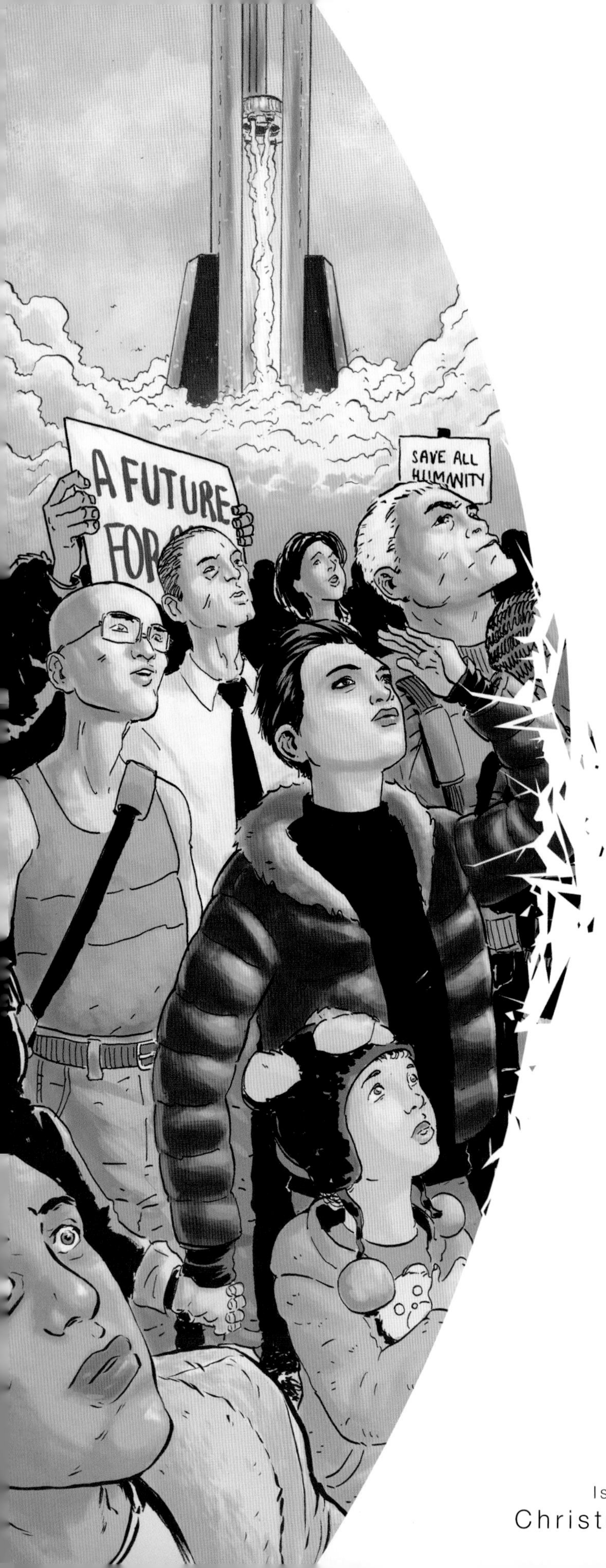
A FUTURE
FOR
SAVE ALL
HUMANITY

Issue One Cover
Christopher Peterson

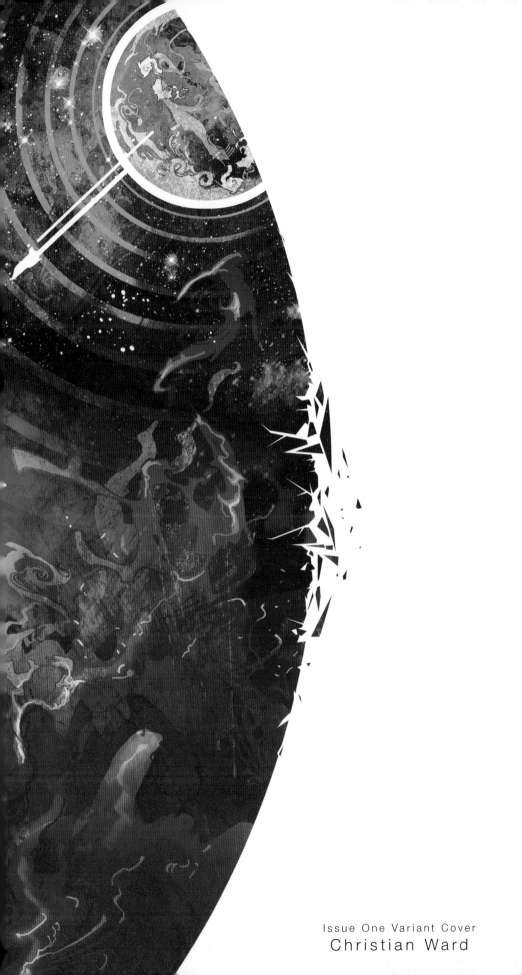

Issue One Variant Cover
Christian Ward

Issue One BOOM! Ten Years Variant Cover
Frazer Irving

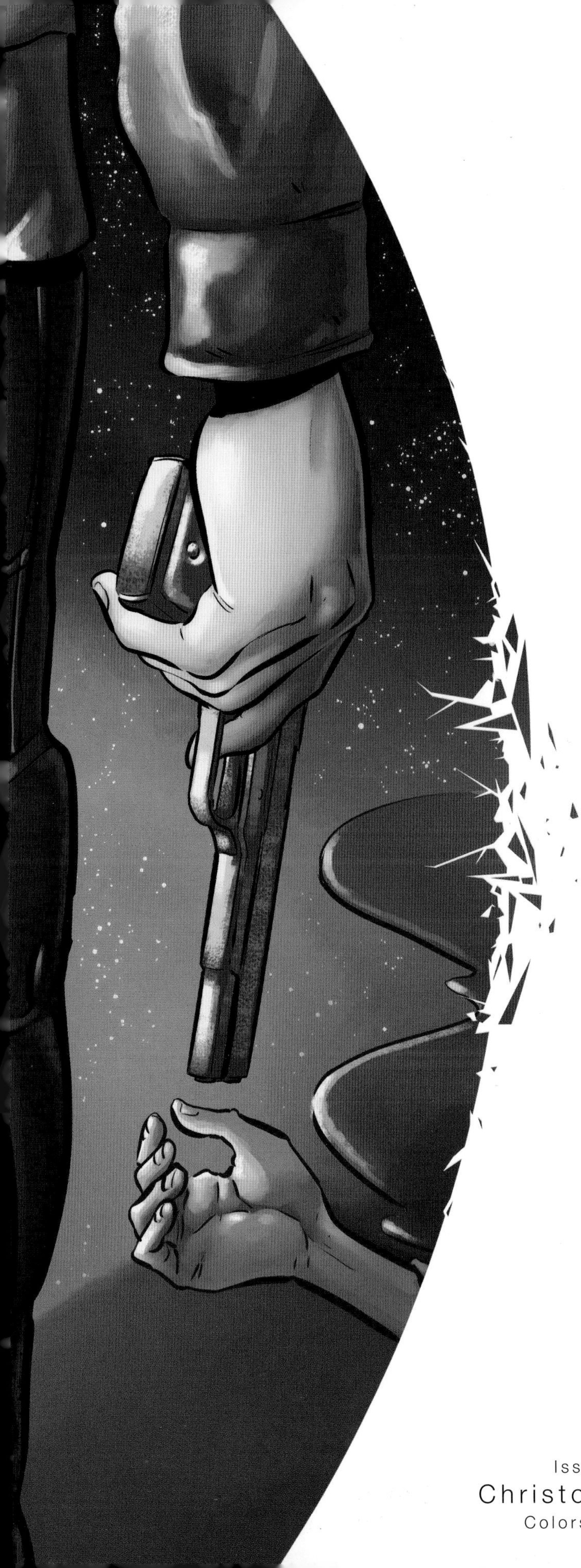

Issue Four Cover
Christopher Peterson
Colors by Jordan Boyd

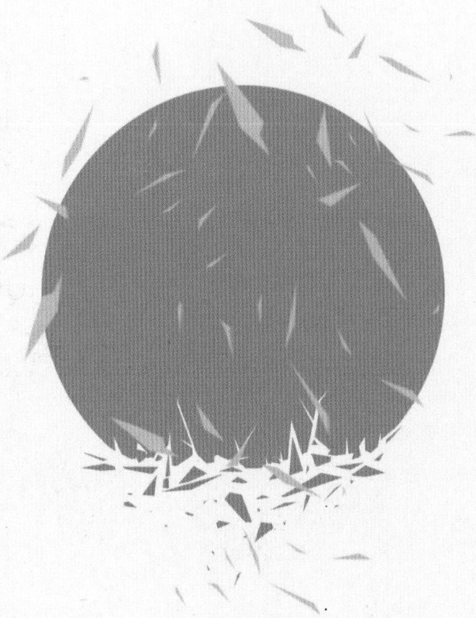